MW00353254

PROFITING FROM MARKET TRENDS

Founded in 1807, John Wiley & Sons is the oldest independent publishing company in the United States. With offices in North America, Europe, Australia, and Asia, Wiley is globally committed to developing and marketing print and electronic products and services for our customers' professional and personal knowledge and understanding.

The Wiley Trading series features books by traders who have survived the market's ever-changing temperament and have prospered—some by reinventing systems, others by getting back to basics. Whether a novice trader, professional, or somewhere in-between, these books will provide the advice and strategies needed to prosper today and well into the future.

For more on this series, visit our website at www.WileyTrading.com.

PROFITING FROM MARKET TRENDS

Simple Tools and Techniques for Mastering Trend Analysis

Tina Logan

WILEY

Cover image: © iStockphoto.com/E_Y_E
Cover design: Wiley

Published by John Wiley & Sons, Inc., Hoboken, New Jersey.
Published simultaneously in Canada.

For general information on our other products and services or for technical support, please contact our Customer Care Department within the United States at (800) 762-2974, outside the United States at (317) 572-3993, or fax (317) 572-4002.

Wiley publishes in a variety of print and electronic formats and by print-on-demand. Some material included with standard print versions of this book may not be included in e-books or in print-on-demand. If this book refers to media such as a CD or DVD that is not included in the version you purchased, you may download this material at http://booksupport.wiley.com. For more information about Wiley products, visit www.wiley.com.

Library of Congress Cataloging-in-Publication Data:

Logan, Tina.
Profiting from market trends : simple tools and techniques for mastering trend analysis/Tina Logan.
pages cm.—(Wiley trading series)
ISBN 978-1-118-51671-3 (cloth); ISBN 978-1-118-72698-3 (ePDF);
ISBN 978-1-118-72700-3 (ePub)
1. Technical analysis (Investment analysis) 2. Investment analysis. I. Title.
HG4529.L64 2014
332.63'2042—dc23

2013034305

Printed in the United States of America.
10 9 8 7 6 5 4 3 2 1

CONTENTS

Preface vii
Acknowledgments xiii

PART I **Trend Development** 1

CHAPTER 1 **Introduction to Trend Analysis** 3

CHAPTER 2 **Trend Direction** 9

CHAPTER 3 **Trend Duration** 27

CHAPTER 4 **Trend Interruptions** 59

CHAPTER 5 **Early Trend Reversal Warnings** 93

CHAPTER 6 **Later Trend Reversal Warnings** 119

PART II **Putting Trend Analysis to Work** 143

CHAPTER 7 **The Broad Market** 145

CHAPTER 8 **Bull Markets** 163

CHAPTER 9 **Bear Markets** 183

CHAPTER 10 **Monitoring the Market Trends** 195

CHAPTER 11 Current Bull Market–Case Study 229

CHAPTER 12 Conclusion 271

Bibliography 275
About the Author 277
Index 279

PREFACE

During trending phases, market participants can really boost their returns. Thus, analyzing trends effectively is one of the most important and relevant skills a trader can develop. That's what you will learn from this unique book. You'll be shown how a trend begins and progresses through its life span offering traders myriad opportunities to generate profits. You'll learn how to monitor the strength of a trend in order to take full advantage of it while it lasts, and recognize signs that suggest when it may be coming to an end.

The principal purpose of this instruction is to help novices build a strong base of knowledge in trend analysis in order to increase profitability. This book is a crucial part of the charting instruction I offer, and is part of the foundation from which successful trading strategies may be developed and implemented. This text will help you progress down the path to becoming a master trader.

The primary reasons for learning how to analyze trends efficiently are threefold:

1. To generate profits by implementing strategies that take advantage of a trend.
2. To protect the initial capital invested, as well as the gains accrued during a trend.
3. To prepare to participate in a new trend in the opposite direction when a trend reversal occurs.

Understanding how trends evolve is very important because a large number of trading strategies are designed to capitalize on lucrative trending phases. By carefully reviewing this instruction, beginner to intermediate-level traders will gain the knowledge and understanding of market movement that will help them successfully implement various strategies they may be shown, or to develop their own unique strategies if they choose.

What Makes This Book So Valuable?

I want to thank you in advance for putting your confidence in me to help you develop or expand your charting knowledge and trading skills. I realize this book is not only an investment of your money, but also of your time. I understand and respect the value of both. Therefore, you can rest assured that I have worked tirelessly for several years developing my training content in a manner worthy of your investment.

This is not just another technical analysis reference book. Rather, it is a lively publication that reveals my passion for the subject matter and capitalizes on the following training characteristics I am known for:

- *It's an easy read*—Although the content is technical, and gets progressively more advanced as the chapters unfold, it is easy to understand and it keeps the readers engaged.
- *Well-organized material*—The content of each chapter is categorized in ways to make it easy to learn. Each chapter builds upon the prior chapter with smooth transitions from one topic to the next.
- *Details matter*—The content goes far beyond just the broad strokes of technical analysis. You will appreciate the fine details and nuances, combined with plenty of helpful chart illustrations.
- *Application of the content*—You will be shown how to apply the information provided. Throughout the book you'll be given suggestions for applying your newfound knowledge to generate profits and protect capital.

Definitions are provided and technical topics are dissected, but I strive to put a conversational tone to my writing. I write for you like I'd talk to you if we were sitting elbow to elbow at my trading desk analyzing charts, including injecting a bit of geeky trader humor where appropriate. I tell you about my chart analysis and trading activities, and share with you some of the struggles I've experienced, and lessons learned, during my years in this industry.

Who Will Benefit from This Book?

This book will appeal to intermediate-level traders, many of whom, in spite of having some knowledge and experience, struggle to achieve consistent success. They just can't quite get their arms around it all and get their trading activities running smoothly. If this describes you, I believe you'll find this instruction provides important pieces of the puzzle that you've been missing.

For newcomers to the stock market, this book will prove to be invaluable. It will save them a significant amount of time and frustration; and for most, it will save them a lot of money that otherwise would be lost in the marketplace. The biggest danger to beginners is that they'll lose their capital and/or confidence before they learn what they need to know. And unfortunately, they don't know yet what they don't know! Analyzing trends effectively is one of the skills that most novices don't realize the importance of early in their trading careers; so it is my job to see to it that they acquire this critical knowledge early on.

It took me many years to develop my knowledge. But you can shave several months, and for some of you a few to several years, off your own learning curve by carefully studying, and then applying with discipline, the information presented in this book.

I make no apologies for defining technical terms and describing concepts that experienced traders might consider familiar territory. In fact, advanced traders may find parts of this book to be elementary relative to their level of knowledge. My primary audience is beginner to intermediate-level traders, so I feel I must direct my instruction in a manner that assures their understanding of it.

With that said, even highly skilled chartists who read this book should appreciate the painstaking attention to detail and earnest approach to providing important insights for readers of all skill levels. Seasoned technicians understand the value in acquiring at least one helpful trading tip or tool that adds to their knowledge, or helps to make or save them time or money. It can pay for the price of a book, seminar, or other training resource many times over.

Format of This Instruction

This book is broken into two segments, each containing several chapters:

- Part I: Trend Development
- Part II: Putting Trend Analysis to Work

Part I outlines in detail some key tenets of charting, and provides fairly simple yet effective tools and techniques for analyzing trends in general. That is, the information applies to the charts of stocks, indices, sectors, and so on. Those chapters provide the important foundation of knowledge for analyzing trends, which sets the stage for more advanced discussion in the later chapters.

Part II puts those analysis techniques, plus some additional tools, to work demonstrating how to analyze the charts of market averages to help guide your overall trading activities. Chapter 11 includes one of the most extensive case studies you will likely ever come across. It is a detailed analysis of the current bull market, which has been included in order to really drill the information into your brain.

To help you absorb the wealth of information included in this text, and to make it easier for you to remember the concepts, bulleted and numbered lists, and tables, have been included throughout for quick reference.

During your review of the chapters, you should notice that certain concepts are reiterated, sometimes several times throughout the book. That is not done because I forgot that I already mentioned it in a prior chapter! But rather, because repeatedly bringing important concepts back into the discussion helps readers retain the information. A concept stated one way may not be assimilated; but the reader may fully understand it, and/or recognize its importance, when it is stated again later with a different example or when applying that information.

Since I use candlesticks in lieu of standard bar charts, I often refer to a specific candlestick line or pattern throughout this text. Those who are new to candlestick charting will find this aids in their understanding of the sentiment they reveal, as well as learning to recognize some of the reversal patterns that often form on charts. Those of you who read my first book, *Getting Started in Candlestick Charting* (John Wiley & Sons, 2008), will appreciate that I've included plenty of candlestick references that will build upon that instruction. *Note:* The terms *candles* and *candlesticks* are often used to refer to candlestick charting.

Time Frames

Most of the charting concepts and analysis techniques described are demonstrated utilizing the daily time frame. However, they may also be applied to other time frames. Short-, intermediate-, and long-term trends form on charts from yearly down to one minute; as do pullbacks, corrections, reversal patterns, and periods of consolidation. The implication is the same as the concepts shown on the daily charts, but relative to the time frame being analyzed. For instance, a short-term trend on the daily chart may last for several days, whereas on the hourly chart, a short-term trend may last for several hours.

Chart Examples

In the first several chapters, the chart examples provided are of clean and orderly trends and patterns. That was done intentionally to make sure readers fully absorb the concepts. However, in real-time analysis not all trends and patterns are ideally formed or shaped. Thus, as readers progress to the later chapters, not-so-clean examples, and variations, may be observed.

In many of the chart illustrations, only price bars are shown. That is, they may not have volume bars or technical indicators displayed. This should not be construed to mean that I do not utilize volume or indicators. I do use those tools regularly. However, when introducing a concept, I want readers to hone in on the price action being described and not be distracted by other technical tools. When indicators or volume are discussed, those chart examples will include them since they will be significant to that particular discussion.

All chart examples within this text are produced by TC2000®, which is a registered trademark of Worden Brothers, Inc., Five Oaks Office Park, 4905 Pine Cone Drive, Durham, NC 27707; phone (800) 776-4940 or (919) 408-0542, www.worden.com. Version 7 of the platform (known to long time users as TeleChart®) was used for ease of instruction and in order to perform the multi-year analysis required for completion of the extensive case study in Chapter 11. TC2000 users may also wish to explore version 12 of the platform, which, while it includes limited historical data, incorporates some new tools and features.

Chart Symbols

The symbols for charts of stocks and exchange-traded funds (ETFs) that are illustrated are universal. However, the symbols for the index charts shown may vary from one charting platform to another. For instance, in TC2000, the symbol for the Dow Jones Industrial Average is DJ-30. On the popular website StockCharts.com, the symbol is $INDU.

For many indices, the core of the symbol is common to all platforms, but there may be additional lettering or characters before or after it. For instance, the symbol for the Philadelphia Housing Sector Index in TC2000 is HGX--X and is $HGX on StockCharts.com. The Philadelphia Semiconductor Sector Index is SOX--X in TC2000 and $SOX on StockCharts.com.

Additional Information

Readers should be aware of the following:

- The discussion in this book, and the illustrations, represent the U.S. stock market. However, trends occur in all markets as they are necessary for a market's long-term survival. Thus, the basic precepts of trend analysis can be used for a wide range of trading instruments.
- The pronoun *he* is used generically to reference traders of either gender. No offense is intended to lady traders, for I am one myself.
- The terms *trader* and *investor* may be used generically throughout the text to refer to all market participants, whether they be active traders or long-term investors. However, when applied specifically, as a general rule traders tend to take a more active role than investors.
- The word *price* is used generically to refer either to prices of stocks or values of indices shown in the price column.
- When a topic is introduced, if there is more than one term that tends to be used, I provide the various labels that I am aware of. This helps beginners avoid confusion since they may come across different labels in various texts.
- The terms *index* and *average* may be used interchangeably throughout this book in reference to the chart of an index or market average.

ACKNOWLEDGMENTS

I've had the great fortune of being influenced and motivated by several remarkable individuals during my life's journey. I wish I could thank them all sufficiently, but how does one do so with mere words? Those individuals who have left an imprint on my life range from family members and friends to special teachers from high school, college, and beyond. And if not for the years I spent working at the Anthony Robbins Companies, I'm certain I would not have become a trader, for it was there that my interest in the stock market was first sparked. From there, I had the privilege of working with Chris Manning of Manning Advanced Trading Seminars for a few years, which was an integral step in helping me develop a strong knowledge base of technical analysis.

There are many trading books on my shelf that I could not imagine parting with. I wish to thank the authors of those great, classic books—including works by Victor Sperandeo, Steve Nison, Alan Farley, Dr. Alexander Elder, Dr. Van Tharp, Thomas Bulkowski, Oliver Velez, Gregory Morris, John Murphy, Martin Pring, and Martin Zweig. The contributions they have made to me, and to so many others, by sharing their vast knowledge and insights are very much appreciated. Special recognition goes to Herbert Otto, a skilled trader and chartist with more than four decades of experience. I was fortunate to be introduced to him in the trading community over 10 years ago and have gleaned much from his vast knowledge and trading wisdom.

I would like to thank my family, of course, and my close friends for their seemingly never-ending patience and support. They may not understand why I'm so obsessed with the stock market and helping others navigate in this business, but they respect that I feel compelled to do so. I must recognize three of my great, long time friends, Jelaine Whipple, Debbie Hagan, and Michelle Becker. They have stood by me without wavering through all my challenges and successes over the years. Thanks goes to Billie Sandoval and Solveig Perry, who care enough to give me a gentle push, and sometimes even a good shove, just when I need it most.

Thank you to the fine folks at John Wiley & Sons, especially my editor, Kevin Commins, who agreed it was time for me to write another book (what was I thinking?). Special thanks to Senior Development Editor, Meg Freeborn, for patiently waiting and waiting for the manuscript and for fielding my many questions. Thanks also go to Tiffany Charbonier and her colleagues for their contributions, including designing the fantastic cover, and to Steven Kyritz for guiding me through the final editing process. It really takes tremendous teamwork and persistence to get a book to its finale.

PART I

TREND DEVELOPMENT

CHAPTER 1

Introduction to Trend Analysis

Markets move in trends. This phenomenon is one of the major organizing principles of market behavior and one of the tenets of the Dow Theory. Some well-known axioms have been coined over the decades regarding market trends, such as "The trend is your friend" and "Don't fight the trend." Numerous trading and investment strategies have been developed around the fact that markets move in trends. Most traders find it easier to profit when a market is trending than while it is in a period of prolonged consolidation.

What Is a Market Trend?

A simplistic definition of a market trend is a directional price move—either up or down. An uptrend is a price move that starts from a specific low point. A downtrend is a price move starting from a certain high point.

Traders ask many questions about the trend, such as the following:

- Which direction is it moving?
- How long might it last?
- How strong is it?
- How can I spot opportunities to participate in a trend's movement?
- What signs should I look for that suggest the trend may be weakening or changing direction?

- Is this a good time to get aboard the trend?
- When should I exit the trend?

My answers to these questions fill the chapters of this book. The charting tools and techniques described herein are intended for the purpose of identifying and participating in a trend, gauging its strength, and responding to changes in its direction. In my opinion, these trend analysis tasks are *among the most important activities* an active trader or investor will perform.

Trends are an integral part of market analysis, whether it is technical analysis, fundamental analysis, or analyzing market breadth. Although the primary focus of this book is analyzing *price trends*, in market analysis the word "trend" is not limited to describing price movement. It may also be used to refer to other analysis concepts. Following are some examples where an analyst may notice an upward or downward trend, or a change in trend direction:

- A trend in volume.
- A trend in the market internals. For example, the number of stocks making new highs versus new lows.
- A trend in the number of stocks meeting the criteria of a specific filter (e.g., the number of stocks trading above or below their 200-period moving average).
- A trend in the quarterly earnings growth rate of a company.
- A trend in the growth rate of the economy or the employment numbers.

It's All About the Trend

A common challenge for aspiring traders is that they don't fully understand the essential constructs of technical analysis (charting) before attempting to move on to more advanced study and practice. I fell into that trap myself early in my trading career. When I first began my charting studies many years ago, I felt a bit overwhelmed. I found I was spinning my wheels and feeling that there was so much to learn. I was studying various charting-related topics—gaps, support-resistance, candlesticks, chart patterns, technical indicators, and so on—each in isolation. That is, I studied each area of charting as if it was a stand-alone topic. Hence, it is not surprising I felt overwhelmed. There are so many *different* topics to learn, or so I thought.

Then one day I had one of those crucial "aha moments." I realized that all those topics I had been studying were actually directly related to the development of market trends. It was then that I recognized the study of trends is the *primary role* of technical analysis. It was so much easier to really understand and implement the various charting concepts when I put them *in the context of how they contributed to the development of a trend.* That realization simplified and streamlined my studies; and significantly impacted my trading activities and strategy development going forward.

Most everything in technical analysis relates to the concept of trends in some fashion; you'll see that clearly demonstrated throughout this book. Table 1.1 lists several charting concepts directly related to the start, advancement, or conclusion of a trend.

TABLE 1.1 Trend Development

Charting Topic	Role in Trend Analysis
Gaps	Gaps often occur at the beginning (breakaway gap), middle (continuation gap), or end (exhaustion gap) of a trend. Those gaps reflect the start, acceleration, or end of a trend, respectively. Morning gaps play a significant role in short-term trends.
Volume and Volatility	Both volume and volatility often tend to increase during trending periods and decrease during periods of consolidation.
Classic Reversal Patterns	It is common to see a reversal pattern form at the end of a trend. For instance, a double top or head-and-shoulders top may form at the end of an uptrend. The inverse of those patterns may form at the end of a downtrend. Such patterns signal a potential trend reversal.
Classic Continuation Patterns	Continuation patterns may form within a trend stalling its movement for a short period of time (e.g., a flag or pennant) or for a longer duration (e.g., a triangle or trading range).
Candlestick Lines and Patterns	Candlestick lines reveal the sentiment of market participants as a trend develops. A bearish or bullish candlestick reversal pattern may form at the end of an up or down trend, respectively.
Price Swings	Minor, wavelike price movements create the peaks and bottoms that are the building blocks of intermediate-term trends. Those price swings may provide opportunities for short-term trades and profit-taking opportunities for long-term positions.
Corrections	Corrections are retracements of the prior trend.
Trendlines	Trendlines are used to determine the direction, slope, and duration of a trend (sloped lines), as well as to highlight support and resistance areas (horizontal lines). The break of a strong trendline can provide an important signal about the potential continuation or reversal of a trend.

(Continued)

TABLE 1.1 *(Continued)*

Charting Topic	Role in Trend Analysis
Technical Indicators	There are many technical indicators designed for analyzing trends (e.g., to determine the direction and/or momentum of a trend). Some indicators can help identify when a trend may be weakening. For example, a divergence between price and a strong indicator may occur, warning of a potential trend reversal.
Market Indicators	Experienced traders may consult market breadth readings (market internals) to gauge the day-to-day strength of the market trend, as well as cumulative market indicators for monitoring longer trends.
Trading Strategies	Many trading strategies are developed around the fact that markets trend. Trend-following strategies take advantage of a trending market. The success of setups traded, and strategies employed, at any given time may depend greatly on the trend (or lack of) of the broad market.

■ Profiting from Market Trends

Because the phenomenon of trends is so pivotal, much of technical analysis is devoted to the identification of trends and gauging their strength, so chartists can implement appropriate trading strategies. A significant amount of the chart analysis I perform is dedicated to monitoring the trends of the stocks I trade, as well as the major market averages, sectors, and industry groups.

Clearly, it is essential to learn how to analyze trends effectively in order to become a proficient chartist, and for determining which trading methods to employ. Listed below are some of the key skills traders should learn in order to achieve those goals. Helping you develop those skills, and subsequently profiting from market trends, is the primary purpose of this book.

- Identify a trend as early as possible in its development in order to profit from as much of that trend's movement as possible.
- Determine a trend's strength and potential duration. Continually monitor the strength of the trend.
- Recognize technical events and price formations that occur within a trend that may offer trading opportunities.
- Understand the concept of support and resistance and its role in a trend's evolution.
- Identify signs that a trend may be weakening or reversing direction in order to protect profits and/or get aboard a new trend when a change in direction occurs.

Let's Build a Clock

I've been providing private tutoring for traders for almost 12 years. I've sat side-by-side with numerous traders of varying skill levels. I'm sure if you asked any of them, or the hundreds of individuals who have read my books, e-books, or attended my webinars, they'd tell you I'm ridiculously organized, very detail oriented, and probably too verbose. A client once said to me, "I asked you what time it is and you showed me how to build a clock!" I'd say he summed up my training style. I err on the side of providing tremendous detail rather than risk leaving questions unanswered.

As you review this book, I hope you'll appreciate the pains taken to ensure that readers are provided the fine points needed to actually put the information to work. But if, after reading all the chapters at least once, you find anything confusing, you are welcome to e-mail me your question at tina@tinalogan.com. Please keep inquiries to a question or two and not a lengthy questionnaire, or I'll challenge whether you've reviewed the material enough times! But with that said, I am accessible and attempt to respond to e-mails in a timely manner.

Repeated Study Leads to Proficiency

It has been said that "Repetition is the mother of skill." There is a lot of information in this text. Therefore, I encourage readers to review the content over and over again, as many times as it takes to absorb the information. Afterward, put that knowledge to work through vigorous application using real-time analysis, and effective trade selection and management, in order to generate profits.

There are several great trading books on my shelves that I've reviewed many times each. A couple of them have broken spines due to so much use. Thus, I wouldn't ask you to do anything I haven't done, or wouldn't be willing to do. True understanding of the content comes from repeated study and persistent application.

Develop a Strong Foundation of Knowledge

The first book I wrote was *Getting Started in Candlestick Charting* (John Wiley & Sons, 2008). I'm hooked on candlesticks and cannot imagine going back to using a standard bar chart. It is my opinion that candlesticks should be utilized in conjunction with other technical events that develop on charts.

Candlestick charts are used exclusively in the illustrations provided in this publication. You'll see references to specific candlestick lines (e.g., the size of a bar's body), and several commonly formed reversal patterns are identified. If you don't already have some familiarity with the basics of candlesticks, I suggest a quick review of Part I of *Getting Started in Candlestick Charting*.

A brief introduction to Western chart analysis was provided in *Getting Started in Candlestick Charting*. In *Profiting from Market Trends,* you'll see some of those core tenets of chart analysis revisited, but covered much more extensively here. This book delves deeply into trend analysis, and adds the important task of continually monitoring the trend of the broad market. As the title suggests, a thorough understanding of trends, and utilizing that information regularly in analysis and trading strategy development, can result in significant profits for those who do so with consistency and discipline.

There is much to learn in order to become a skilled chartist and a master trader. Enthusiastic students of the markets can quickly become overwhelmed and discouraged if they fail to develop a crucial knowledge base of chart analysis. The markets are unforgiving to those who dive in without adequate knowledge. Be patient and committed to your study of the material in this book and you'll reap the rewards that attract, but elude, so many who attempt to extract profits from the markets.

CHAPTER 2

Trend Direction

The trend indicates the direction the market is moving. There are only two directions in which markets can trend—up or down. There will also be phases where no trend is present and price moves primarily sideways for a period of time. Those trendless periods are often referred to as consolidation, or a trading range.

Personally, I like to stay informed as to the fundamental reasons why the market may be trending or consolidating; and I find that doing so helps to explain certain charting phenomena. However, it is not necessary to know what's driving the market up or down *in order to profit* from that trend. In his book *The Visual Investor* (John Wiley & Sons, 1996, p. 5), John Murphy states, "Knowing the reasons behind a stock's movement is interesting, but not critical. If your stock goes up on a given day, they won't take the money away from you if you don't know why it went up. And if you can explain why it went down, they won't give you back your lost money." He goes on to say, "The trick to visual investing is learning to tell the difference between what is going up and what is going down." Making that determination is the focus of this chapter.

A stock's price, or a market's value, cannot trend, nor can it move sideways, without the movement being imprinted on its chart. The effective analysis of that movement, and taking prudent action based upon it, can give a trader an edge. This chapter provides instruction on how to quickly and easily determine the direction of the trend. Following are three simple charting concepts that will be used to determine trend direction:

1. Price peaks and bottoms
2. Moving averages
3. Trendlines

Price Peaks and Bottoms

Price peaks and bottoms are pivots that form on charts. They show where price turned resulting in at least a temporary change in direction. Peaks and bottoms may be simple in their concept and construct, but don't underestimate their importance. They play a significant role in the development of trends, as well as in the selection and management of trades.

A peak is formed after an advance when price stops making higher highs from one bar to the next and makes a lower high. A peak consists of three bars with the middle bar's *high* being higher than the highs of the bars on either side of it (Figure 2.1). The very high of that middle bar indicates the precise point where price stopped its rise followed by a change in direction.

A bottom is formed after a decline when price stops making lower lows from one bar to the next and makes a higher low. It consists of three bars with the middle bar's *low* being lower than the lows of the bars on either side of it (Figure 2.2). The very low of that middle bar indicates the precise point where price stopped its decline followed by a change in direction.

There are instances, though infrequent, when the pivoting action is formed from more than three bars. After a price advance, the high of two or more *consecutive* bars may be exactly the same price. In candlestick charting this is referred to as a Tweezers Top. As long as there are lower highs on each side of those consecutive highs, there is a peak present. After a price decline, if the low of two or more consecutive bars is exactly the same price it is a Tweezers Bottom. As long as there are higher lows on each side of those consecutive lows, a bottom is present. Figure 2.3 shows a Tweezers Bottom. The bars numbered 1 through 3 have exactly the same low with higher lows on either side.

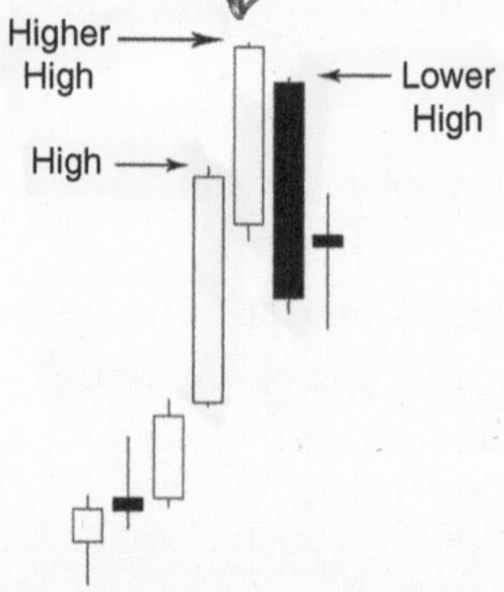

FIGURE 2.1 **Peak**

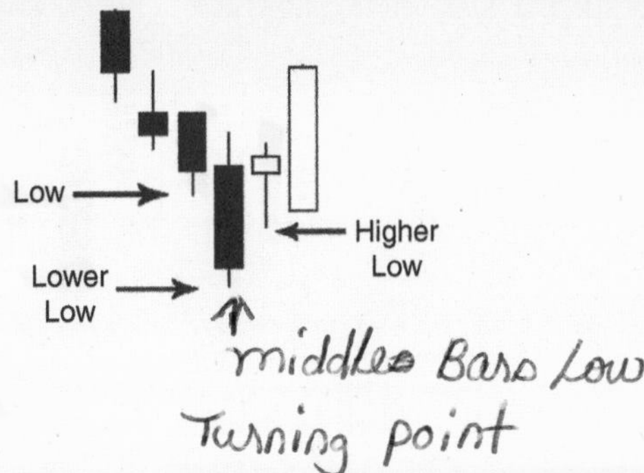

FIGURE 2.2 Bottom

These price pivots are basic elements of charting; however, many novices are not clear on their construct. That may be partially due to the fact that there are several different terms used to label those turning points. When I first began my study of technical analysis, I was not aware that a peak and a swing high were the same thing; so I set out to find the definitions for each term. After some frustration, I realized what was called a swing high in one text was called a peak in another and a rally high in yet another! To help you avoid the same confusion, listed below are all the terms I am aware of:

- A peak may also be referred to by any of the following terms: swing high, pivot high, reaction high, rally high, rally top, rally peak, top, or fractal.
- A bottom may also be referred to by any of the following terms: swing low, pivot low, reaction low, rally low, trough, valley, or fractal.

Note: I may refer to a peak or a bottom as a pivot because of the pivoting action that occurs when one is formed. However, that reference should not be confused with pivot points as defined on the website www.investopedia.com or with pivot point analysis, such as the techniques described in John Person's book *Candlestick and Pivot Point Trading Triggers* (John Wiley & Sons, 2007).

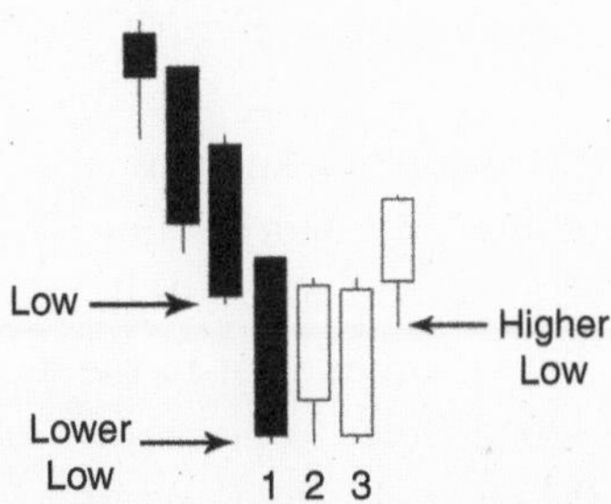

FIGURE 2.3 Tweezers Bottom

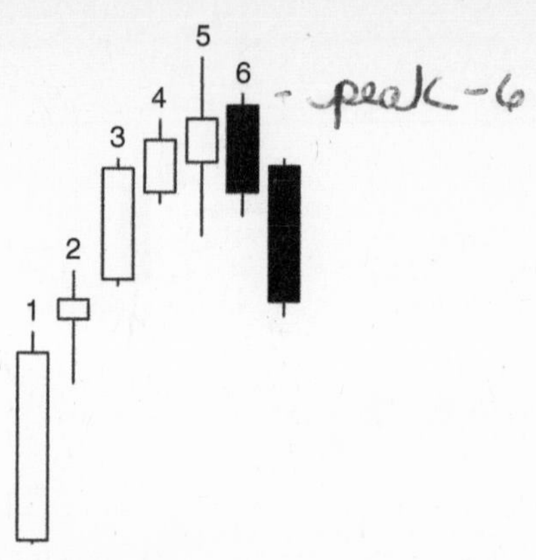

FIGURE 2.4 A Peak Was Formed on Bar 6

It is important to understand the difference between a peak and the high of a price bar. The high of a price bar is the highest price reached during a single, daily trading session; or during one time increment on other time frames. If a stock is making higher highs from one bar to the next (numbers 1 through 5 in Figure 2.4), there is no peak until a lower high is formed (bar 6). Likewise, there is a difference between a bottom and a low of a price bar. The low of a price bar is the lowest price reached during the trading period. If a stock is making lower lows from one bar to the next (numbers 1 through 6 in Figure 2.5), there is no bottom until a higher low is formed (bar 7).

I recall once listening to an audio presentation created by a well-known trainer in this industry. He indicated the definition of an uptrend was one making "higher highs and higher lows." I've also seen a similar definition in a few books on technical analysis. It occurred to me that, even though the statement was "higher highs and higher lows," an experienced trader would interpret that to mean higher *swing highs* (peaks) and higher *swing lows* (bottoms). This may seem like an obvious conclusion to a seasoned chartist; however, new chartists may not know enough yet to make that important distinction.

If inexperienced chartists were to take the words "higher highs and higher lows" literally, they might interpret the rise shown in the boxed area of Peabody Energy (BTU) in Figure 2.6 as an uptrend. The stock did indeed make higher highs and higher lows from one bar to the next for a short period of time from March 5 to 8, 2013 (refer to the arrows in Figure 2.6). However, as the bigger picture of the chart clearly shows, this stock is in a downtrend. The stock was forming lower peaks and lower bottoms. The price advance

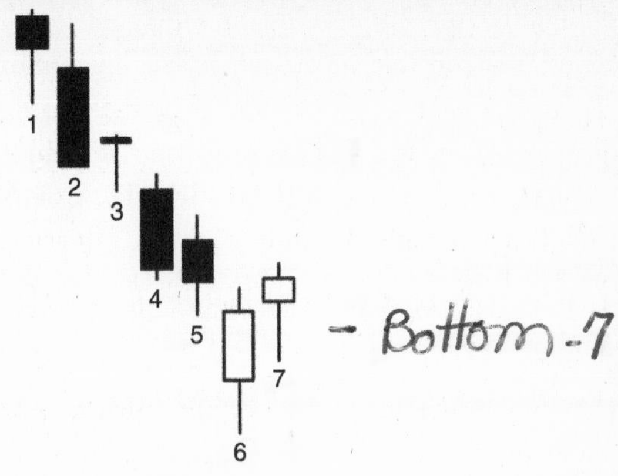

FIGURE 2.5 A Bottom Was Formed on Bar 7

that occurred from March 5 to 8 was just a temporary relief rally. That is, it was a short-term uptrend within the longer downtrend. If I were asked the direction of the trend in Figure 2.6, I'd respond, "The short-term trend shown at the right edge of the chart is up, but the intermediate-term trend is down." The downtrend continued (not shown) after that relief rally. In Chapter 3 you'll learn more about short-, intermediate-, and long-term trends.

FIGURE 2.6 A Relief Rally within a Downtrend
Source: TC2000® chart courtesy of Worden Brothers, Inc.

Hopefully, this emphasizes the importance of making sure to be clear on the *semantics* and the *context* when learning about charting concepts. Read the text carefully and look closely at the accompanying chart or illustration if one is provided. Make sure you really understand what the author is attempting to get across to the readers. For example, if it is stated that price has made a new high, the author may be referring to one of the following:

- A new high of day—The highest price reached during a single daily trading session.
- A new swing high (peak)—A pivot that forms after a price advance (see Figure 2.1).
- A new 52-week high—The highest price reached in the past year.
- A new all-time high—The highest price ever achieved by that stock or index.

Price Pivots Are the Building Blocks of Trends

Throughout this book you'll see how price pivots play an important role in the development of a trend. As price moves up and down in the general direction of the trend, a series of peaks and bottoms will form on the chart (Figure 2.7). Some of those price pivots will be prominent (obvious to

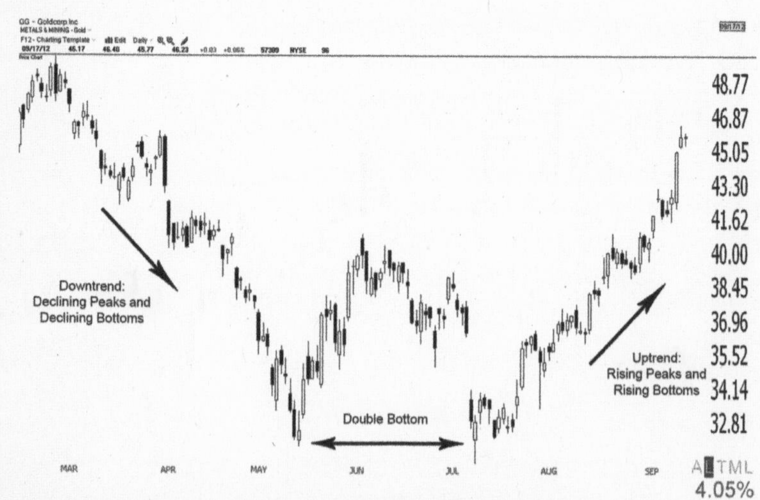

FIGURE 2.7 Peaks and Bottoms Form within a Trend
Source: TC2000® chart courtesy of Worden Brothers, Inc.

many traders), while others will be minor. The prominent formations draw attention to the direction of the trend.

Price pivots also comprise the formation of classic chart patterns that tend to either interrupt (continuation patterns) or reverse (reversal patterns) a trend. For instance, note the double bottom bullish reversal pattern that formed on the chart in Figure 2.7. Two prominent bottoms formed at approximately the same price level, making the pattern very recognizable.

If you look at a triangle or trading range that forms on a chart, you'll see that it is formed from peaks and bottoms as price swings back and forth across the pattern. Those price pivots create the upper and lower boundaries of the consolidation pattern. Head-and-shoulders bottoms and tops are common reversal patterns. The head and the shoulders are comprised of pivots that define the setup of the potential reversal pattern.

Roles of Price Pivots

Price pivots are extremely important in trend analysis. They allow traders to perform tasks such as the following, all of which will be addressed within the chapters of this book:

- Determine the direction of the trend. An uptrend is comprised of rising peaks and rising bottoms; and a downtrend is formed from declining peaks and declining bottoms.
- Draw trendlines to identify the direction, slope, and duration of the trend. Trendlines connect price pivots.
- Identify support and resistance levels that form within trends.
- Recognize when the trend may be losing momentum. For example, a divergence is present; or price is unable to surpass the prior peak (uptrend) or bottom (downtrend).
- Determine when a trend may be changing direction (e.g., price breaks support or resistance).
- Define the precise starting and ending points of a trend.
- Calculate the amount of gain or loss during a trend. That is, determine the distance price traveled either in points or percentage (or both).

Price pivots are also crucial for trade management decisions for many trading strategies. For instance, they may be utilized as setups for entering trades, for determining targets for taking profits, and for setting stop loss orders to protect capital.

Trendlines

One of the simplest tools available to chartists is the trendline. Its simplicity should not diminish its value, though. Trendlines can be very helpful for determining the direction, slope, and length of the trend, as well as alerting to a potential reversal of the trend when an important line is broken. Most charting programs offer a trendline drawing tool among their basic features.

A trendline is drawn touching the turning points of peaks or bottoms as follows:

- Resistance trendline—The downward sloping trendline is drawn across and connecting the declining peaks (numbered 1 through 4 in Figure 2.8) trapping the price action below the line.
- Support trendline—The upward sloping trendline is drawn across and connecting the rising bottoms (numbered 1 through 3 in Figure 2.9) trapping the price action above the line.

There must be at least two peaks or bottoms present in order to draw a resistance or support trendline, respectively. Some chartists require a third touch before they consider the line to be valid. The more times price pivots at/near a trendline, the stronger the line is and the more meaningful when broken.

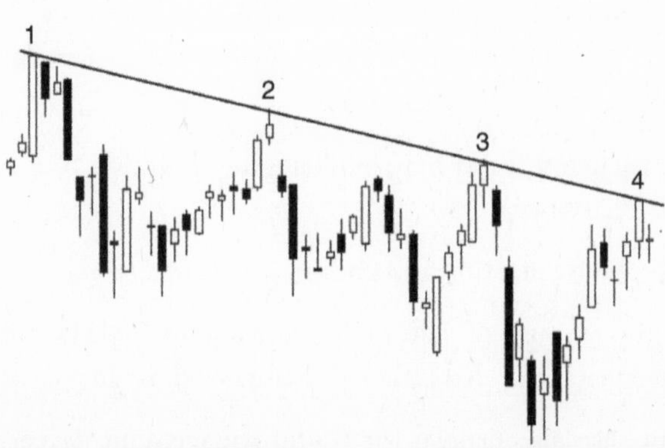

FIGURE 2.8 Resistance Trendline

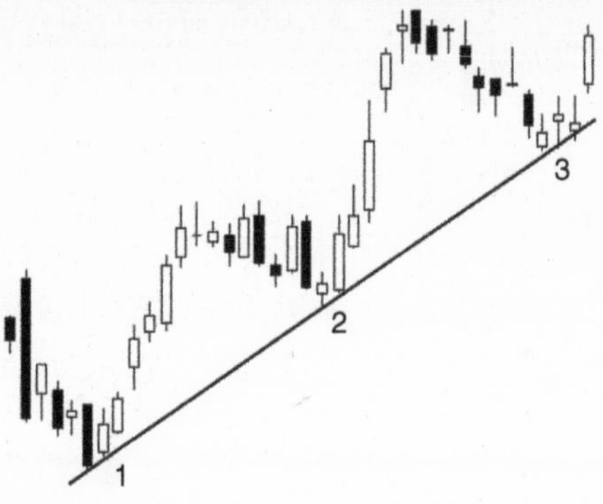

FIGURE 2.9 **Support Trendline**

In most technical analysis texts, the word "trendline" is used in reference to an upward or downward sloping line. However, horizontal lines can also be drawn on charts to identify important support and resistance levels formed by prior peaks and/or bottoms, and extended to the right edge of the chart to identify when price is approaching those levels again. I draw as many, if not more, horizontal lines on charts as sloped lines. Thus, when I refer to the practice of utilizing trendlines, it includes drawing sloped trendlines as well as horizontal support-resistance lines in the chart window for the purpose of assisting with chart analysis. You'll see many examples of both types of lines drawn throughout this text.

External and Internal Trendlines

There are often debates among traders regarding how to draw trendlines. I'd say the most common argument is whether or not to clip the shadows of price bars when touching the lines to the price pivots. An external trendline rests on the *very edges* of the pivots—at the highest point of a peak (Figure 2.10) and the lowest point of a bottom (Figure 2.11). External lines do not cut through any price points. This is the traditional method of drawing trendlines described in many technical analysis books.

An internal trendline rests on the *bodies* of the peaks and bottoms. For a peak, it rests on the top of the highest body in the pivot (Figure 2.10). For a bottom, it touches the bottom of the lowest body in the pivot (Figure 2.11). The line can slice off the shadow(s) of a pivot, but it should not cut through the body of a bar. The shadows represent the extreme prices, or outliers. Many experienced chartists use this method.

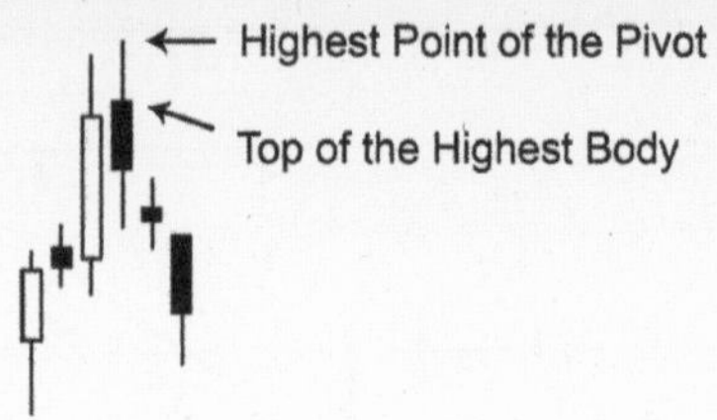

FIGURE 2.10 **Peak**

Note: The body is the boxed area of the candlestick line representing the area between the opening and closing prices. The shadows are the thin, vertical lines above and below the body. The upper and lower shadows represent the distance from the top of the body to the high of the bar and from the bottom of the body to the low of the bar, respectively.

In his book *Getting Started in Chart Patterns* (John Wiley & Sons, 2006, p. 18), Thomas Bulkowski provides the following easy-to-understand distinction: "If the price peak were a hill, an internal trendline would rest on the ground. An external trendline, by contrast, would only connect the tops of the tallest trees."

Figure 2.12 illustrates the difference between an external and internal trendline. Which is best to use? Chartists will argue for their preference. As a general rule, I favor internal trendlines. I feel they show where most of the price action occurred; whereas the edges of the shadows (the external line) represent the extreme prices where there may have only been a few trades executed. However, I consider both lines to be valid; and the area between the two is a zone of support or resistance. As a general rule, though, when

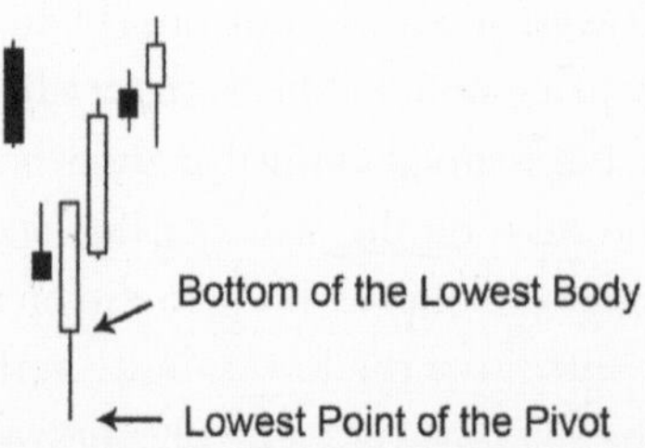

FIGURE 2.11 **Bottom**

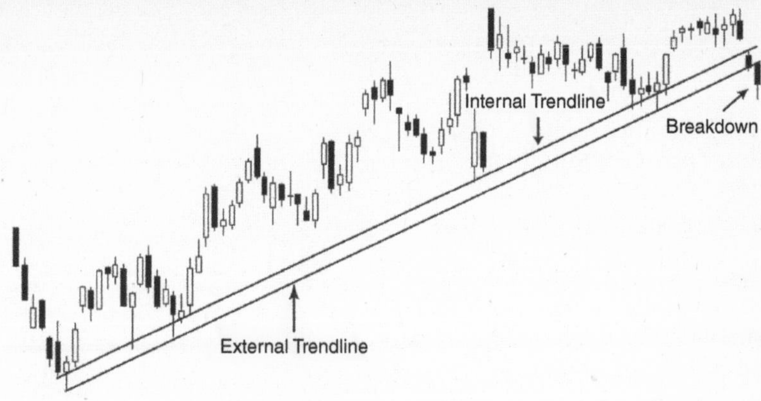

FIGURE 2.12 External versus Internal Trendline

it comes to determining the actual break point, in most cases I'd suggest requiring price close beyond the external line to consider it a valid trendline break—especially when there is not much distance between the two lines as illustrated in Figure 2.12. Doing so puts price clearly outside that zone of support (up trendline) or resistance (down trendline).

■ Moving Averages

Moving averages are trending indicators that are plotted over price. They help take some of the noise out of price movement. Plotting a moving average over price helps to smooth out the fluctuations and distortions that are inherent in most trends and draw the trader's eye to the primary direction of the trend. As a general rule, a rising moving average indicates an uptrend and a declining moving average indicates a downtrend. Think of a moving average as sort of a moving trendline.

The 20-period is a good moving average length to use for the purpose of determining the direction of an intermediate-term or longer trend (other moving average lengths will be discussed later). It is a fairly robust setting and works well on all time frames. During a strong upward move, the 20-period simple moving average (SMA) will be rising most of the time, and vice versa during a decline. When price moves sideways for a prolonged period of time (a trendless phase), the 20-period moving average will move sideways or exhibit a rolling motion until price begins to trend again. The daily chart

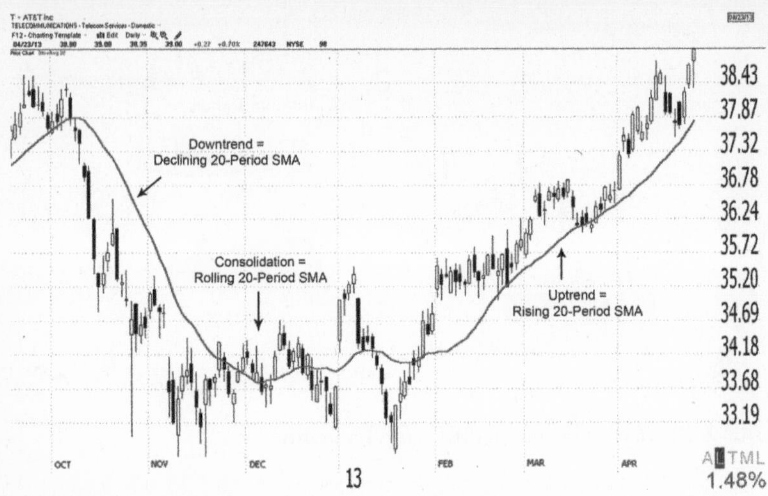

FIGURE 2.13 The 20-Period SMA Helps Identify the Trend Direction
Source: TC2000® chart courtesy of Worden Brothers, Inc.

of AT&T, Inc. (T) in Figure 2.13 illustrates all three scenarios. *Note:* The moving average will lag behind price, so it does not provide precise timing signals for trend reversals.

Another way to use moving averages to determine trend direction is to plot two short-term moving averages over price, for example a 10- and 20-period moving average. During an uptrend, the faster 10-period moving average will remain above the slower 20-period moving average during most of the uptrend, and vice versa in a downtrend. During a trendless phase, the two moving averages will flatten out or roll, so they may intertwine until price begins trending again.

Determining Trend Direction

Since a stock or market may only trend up or down, it might seem as if the direction of the trend should be quite obvious; and often that is the case. However, trends do not develop in a straight line. Rather, price tends to zig and zag its way in the general direction of the longer trend, and may be in transition at the time of analysis.

With the help of price peaks and bottoms, trendlines and moving averages, we have the necessary tools to quickly determine the direction of the trend. The techniques described below can be used to determine the direction of intermediate-term trends and many long-term trends; however, trying to apply them to short-term trends may be futile because short price moves often don't last long enough to form two or more price pivots. You'll learn more about short-, intermediate-, and long-term trends in Chapter 3.

Criteria for an Uptrend

An uptrend can be identified by the technical events listed in Table 2.1.

TABLE 2.1 Criteria for an Uptrend

Peaks and Bottoms	An uptrend is formed from primarily rising peaks and rising bottoms.
Moving Averages	The 20-period moving average will be rising, and price will remain above it, much of the time during the uptrend. If using two short-term moving averages, the faster one (e.g., 10-period) will remain above the slower one (e.g., 20-period) throughout much of the uptrend.
Support Trendline	An upward sloping trendline can often be drawn below and connecting the prominent rising bottoms.

During an uptrend, the upward price swings typically consist of primarily bullish candles. The magnitude of those upswings is usually greater than that of dips that follow; otherwise the uptrend could not continue. If price pulls back deeply enough, price may temporarily decline below the rising 20-period SMA. Price will move back above it when the uptrend resumes. In some cases, a pullback will be deep enough for the moving average to turn down temporarily; it will turn back up as price resumes the uptrend.

There must be at least one new, prominent rising bottom after the stock changes direction from a downtrend to an uptrend before a rising support trendline can be drawn. The trendline should touch the bottom that was the reversal point of the prior downtrend, and a higher bottom (labeled B1 and B2 in Figure 2.14). There may not be one specific price pivot that marks the precise reversal point; instead, there will often be some type of bottoming price action followed by rising bottoms. For instance, price may form a double bottom (see Figure 2.7) or a rounded or rectangular-type bottom before a new uptrend emerges. But at some point, rising bottoms will be present allowing for an up trendline to be drawn.

Figure 2.14 shows a daily chart of Zumiez, Inc. (ZUMZ). The shift from downtrend to uptrend began off the December 2012 bottom (labeled B1). The rising bottoms (labeled B2 through B4) represent the upward shift. The prominent peaks (labeled P1 through P4) are rising. The 20-period simple

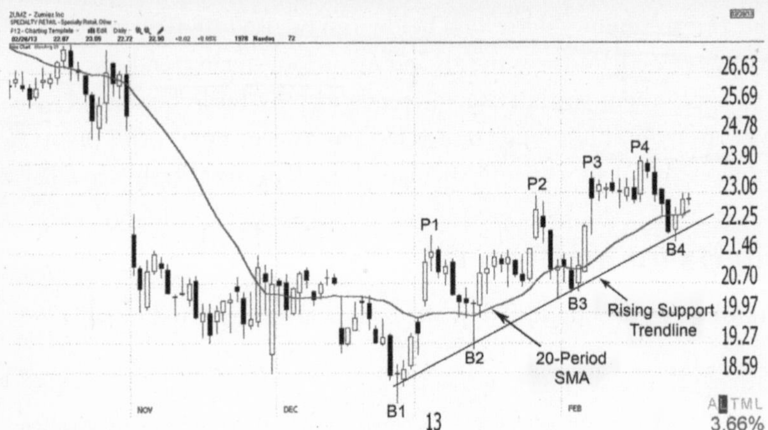

FIGURE 2.14 A Stock in an Uptrend
Source: TC2000® chart courtesy of Worden Brothers, Inc.

moving average (SMA) turned up and is rising. Additionally, a support trendline can be drawn connecting the rising bottoms (an internal trendline is illustrated). In fact, if desired, a parallel resistance trendline could also be drawn across the rising peaks identifying what is referred to as an *ascending price channel*.

Criteria for a Downtrend

A downtrend can be identified by the technical events listed in Table 2.2.

TABLE 2.2 Criteria for a Downtrend

Peaks and Bottoms	A downtrend is formed from primarily declining peaks and declining bottoms.
Moving Averages	The 20-period moving average will be declining, and price will remain below it, much of the time during the downtrend. If using two short-term moving averages, the faster one (e.g., 10-period) will remain below the slower one (e.g., 20-period) throughout much of the downtrend.
Resistance Trendline	A downward sloping trendline can often be drawn above and connecting the prominent declining peaks.

During a downtrend, the downward price swings typically consist of primarily bearish candles. The magnitude of those downswings is usually greater than that of relief rallies (bounces) that follow; otherwise the

FIGURE 2.15 **A Stock in a Downtrend**
Source: TC2000® chart courtesy of Worden Brothers, Inc.

downtrend could not continue. If price bounces high enough, price may temporarily rise above the declining 20-period SMA. Price will move back below it when the downtrend resumes. In some cases, price will bounce strongly enough for the moving average to turn up temporarily; it will turn back down as price resumes the downtrend.

There must be at least one new, prominent declining peak after the stock changes direction from an uptrend to a downtrend before a declining resistance trendline can be drawn. The trendline should touch the peak that was the reversal point of the prior uptrend, and a lower peak. The downward shift may not occur from one specific price pivot; instead, there may be some type of topping price action followed by declining peaks. For instance, in Figure 2.15, price formed a double top before a new downtrend emerged. In that case, the second top of the double top (labeled P1) was the starting point for the down trendline.

Figure 2.15 illustrates a daily chart of Citrix Systems, Inc. (CTXS). The declining peaks (labeled P2 through P4) and declining bottoms (B1 through B3) suggest price is in an intermediate-term downtrend. The 20-period SMA turned from up to down as price reversed direction from the bearish double top pattern that formed at the January and March 2013 highs. A resistance trendline connects the declining peaks.

Note that the down trendline in Figure 2.15 does not quite touch the peak labeled P2. At one time it would have, though. Imagine this chart had you viewed it *before* the peak labeled P3 had formed. At that time, a down trendline would have connected the peaks labeled P1 and P2. However, when peak 3 was formed (P3), that trendline was broken, but price immediately turned down again, requiring the line be adjusted slightly upward to touch that new peak. Otherwise, the line would have been extended downward, cutting through the bodies of the bars in peak 3. It is okay for an internal trendline to clip the *shadows* of one or more price bars, but it should not be drawn through the *bodies* of the price bars.

As a trend evolves, the trendline may need to be adjusted and lengthened, sometimes several times, in order to reflect the current slope and duration of the trend until such time as that trend changes direction. There may also be instances where there is more than one valid trendline. For example, price may be rising at a certain slope and then accelerate upward. That price action may necessitate drawing two trendlines at different slopes. You'll see some examples in later chapters.

Sideways (No Trend)

A sideways move is commonly referred to as consolidation or a trading range. Those trendless phases can be identified by the technical events listed in Table 2.3.

Figure 2.16 illustrates a daily chart of Hornbeck Offshore Services, Inc. (HOS) compressed so several months of data are visible. This uptrend was interrupted by consolidation, in the form of a symmetrical triangle, from November 2011 to mid-January 2012. Converging trendlines were drawn to identify the pattern. The uptrend stalled again during March and April 2012 as price moved sideways for several weeks. Parallel, horizontal lines were drawn in this case to identify the upper and lower boundaries of the trading range. Note how the 20-period simple moving average (SMA) flattened out during those periods of sideways movement.

TABLE 2.3 Criteria for a Trendless Phase

Peaks and Bottoms	There is no clear direction indicated by the peaks and bottoms. The price movement is primarily sideways. Price may be confined within a trading range or a triangle.
Moving Averages	The 20-period moving average will flatten out or move sideways in a rolling motion. If using two short-term moving averages (e.g., 10- and 20-period), they may intertwine as price moves sideways.
Support and Resistance Trendlines	The sideways price movement can often be trapped between support and resistance lines. The lines may be parallel, horizontal lines; or they may be converging if price is forming a triangle.

FIGURE 2.16 Periods of Consolidation within an Uptrend
Source: TC2000® chart courtesy of Worden Brothers, Inc.

Building upon the Basics

Three basic charting concepts were introduced in this chapter: peaks and bottoms, moving averages, and trendlines. Those concepts were used to demonstrate how to determine the direction of a trend, but that is not their only role. As you review each subsequent chapter, you'll see those important tenets of charting come up over and over again (e.g., their roles as support and resistance) as we delve deeper into the process of analyzing trends.

Most of the chapters in this book include references and/or discussion of support and resistance levels. Therefore, you should have a good understanding of what constitutes support and resistance by the time you reach the final chapter.

Some classic chart patterns were illustrated in this chapter: a double bottom (Figure 2.7), a double top (Figure 2.15), a symmetrical triangle, and a trading range (Figure 2.16). You'll see more classic patterns demonstrated throughout this text. However, due to space limitations, and not wanting to veer too far off the primary focus of trend analysis, I've only provided cursory information about specific patterns. If you would like to venture further down this path, I consider Thomas Bulkowski to be one of the most trustworthy sources when it comes to understanding the various chart patterns and testing their efficacy. He has published his extensive testing results in a series of books. For novices, I recommend reading *Getting Started in Chart Patterns* (John Wiley & Sons, 2006) first.

Some instruction on drawing trendlines was included in this chapter, and more tips will follow. I'm an advocate of using sloped trendlines and horizontal support-resistance lines to assist with chart analysis, and both are used extensively throughout this text. However, if I were to really dive into the many nuances and distinctions of using trendlines for analysis, trade selection, and trade management, it would take up a considerable portion of this book and I would have had to exclude some other information I consider to be very important to the topic of trend analysis. Thus, I had to be selective in what information I provided in this publication. Nonetheless, I've included plenty of information on trendlines to provide what is needed for effective trend analysis.

Note: I've written detailed e-books on classic chart patterns and utilizing trendlines. If you wish to find out more about those and other training topics I offer, visit my website at www.tinalogan.com.

CHAPTER 3

Trend Duration

The origins of modern Western technical analysis can be traced back to the work of Charles Henry Dow in the late 1800s. Dow was a businessman, journalist, and member of the New York Stock Exchange. He created the Dow Jones Industrial Average and co-founded Dow Jones & Company. If you have read a few books on technical analysis, you've probably been introduced to Dow Theory in at least one of them. The tenets of Dow Theory have largely stood the test of time.

One of the basic principles of Dow Theory states that the market moves in trends. Dow recognized that trends provide the key to anticipating price movements. He observed three distinct market trends that he categorized by their duration. These classifications of trend duration have been widely accepted in technical analysis:

1. Long-term trend
2. Intermediate-term trend
3. Short-term trend

Trend analysis is a broad topic. It helps to categorize extensive subject matter in order to thoroughly present the information without overwhelming the recipients. In Chapter 2, the categorization was of the trend direction—up, down, or sideways. In this chapter, trends will be categorized by their duration—long, intermediate, and short. You'll learn the definition of these market trends and how to identify them on charts, and gain an understanding of their implications.

■ Long-Term Trend

A long-term trend may also be called the major or primary trend. Dow Theory suggests that a long-term trend is one that lasts up to a year or more. Many traders (including me) consider a trend that has been in force at least six months or longer to fall into this category. Some long-term trends go on for many years. Always assume that the major trend is in force until there is clear evidence to the contrary.

There may be instances when a long-term trend is quite smooth and experiences only brief, minor interruptions; however, that is the exception rather than the rule. More often, a long-term trend is formed as price zigs and zags its way in the general direction of the trend. It is common for a move in the direction of the major trend to be followed by a notable interruption of the trend as illustrated on the daily chart of the Dow Jones Industrial Average in Figure 3.1. The chart has been tightly compressed to show a 15-month span (March 2012 to June 2013) of the bull market that is still in force.

Interruptions of the long-term trend may last from several days to several weeks, and several months in some cases. They may be in the form of a correction where price moves against the long-term trend, or consolidation where price moves mostly sideways. Thus, *most long-term trends are actually strung together by several price moves of shorter duration*. The major trend resumes after each interruption until it finally ends and reverses direction.

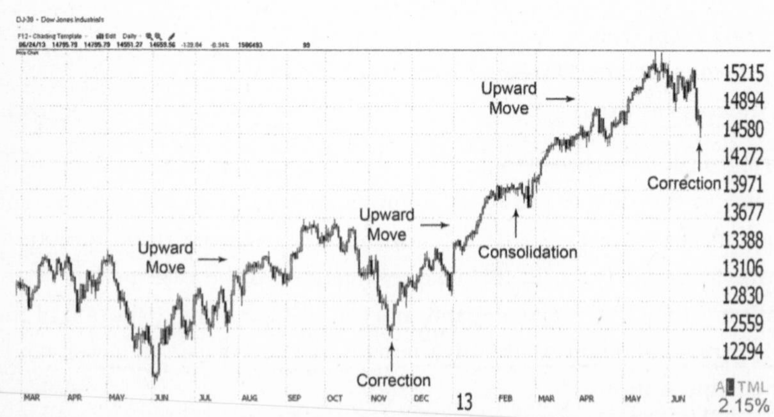

FIGURE 3.1 A Long-Term Uptrend on the Dow Jones Industrial Average
Source: TC2000® chart courtesy of Worden Brothers, Inc.

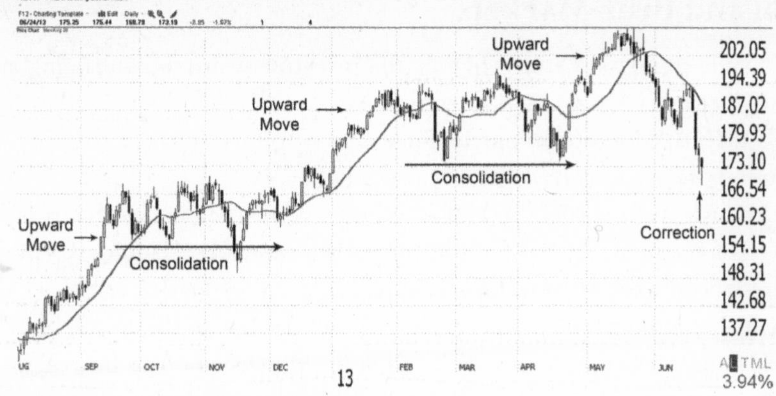

FIGURE 3.2 A Long-Term Uptrend on the Housing Sector Index
Source: TC2000® chart courtesy of Worden Brothers, Inc.

This phenomenon is not only applicable to charts of the major market averages; you'll also see that type of zigzag movement on the charts of other indices, as well as many individual stocks. Look closely at the long-term uptrend of the Philadelphia Housing Sector Index on the daily chart illustrated in Figure 3.2. During the time span shown (August 2012 to late June 2013) there were upward moves and periods of consolidation, each lasting from several weeks to a few months. Note how the 20-period simple moving average flattened out or exhibited a rolling motion during the consolidation phases.

At the right edge of the chart, the index is experiencing a correction of the trend that has lasted five weeks so far. However, if you look across the entirety of the chart, it is clear from the prominent rising peaks and rising bottoms that the index is in a prolonged uptrend. This chart shows the zigzag movement that is common in the formation of major trends.

The major trend is very important to investors who have a long-term focus for their investment portfolios. That's not to say that active traders should ignore the major trend—quite the contrary. Although their activities may be directed toward short- or intermediate-term trends, the long-term trend may have a considerable influence on their trading activities. For instance, the major market trend may dictate which strategy (or strategies) they trade.

Bull and Bear Markets

The major trend shows us whether the investment instrument being analyzed (e.g., a market average, currency, stock, and so on) is in a bull or bear market. Thus, a long-term uptrend may also be referred to as a bull market, and a long-term downtrend as a bear market.

Although we typically think of a bull or bear market as one that remains in force for a prolonged period of time, there may be periodic exceptions where it occurs relatively quickly (e.g., the 1987 stock market crash). Therefore, it should be noted that it is not only the *duration* of the trend, but also its *magnitude* that may encourage its identification as a bull or bear market. For instance, in May and June 2013, the Tokyo Nikkei Index plunged over 20 percent during a period of just 15 trading days. The duration of that decline was not nearly enough to categorize it as a long-term downtrend; however, a decline of 20 percent is widely construed as the dividing line for entering a bear market. Thus, if you were listening to the financial talk shows and/or paying attention to news releases in June, undoubtedly you heard references to the Nikkei entering bear market territory.

Had you looked at the chart several weeks later, though, it showed the sharp selloff bottomed out in mid-June and much of the decline had been recovered by mid-July. In hindsight, it appeared to have behaved more like a market crash with a relatively quick recovery instead of extending deeper into bear market territory. I encourage you to look at the Nikkei's chart periodically to see how it ultimately turns out (the symbol in TC2000 is NIKI-X).

Intermediate-Term Trend

Intermediate-term trends are the building blocks of most long-term trends. Hence, let's first look at the role of intermediate-length trends in that context.

The Intermediate-Term Trend's Role in the Major Trend

It is common for an intermediate-term trend to be identified in many technical analysis books as a movement *against* the major (long-term) trend. A movement against the major trend may also be referred to as a secondary trend, a correction, or a reaction. A major trend may experience a few to several corrections during its lifespan. Now let me be very clear before continuing: I am *not* arguing against this classic definition, but I do wish to expand upon it.

Over the many years that I've analyzed market trends, and also had the privilege of training others to do the same, I've devised my own manner of describing how long-term trends develop. I have found that it helps to look at the long-term trend as one that is typically strung together by a number of intermediate-length movements as follows:

- Extension of the Trend—Price moves *in the direction of* the long-term trend for what would be considered an intermediate-term period of time. This movement extends (lengthens) the major trend. There may be a few to several such movements during the life cycle of a typical long-term trend.
- Correction of the Trend—Price moves *against* the long-term trend for an intermediate-term period of time. That is, price retraces a portion of the prior intermediate-term upward move (bull market correction) or downward move (bear market correction). There may be a few to several of these corrective moves during the life span of a typical long-term trend.

By my definition, the expression "intermediate-term trend" is not restricted to describing a movement against a major trend. Rather, it can also be used to describe a movement in the direction of the major trend.

An intermediate-term trend usually lasts from a few weeks to a few months, and up to several months in some cases. That's a pretty wide range, so I'll clarify: Most of the movements in the direction of the long-term trend tend to last longer than those that correct the trend. I have seen instances where price moves in the direction of the major trend for just a few weeks. However, more frequently those movements that extend the major trend tend to last for a few months; and some may last as long as four to six months (but seldom much longer).

In Chapter 11, you'll find a table showing the duration of each of the 10 completed intermediate-term upward movements I've identified that occurred so far during the current bull market. Only one of those lasted less than a month. It was 19 trading days, and the average trading month includes 21 days. Five of those upward movements lasted from three to about six months. The rest were in the one-to-three-month range.

Chapter 11 also includes a table showing the duration of each of the 10 standard (or deeper) corrections I've identified that have occurred so far during the current bull market. Most of them lasted from three to six weeks. Only two lasted longer than two months. This shows that the intermediate-term movements in the direction of the major trend have tended to last longer, and some were significantly longer, than the market corrections.

Now let's shift the focus from the duration to the *magnitude* of intermediate-term trends. The intermediate-term movements in the direction of the long-term trend tend to be of greater magnitude than those that move against the trend. This must occur regularly or a long-term trend could not evolve—there must be extensions of that trend to further its movement.

When price turns against the trend, it tends to retrace from about one-third to two-thirds of the prior movement. The correction, while it is against the long-term trend's direction, is not typically a correction of the entire long-term trend. Rather, price retraces a portion of the prior intermediate-term upward move (bull market correction) or downward move (bear market correction). Look again at Figure 3.1 and this will be clear.

Figure 3.1 shows an intermediate-term uptrend from June to September 2012 on the Dow, followed by a significant retracement (a bit more than two-thirds) of that trend. That was followed by another intermediate-term uptrend from November 2012 to May 2013, and then a retracement of that trend during May to June.

In addition to corrections against the trend, there may also be instances when price moves primarily sideways for an intermediate-term period of time. Such phases are referred to as consolidation. Consolidation may stall a trend's movement from a few weeks to several months (see Figure 3.2).

If you are wondering why market corrections and periods of consolidation occur, it may help to think of it in this way. During a long-term trend, there will be periods where price moves with the major trend extending it. However, that move gets exhausted on an *intermediate-term basis*. That is, the market gets overbought (uptrend) or oversold (downtrend). It's like pressure building up inside a pipeline.

The market then experiences a setback—a correction against the trend; or price stops for a while and moves sideways allowing the trend to rest. Those corrections and sideways moves serve to alleviate the prior overbought or oversold condition. They relieve much of the pressure that was building up inside the pipeline. This allows price to move again for a while in the direction of the major trend until such time as it becomes overextended again. This can go on and on, sometimes for years. The result is a long-term trend, but it develops through a series of pushes forward and steps back, or sideways shuffles, as illustrated in Figures 3.1 and 3.2.

The Construct of Intermediate-Term Trends

Now let's take a closer look at an intermediate-term trend by itself, rather than in the context of the major trend. Just as many long-term trends are strung together by a series of intermediate-length moves, an intermediate-term trend may be strung together by a series of relatively short price swings. Those short directional moves are separated by brief interruptions of the intermediate-term trend.

Figure 3.3 shows a daily chart of the Philadelphia Housing Sector Index again, but in this example focusing on a several-week period that comprised just one intermediate-term upward leg of that bull market. The uptrend from mid-November 2012 to about mid-February 2013 was comprised of upward swings separated by pullbacks against the prior upward swing, and a sideways move (labeled minor consolidation).

Some chartists may refer to the pullback nearest the right edge of the chart in Figure 3.3 as consolidation. I have no problem with identifying it as such; it just comes down to semantics and reminds us there is some subjectivity in chart analysis. In order to aid in training novices (my primary audience), I find it helps to differentiate between a dip back against the trend and a lateral move. Therefore, I referred to this instance as a pullback because the price action had a slight downward slant.

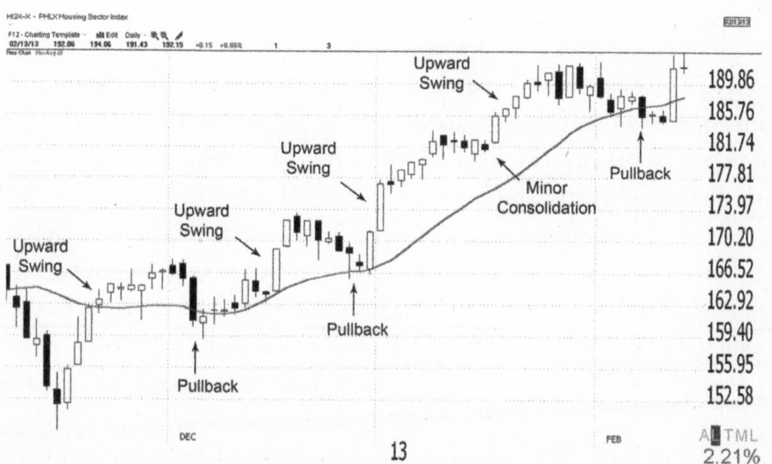

FIGURE 3.3 An Intermediate-Term Uptrend on the Housing Sector Index
Source: TC2000® chart courtesy of Worden Brothers, Inc.

It is rare to see a long-term trend that made its move along a straight path. There is just too much time span for the trend to experience no interruptions along the way. There's more chance of a smooth, uninterrupted run occurring with an intermediate-term trend because it is much shorter in duration. And you will periodically see essentially uninterrupted intermediate-length trends. However, that scenario is not the norm either. There are many swing traders in the marketplace taking profits after short-term price swings. Hence, most intermediate-term trends will develop in sort of a zigzag fashion strung together by a series of short-term moves.

Short-Term Trend

A short-term trend may also be called a minor trend or a swing. It typically lasts from a few days to a couple of weeks, but seldom longer than three weeks. In my experience, the average price swing lasts from about three to five bars before experiencing at least a brief pause. This is a general rule. There will be instances when a price swing lasts longer than average, and there will be shorter than average price swings as well.

The long-term trend shows a big picture view of the market action. The intermediate-term trend takes it a step lower, revealing the movements within the major trend. If you wish to see more detail on how the intermediate-term trend is developing, take the analysis another step lower and study the smaller trends within it. Short-term trends are very important for swing trading.

Short-term price moves are the building blocks of most intermediate-term trends. There may be a few to several short-term movements within an intermediate-term up- or downtrend. A short-term trend can move *in the direction of* the intermediate-term trend (extending it), or it can move *against* the trend (retracing a portion of it). When price moves against an intermediate-term uptrend, it is referred to as a pullback or a dip. When price moves against an intermediate-term downtrend, it is referred to as a bounce or a relief rally. You may also hear it referred to as a short-covering rally since bearish traders covering their positions can fuel a rally.

It doesn't usually take too long before a short-term trend gets exhausted. An upward swing gets overbought, or a downward swing gets oversold, on a *short-term basis.* The intermediate-term trend then experiences a relatively minor setback, or in some cases a period of sideways movement. That minor interruption of the trend serves to alleviate the prior overbought

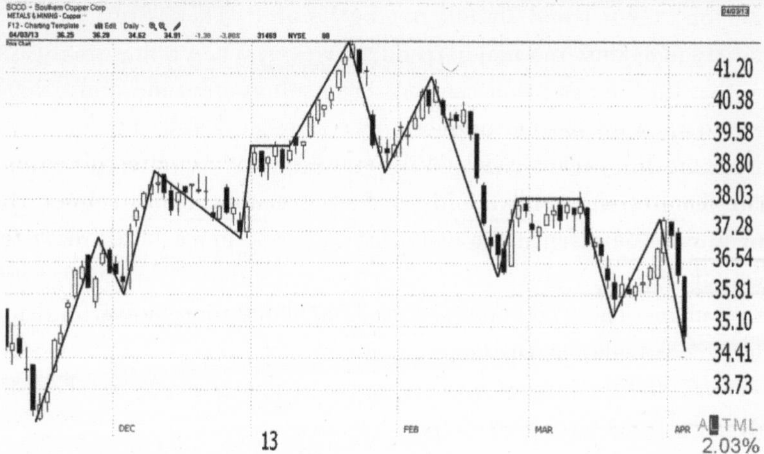

FIGURE 3.4 Short-Term Price Moves within Intermediate-Term Uptrends and Downtrends
Source: TC2000® chart courtesy of Worden Brothers, Inc.

or oversold condition allowing for another price swing in the direction of the intermediate-term trend. The result is an intermediate-term trend that develops through a series of brief pushes forward and minor backward steps or sideways shuffles as illustrated in Figures 3.3 and 3.4.

Figure 3.4 shows a daily chart of Southern Copper Corp. (SCCO). The lines on the chart trace the path of the short-term price moves while the stock was trending up and then down. During the intermediate-length uptrend, the short-term upswings were stronger than the pullbacks and period of consolidation, allowing the uptrend to develop. Likewise, the bounces during the intermediate-length decline were minimal enough to allow the downtrend to continue.

■ Longer Trends Are Dominant

There will be times when you analyze a chart and observe that the three trend lengths—the long-, intermediate-, and short-term—are all moving in the same direction. At other times, there will be conflicting stories among the three trends. For instance, price may be in a short-term decline, with the intermediate-term trend also moving down, but the long-term trend is up (see Figure 3.1).

The long-term trend should not be ignored. That is not to say you cannot trade against the major trend; however, when doing so always be aware that the longer trend can reassert itself at any time. I also suggest paying close attention to support and resistance levels that have developed on the long-term chart. When trading the short-term trend, the intermediate-term trend should not be ignored as it may reassert itself at any time. Pay attention to support and resistance levels within the intermediate-term trend.

In summary: The trend one magnitude higher is more powerful than the shorter trends within it. The long-term trend may override the intermediate-term trend, and the intermediate-term trend may override the short-term trend.

Note: Be aware that when I refer to the "longer trend" during a discussion, I'm not necessarily talking about the long-term trend. For instance, I may refer to a short-term price swing within the longer trend, meaning within the intermediate-length trend, which is longer than a short-term trend. When I am specifically referring to the long-term trend, I will use the term long-term, major, or primary trend.

Trends within a Trading Range

In addition to forming within a longer up- or downtrend, short-term trends are also present when a stock is confined within a trading range as shown on the daily chart of Zimmer Holdings (ZMH) in Figure 3.5. In this case, the intermediate-length move was sideways and comprised of a series of short-term up- and downtrends. The price action can be trapped between an upper resistance line and a lower support line to identify the ceiling and floor, respectively. Because of its shape, a trading range may also be called a horizontal channel or a rectangle.

Price may get trapped in a much wider trading range as shown on the daily chart of Toll Brothers, Inc. (TOL) in Figure 3.6. After a long-term uptrend (not shown), price started trending back and forth in a wide trading range. The dotted lines show the approximate resistance and support levels. The distance from ceiling to floor is about 20 percent. It took from a few to several weeks to complete each traverse across the deep channel. Thus, those are *intermediate-length* up- and downtrends between the channel boundaries rather than the short-term price swings that occurred in the narrower trading range shown in Figure 3.5.

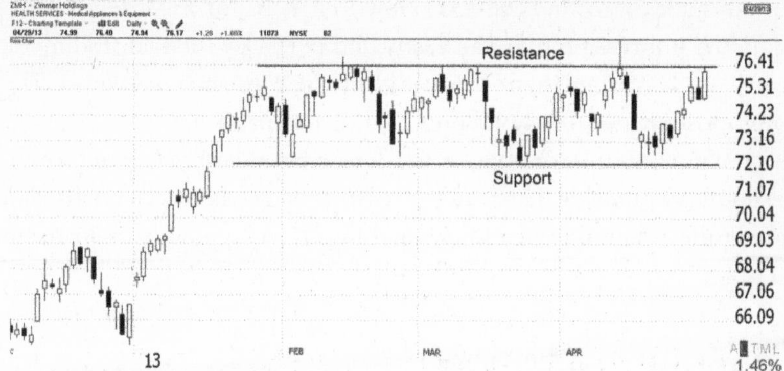

FIGURE 3.5 A Trading Range Comprised of Short-Term Up and Down Moves
Source: TC2000® chart courtesy of Worden Brothers, Inc.

It may take several weeks, or months in some cases, for a stock to move from one side of a wide trading range to the other. In fact, in a standard view on a daily chart (e.g., five to eight months of data), the channel may not even be apparent. It may only be obvious when the daily price bars are compressed tightly to show more data in the chart window (e.g., one to two years), or by shifting the time frame up to a weekly chart.

The examples illustrated in Figures 3.5 and 3.6 are very clear examples chosen in order to make sure readers fully understand the concept

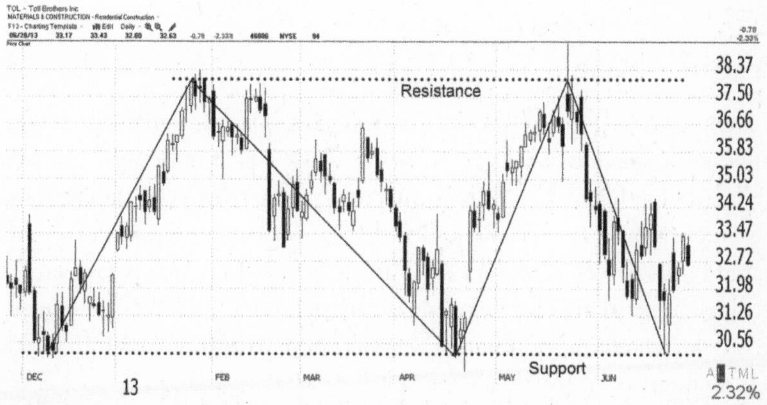

FIGURE 3.6 A Wide Trading Range Comprised of Intermediate-Term Uptrends and Downtrends
Source: TC2000® chart courtesy of Worden Brothers, Inc.

of trend duration in this context. However, it is not my intention to give novices the impression they can easily find perfectly formed trading ranges and just trade within them from bottom to top, and vice versa. Trading ranges are rarely perfectly formed. All of the price action may not be so well contained within the upper and lower boundaries—sometimes price overshoots a boundary. There may also instances where price falls short of reaching the other side of the channel before whipping back in the other direction.

■ Rapid Price Moves

There will be instances where price moves a great distance in a short period of time. Price can make a percentage move that would be equivalent to the distance covered during an intermediate-term trend, or even a long-term trend, within the amount of time that is usually indicated as a short-term trend (e.g., a few days to a few weeks). It is during those swift moves that you may see a smooth, relatively uninterrupted price run.

It may be difficult to draw a trendline across such a steep trend. In some cases, there are not prominent enough price pivots to connect the line because there are only brief pauses interrupting the trend rather than countertrend moves or sideways movements. In some cases, even if a trendline can be drawn, it will be at such an awkward, steep slope that it would cut through the bodies of one or more price bars, making it an invalid line; and/or the line would be so tight it would be prone to false breaks.

Parabolic Rise

Price may make a parabolic or vertical rise. This designation is typically applied to a specific stock, or in some cases a sector or index, that rises rapidly (a significant percentage increase) in a relatively short period of time. Such moves are usually spurred by rumor or news and can be exacerbated by short-term traders exploiting the opportunity. A fast, steep rise occurred on the daily chart of China Dangdang, Inc. (DANG) in Figure 3.7. The stock gained approximately 119 percent from the April 2013 low to the June high.

A parabolic rise may occur without much interruption; and it may appear, at the right edge of the chart, as if it will never stop climbing. You can rest assured, though, that it will eventually stop. Just as trees don't grow to the

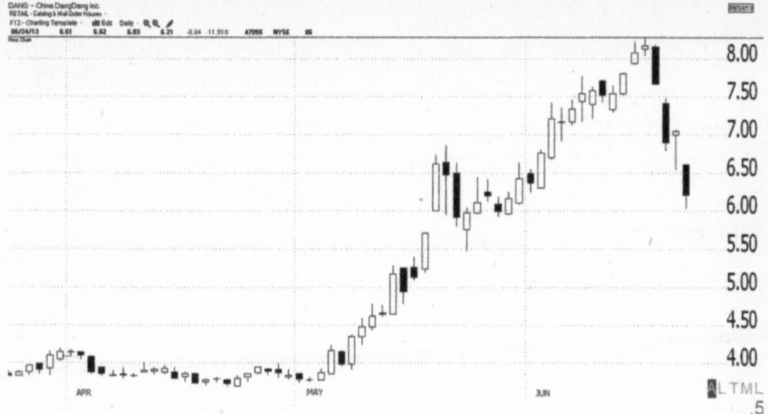

FIGURE 3.7 A Parabolic Rise Followed by a Quick Retracement
Source: TC2000® chart courtesy of Worden Brothers, Inc.

heavens (Jack and the Beanstalk was a fairy tale), a vertical rise cannot be sustained for a long period of time.

Such a swift move up creates a severely overbought condition that must, at some point, be alleviated. Because of the rapid price advance, upon the first signs that the move has run out of steam, astute traders start hitting the sell button in order to lock in their profits. The selloff accelerates as layers of protective sell stop orders are triggered. Thus, a retracement move can be sharp and fast and may result in a significant decline. In Figure 3.7, price retraced about 50 percent of the parabolic move in only four days.

Note: In Figure 3.7, the price scale is set for arithmetic to emphasize the depth of the decline. When price retraces after such a fast move up, if the scale is set for logarithmic it may not appear *visually* that price retraced as much as it did.

A trader who holds a long position in a stock that makes a rapid ascent may consider employing one of the following techniques:

- Proactively exit the entire position (sell into strength) upon the emergence of any indication of a potential reversal. Doing so avoids giving back much of the profits, and also avoids the possibility of severe slippage that may occur when exiting with many other traders during a selloff. If still interested in the stock, watch for a re-entry opportunity once the overbought condition has been alleviated.

- Reduce exposure to a sharp selloff by exiting part of the position to lock in some of the profits. Carefully monitor the protective stop loss order on the remainder of the position. If the rise continues, the trader will benefit with a partial position.

- Remain in the entire position, but trail a stop loss order fairly close to the current price; or shift down to an intraday time frame to manage the stop. A tight stop will be more vulnerable to price manipulation and relatively minor declines in price; however, it will help protect most of the gains achieved during the steep run up. There is still a chance of potentially severe slippage when the stop is triggered.

Volatility is at work here. When a stock accelerates the volatility increases, often dramatically. It may become quite difficult to maintain a close stop loss order when the volatility spikes. A tight stop can easily be triggered by what appears visually to be a minor fluctuation, but when the move is calculated using price percent change, it is actually sizeable on a percentage basis.

The breakdown from a vertical rise may result in a complete reversal of that move (a "pump and dump" scenario); or it may retrace a portion of the prior up move and then start rising again at a more sustainable slope. The initial hype has passed, and cooler heads may now prevail.

Rapid Decline

I've heard it said that stocks fall up to three times faster than they rise; however, I have not seen testing to prove that specific claim. I have observed, though, that stocks do often fall much faster than they rise. This phenomenon becomes very apparent when the broad market declines sharply and a large number of stocks sell off quickly. Traders exit positions, or are stopped out, in order to protect weeks or months of profits. Additionally, traders who sell short into the decline can make quick profits if they get a well-timed entry, assuming they are able to borrow shares to short.

A fast decline may occur due to rumor or the release of news. A rapid decline may also occur after price has made a prior sharp advance (refer to the discussion above on parabolic rises). Figure 3.8 shows a relatively quick 67 percent decline on the daily chart of Infinity Pharmaceuticals, Inc. (INFI). A price advance that took almost five months from November 2012 through March 2013 was wiped out in about two months. The stock fell off a cliff and got shot on the way down!

FIGURE 3.8 A Rapid Price Decline
Source: TC2000® chart courtesy of Worden Brothers, Inc.

Starting and Ending Points of Trends

Price pivots (peaks and bottoms) were introduced in Chapter 2. Pivots mark the starting and ending points of trends as indicated in Table 3.1. Once a trend has ended, it is easy to determine the precise start and end points. However, while a trend is still in force, we don't yet know its ending point. That is to be determined at some point in the future when the trend changes direction again.

TABLE 3.1 Trend Measurement

Trend Duration	Measurement
Long-Term Trend	Measured from one *major* reversal point to the next *major* reversal point. That is, from the prior bear market's closing low to the bull market's final closing high for a major uptrend; and from the prior bull market closing high to the final closing low of the bear market for a major downtrend. For instance, the last bear market on the Dow Jones Industrial Average started from the October 9, 2007, closing high, and ended at the March 9, 2009, closing low.
Intermediate-Term Trend	Measured from one intermediate-term reversal point to the next intermediate-term reversal point. For instance, in a bull market a correction is measured from the prior intermediate-term uptrend's closing high to the correction's closing low (see Figure 3.9).
Short-Term Trend	Measured from one short-term reversal point to the next short-term reversal point. Those points are frequently referred to as a swing high (top of an upswing) and a swing low (bottom of a downswing). For instance, a pullback within an uptrend is from the prior swing's closing high to the pullback's closing low.

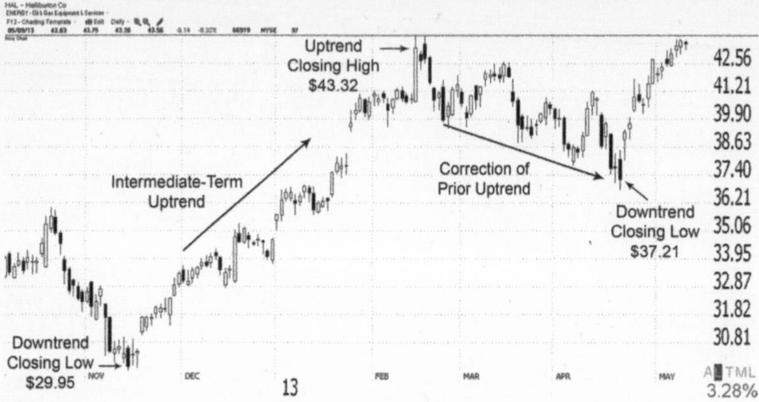

FIGURE 3.9 Price Pivots Identify a Trend's Start and End Points
Source: TC2000® chart courtesy of Worden Brothers, Inc.

Figure 3.9 shows a daily chart of Haliburton Co. (HAL). An intermediate-term uptrend began off the closing low on November 14, 2012, ending three months later at the February 14, 2013, closing high. A correction followed for approximately two months, ending at the closing low on April 19.

Determine a Trend's Percentage Rise or Decline

If you know the starting and ending points of a trend, regardless of whether it is long-, intermediate-, or short-term, you can easily determine the distance price moved during that trend—either in points or as a percentage, or both.

A trend's rise or decline is not typically defined by the extreme highs and extreme lows (the edges of the bars' shadows at start and end points). Rather, it is measured from specific *closing highs and closing lows*. For instance, an uptrend is measured from a specific closing low to a specific closing high, and vice versa for a downtrend (Figure 3.9). If I were to refer to the "April 2013 low" on the chart of Haliburton, I'd mean the lowest close bar of the correction rather than the very low of the lowest shadow at the bottom of the correction.

When determining how far a stock or a market has moved during a specific period of time, traders use the price percent change (PPC) method. For instance, to measure the percentage decline of the correction on Haliburton Co., use the following two values:

1. The closing high of the highest peak prior to the start of the correction = \$43.32 on February 14, 2013.
2. The closing low of the lowest bottom marking the end of the correction = \$37.21 on April 19, 2013.

To convert that decline to a percentage requires some simple math:

- Subtract the closing low of \$37.21 from the closing high of \$43.32 for a difference of 6.11 points.
- Divide the result of 6.11 by the closing high of \$43.32 to get the percentage decline: 43.32 – 37.21 = 6.11/43.32 = 14.10 percent.

Your charting software may provide a tool that makes it easy to quickly make such a determination. In TC2000 (version 7), the "custom date sort" tool can be used to quickly calculate the price percentage change from the close of one specific price bar to another.

Figure 3.10 shows the chart of Haliburton Co. again applying the custom date sort. This tool allows users to simply press the letter *C* on the keyboard, click on a specific bar, and drag the line across the price bars to another location on the chart. Once the mouse is released, the range of bars used in the calculation is clearly identified on the chart with two vertical

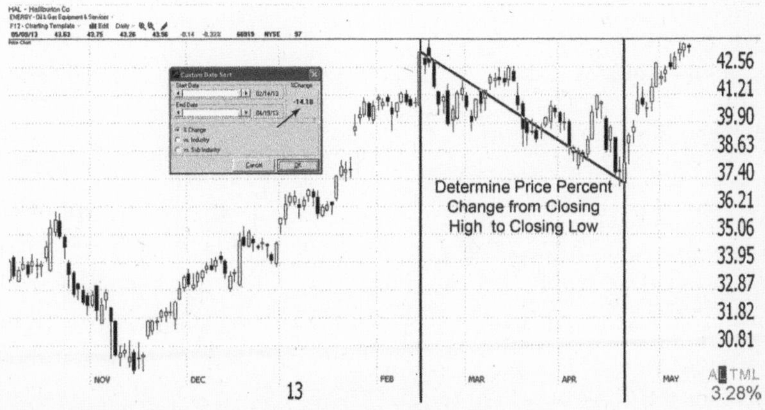

FIGURE 3.10 A Decline Measured Using Price Percent Change
Source: TC2000® chart courtesy of Worden Brothers, Inc.

lines connected by a diagonal line. A pop-up box also shows the specified date range, along with the price percent change during that period. As you can see, using this feature calculates the percentage decline on the chart as 14.10 percent, just as our manual calculation indicates. But it is much faster to use the custom date range tool.

Note: In Chapter 11, tables are provided showing the percentage rise and decline of the intermediate-term trends that have occurred during the current bull market. Those percentages were acquired using the PPC tool described above.

Determine a Trend's Progress While a trend is still in force, traders may wish to monitor its progress (the percentage rise or decline to date). For instance, Figure 3.11 shows the S&P 500 Index during December 2012 as it appeared at the right edge of the chart at that time. After a correction of several weeks, the S&P 500 had turned back up and appeared to be well into the next leg up of the bull market. If you had wanted to know how far the S&P 500 Index had risen from the correction low, you could have run a price percent change calculation using the most recently formed bar's closing high and the closing low of the correction. In this case, the S&P 500 Index had risen 6.91 percent since the end of the correction.

You may be wondering, "How is this helpful to me?" I'm glad you asked. It can be used to compare the move, to date, of a stock or index to that of another stock or index, or to a list of symbols. For instance, let's go back in time when I was watching the market in real time on December 18, 2012. I wanted to see which S&P sectors were *leading upward* at that

FIGURE 3.11 Determine the Percentage Advance of a Trend That Is under Way
Source: TC2000® chart courtesy of Worden Brothers, Inc.

TABLE 3.2	SPDRs Sector ETFs	
Sector	**Symbol**	**Exchange-Traded Fund**
Consumer Discretionary	XLY	SPDRs Select Sector Consumer Discretionary ETF
Consumer Staples	XLP	SPDRs Select Sector Consumer Staples ETF
Energy	XLE	SPDRs Select Sector Energy ETF
Financials	XLF	SPDRs Select Sector Financial ETF
Healthcare	XLV	SPDRs Select Sector Healthcare ETF
Industrials	XLI	SPDRs Select Sector Industrial ETF
Materials	XLB	SPDRs Select Sector Materials ETF
Retail	XRT	SPDR S&P Retail ETF
Technology	XLK	SPDRs Select Sector Technology ETF
Utilities	XLU	SPDRs Select Sector Utilities ETF

particular point in the market's rise. I activated a watchlist I created, shown in Figure 3.11, which includes the symbols of the exchange-traded funds (ETFs) that track the 10 main sectors of the economy. It includes the symbols listed in Table 3.2.

After using the custom date sort feature to determine how far the S&P 500 Index had risen at that point (+6.91 percent as of December 18), clicking the OK button in the dialog box quickly applied the calculation for that range of dates against all the symbols in the active watchlist. The result of the above steps is shown in Figure 3.12. The price percent change from November 15 through December 18, 2012, for each of the S&P sector ETFs is displayed in the Sort Value column in the watchlist window. As you can see, the Financials and Industrials were leading the pack of sectors at that point with percentage rises of 9.16 and 8.58 percent, respectively.

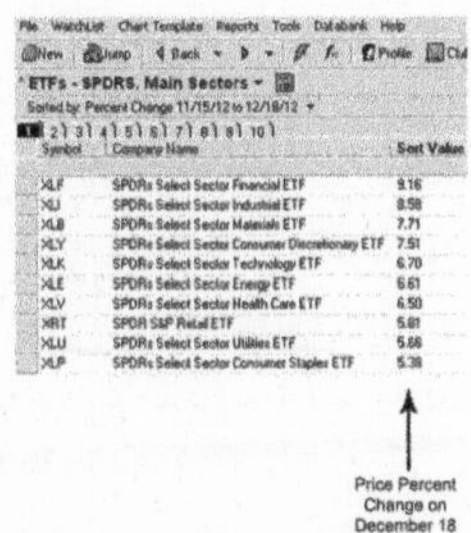

FIGURE 3.12 Price Percent Change Applied to Market Sectors
Source: TC2000® courtesy of Worden Brothers, Inc.

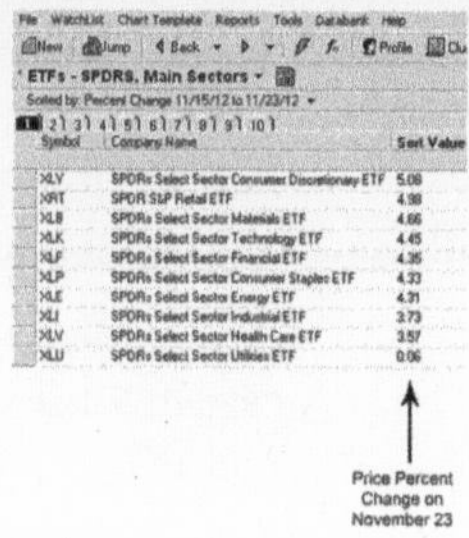

FIGURE 3.13 Price Percent Change Applied to Market Sectors
Source: TC2000® courtesy of Worden Brothers, Inc.

Had I run this calculation, say, on November 23, 2012, much earlier in the new up move, at that time the S&P 500 Index was up 4.12 percent and the top two sectors were Consumer Discretionary and Retail showing percentage rises by that date of 5.08 and 4.98 percent, respectively, as illustrated in Figure 3.13.

Using this technique, at any time during a market's rise or decline, you can check the price percent change to determine which sectors are leading and which are lagging. For instance, as of November 23, with the S&P 500 Index up over 4 percent, the Utilities were only up .06 percent, barely in positive territory and clearly lagging the other sectors.

Let's come back to the present now. At the time I was completing a final review of this book for publication (July 2013), another correction had ended and the bull market was well into its next leg up. Since the time it had become clear to me that a new intermediate-term up move was likely under way (you'll learn how I make that interpretation later), I began running the PPC calculation indicated above on a regular basis to monitor the leading and lagging sectors. As of July 19, the S&P 500 Index was up 7.56 percent from the June correction low. The Financials were in the lead with a rise of 10.44 percent, and Technology was at the end of the pack with a rise of only 4.31 percent.

Monitoring sectors and industry groups is an important part of my routine. It allows me to see where the money is flowing in the marketplace. That is, to see which stocks, or groups of stocks, are in a leadership role and to identify when money rotates from one group to another. Hence, this is a tool I find very useful. The watchlist shown in Figure 3.11 includes only the ETFs that act as a proxy for the main sectors of the economy. I also use this technique on other watchlists, such as those of industry groups, indices, stocks, and longer lists of ETFs.

Once you start analyzing trends as part of your regular trading routine, you may frequently want to measure the distance of a decline or advance. Therefore, if you are not sure if your charting platform has a similar price percent change (PPC) calculator as the one illustrated above, I advise contacting your provider to inquire. If it does not, the calculations can be done manually by calculator or using a spreadsheet, but it will be more time consuming and less convenient.

A Note about the Shadows It is a common practice to measure a trend from its closing high to its closing low, and vice versa, as demonstrated above. The movement that creates an upper shadow at a peak, and/or a lower shadow at a bottom, are excluded from the PPC calculation. But that does not mean shadows have no relevance. A shadow may be very meaningful to a swing trader. For instance, a stock may close well off its high, leaving a long upper shadow at the top of an upswing. However, during the trading session, at one point that long upper shadow was a long bullish candle. A swing trader holding a long position may have exited into strength while the bar was strongly bullish, and recognized more profits (in some cases significantly more) than a swing trader who waited to take action until the candle body had changed to that of a long upper shadow.

To see an example of this scenario, look at the daily chart for Immunomedics, Inc. (IMMU) in your own charting platform. On July 16, 2013, a bearish Shooting Star formed at the end of an upswing. Price had already formed two long bullish candles in the days prior. Therefore, by the time a third long bullish candle formed (intraday), the stock was overbought on a short-term basis. Some traders chose to lock in profits early in the day. If you were to look at the 15-minute chart for that day, you'd see that the stock reached its high during the first 45 minutes of trading and it was downhill from there. By the close of market, IMMU was almost 10 percent off its high set early in the day.

Swing traders who sold IMMU early during that session recognized much more profit than those who exited near the close of market when the Shooting Star was apparent. Thus, you won't convince a savvy swing trader that upper and lower shadows are not relevant. There was the potential for a lot of extra profits in that particular upper shadow on IMMU, even though a PPC calculation using closing prices would not have revealed it.

For another example showing the relevance of a long shadow, view the charts of the major averages on May 6, 2010. You'll see a very long lower shadow. That was the day of the Flash Crash, when the Dow declined about

1,000 points intraday before recovering much of that decline by the close of market. That long lower shadow tells an important story about the intraday activity.

Drawing Trendlines

Since there are varying lengths of trends, it makes sense that trendlines can be drawn to identify the slope and length of those trends. At least that is the case for most long- and intermediate-term trends. For many short-term trends, a valid trendline cannot be drawn because the trend does not last long enough for two price pivots to form, which is the minimum requirement to draw a trendline.

Note: Recall from Chapter 2 the discussion of external versus internal trendlines. The trendlines in the examples below are internal lines.

Long-Term Trendlines

The long-term trendline starts at the price pivot that marked the reversal of the prior major trend. When analyzing a trend that occurred in the past, the start and end points will be obvious. However, when analyzing a trend as it evolves from the right edge of the chart, during the early stages of a new long-term trend, *it won't actually be a long-term trend yet*. Remember, a long-term trend typically isn't labeled as such until has been in force for at least six months. Hence, at first it will appear to be just another intermediate-term correction against the major trend, as illustrated in Figure 3.14. Because of this, the first trendline drawn on what ultimately becomes a long-term trend will typically be an intermediate-length trendline.

That trendline may be broken during the first significant correction or period of prolonged consolidation that forms within what will ultimately be recognized as a new major trend. Once that correction or consolidation ends, and price makes another move extending the prevailing trend, a new upward or downward sloping trendline can be drawn to represent the current slope and length of the up or down trend, respectively. Eventually, you'll have a long-term trendline drawn as the major trend continues to evolve.

Figure 3.14 shows a tightly compressed daily chart of United Community Banks (UCBI). The first several weeks of this long-term uptrend were actually an intermediate-term up leg against the prior downtrend. A trendline (numbered 1) representing that move up was drawn across the prominent rising bottoms. Price consolidated for three months, breaking the intermediate-term up trendline. Once the consolidation ended and price resumed the uptrend, a new up trendline was drawn (2) representing the new length and slope of the trend. The line was continually extended upward until it was broken during a correction of the uptrend. Once the correction ended and price began to move up again, a new up trendline (3) was drawn to represent the current length and slope of what is now clearly a long-term uptrend. That line will continually be extended upward as the trend goes on until it is broken at some point in the future.

If viewing a long-term trend on the daily chart, it is usually necessary to compress the bars so that over a year of price data can be seen in the window, as illustrated in Figure 3.14. The longer the major trend goes on, the harder it will be to analyze it effectively, or draw long-term trendlines, using the daily chart. The chart would need to be very tightly compressed in order to see the entire duration of the trend. When the chart is compressed so tightly, it becomes a challenge to determine the closing highs and lows at the turning points, and precisely where to connect the long-term trendline. Thus, once the major trend exceeds about a year in length, to gain a full perspective of the duration and slope of the trend, it is often easier to shift up to the weekly chart.

The peaks and bottoms that identify the direction of the long-term trend on the weekly chart are the significant turning points within the trend.

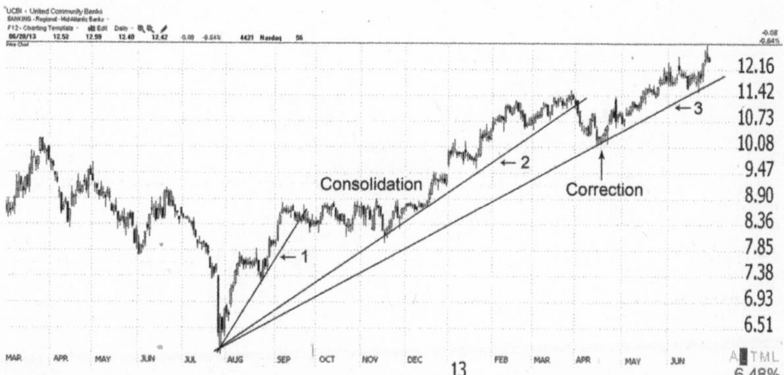

FIGURE 3.14 Trendlines Are Broken and New Trendlines Drawn as the Long-Term Uptrend Evolves

Source: TC2000® chart courtesy of Worden Brothers, Inc.

Recall that most long-term trends are strung together by intermediate-term trends and periods of consolidation. Therefore, in a major uptrend, the rising peaks are the tops of the intermediate-term up legs within the major trend. The rising bottoms are the lows of the corrections or the ends of the periods of consolidation.

Figure 3.15 shows a weekly chart of the SPDRs Select Sector Utilities ETF (XLU). The bottoms used to connect the up trendline are the lows of the significant corrections that have occurred during the past several years of the bull market. *Note:* The very long lower shadow in mid-2010 was from the Flash Crash that occurred on May 6, 2010 (more on that event later).

As the long-term uptrend continues to evolve, the long-term trendline will need to be continually extended up and to the right to reflect the current length of the trend. Additionally, it may need to be adjusted upward or downward periodically to reflect changes to the slope of the trend as additional extension moves and corrections or consolidation phases occur. There may be cases where there is more than one valid long-term trendline of differing slopes. For instance, there may be a very loose trendline and a tighter line drawn if the slope of the trend shifts markedly upward during its evolution.

For long-term downtrends, the first leg down of what ultimately becomes a major trend will appear to be a bull market correction. The first

FIGURE 3.15 A Long-Term Up Trendline Drawn on the Weekly Chart
Source: TC2000® chart courtesy of Worden Brothers, Inc.

FIGURE 3.16 The Tighter Trendline Represents the Current Slope of the Trend
Source: TC2000® chart courtesy of Worden Brothers, Inc.

down trendline will be an intermediate-length line. It will be adjusted and extended (or redrawn) as the downtrend continues its decline, eventually becoming a long-term trendline. There may be more than one valid long-term down trendline as illustrated on the weekly chart of Swift Energy Company (SFY) in Figure 3.16.

For a major downtrend, you may need to shift to the weekly chart to draw the primary trendline. The declining troughs on the weekly chart are the bottoms of the intermediate-term down legs within the bear market. The declining peaks are the tops of the bear market corrections or ends of the periods of consolidation.

Intermediate-Term Trendlines

Recall that many intermediate-term trends are actually strung together by short-term price movements. An intermediate-length up trendline starts at the lowest price pivot of that trend (numbered 1 in Figure 3.17). The rising bottoms used for connecting the support trendline are the prominent price pivots (pullbacks) and periods of minor consolidation formed during the intermediate-term trend (labeled 2 through 5 in Figure 3.17).

There may be more than one trendline that identifies an intermediate-term trend. The trend may move along at a certain slope for a period of time and then accelerate. When that occurs, I draw a second trendline representing the new slope of the trend, as illustrated on the daily chart of TECO

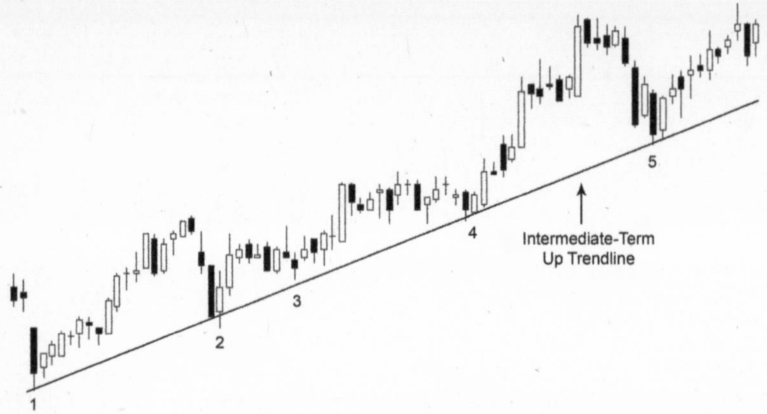

FIGURE 3.17 An Intermediate-Term Up Trendline

Energy, Inc. (TE) in Figure 3.18. The tighter line was more indicative of the more recent price action and was broken quickly as price pulled back. Soon after breaking the trendline, a bearish double top formed and was confirmed. It took a significant retracement before the looser trendline was broken.

When the trend accelerates and a tighter trendline is drawn, it may become quite steep depending on how the uptrend evolves. When that

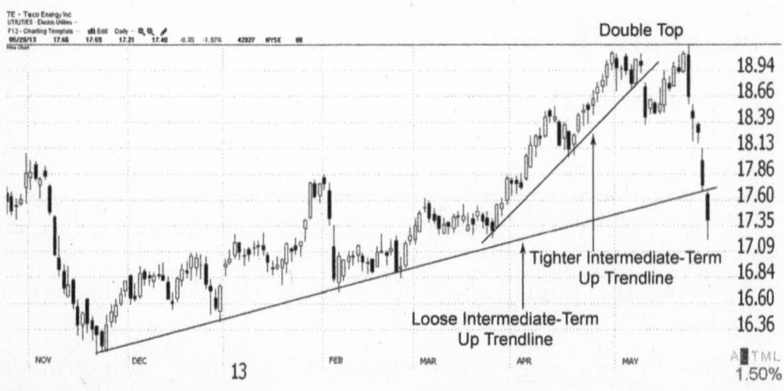

FIGURE 3.18 A Tighter Intermediate-Term Trendline Was Drawn When the Trend Accelerated Upward

Source: TC2000® chart courtesy of Worden Brothers, Inc.

FIGURE 3.19 Intermediate-Term Down Trendlines
Source: TC2000® chart courtesy of Worden Brothers, Inc.

occurs, the line may be quickly broken when a correction begins. Even just a pullback or shift to sideways movement can break a tight line. When it is broken, it may not be a correction starting but just due to a deeper than normal pullback (or even a minor pullback if the line is very tight); or enough sideways movement to break it. Hence, a tight line is susceptible to false breaks. Price may just penetrate the line by a bit and then move again in the direction of the intermediate-term trend. When that occurs, adjust the line to the new slope and length of the trend.

Note: The loose and tight trendlines described above should not be confused with the concept of internal versus external trendlines.

For an intermediate-term downtrend, the declining peaks used to connect the downward-sloping resistance trendline are the tops of the swing highs (the bounces) or the ends of the periods of minor consolidation formed within the downtrend, as illustrated in Figure 3.19. On the daily chart of U.S. Steel Corp. (X) in Figure 3.19, the tighter trendline represents the acceleration of the downtrend. Both lines were broken during May 2013. In June, price tested the May low setting up a potential bullish double bottom pattern. A typical long-term trend will have several intermediate-length trends within it. Therefore, during the life cycle of a major trend, there may be many intermediate-term trendlines drawn and broken.

Short-Term Trendlines

A short-term trend typically lasts from only a few days to a couple of weeks. Thus, it may not be possible to draw a trendline for such a short

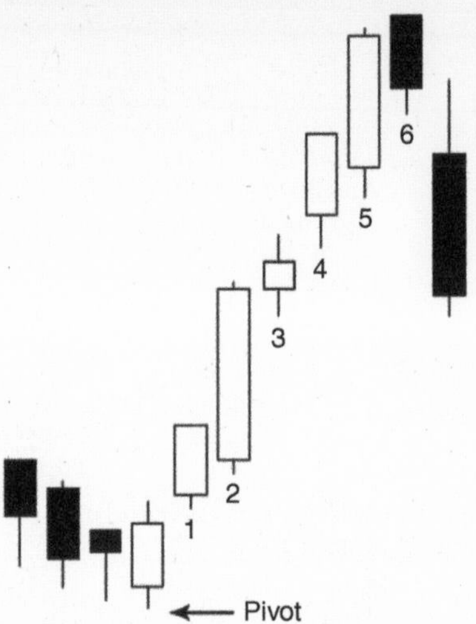

FIGURE 3.20 A Short-Term Trendline Cannot Be Drawn

trend because two price pivots are required to draw the line. Some short-term trends do not even include enough price bars to form two pivots before price changes direction again. Figure 3.20 shows a short-term uptrend with one pivot at the bottom of the upswing. Price formed higher lows from one bar to the next for several days (numbered 1 through 6), then reversed direction, ending that upswing without having formed a higher bottom.

The illustration in Figure 3.21 also shows a short-term uptrend. In this case, a minor pivot did form within the uptrend, allowing a trendline to be drawn. When a short-term trendline can be drawn, it will usually be quite tight because it represents a minor trend. A tight trendline can be broken quickly. It doesn't take much to break such a tight line—often just a minor pullback or period of brief consolidation (e.g., a flag).

A swing trader will typically attempt to profit on the short-term price swings and exit before price reverses direction and takes back part, or all, of those profits. Therefore, a swing trader may utilize short-term trendlines when they can be drawn. A break of a short-term trendline indicates the upswing or downswing may be ending.

A trader who wishes to monitor a trendline on a short-term trend that does not have two price pivots on the *daily* chart may be able to do so using an *intraday* chart. There are more data points on intraday time frames. That increases the likelihood that price pivots will be visible within the trend on

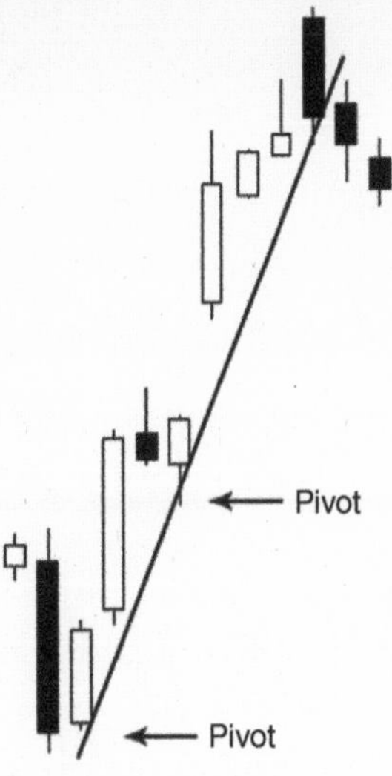

FIGURE 3.21 A Tight Short-Term Up Trendline

that time frame. This brings up the concept of trends within trends, which is described below in more detail.

Trends within Trends

A price *swing* on one time frame is a *trend* on a lower time frame. The price *value* is the same on both time frames, but the *appearance* of the price move is different due to the number of price bars that form during the move. For instance, one price bar on a weekly chart reflects the cumulative price action of five trading days on a daily chart. If price moved up for six consecutive weeks on a weekly chart, it would be a short-term uptrend relative to that time frame. That same upward movement, if viewed on the daily chart, would include 30 price bars forming an intermediate-term uptrend on that time frame.

Let's take that concept down to intraday time frames. Intraday time increments range from hourly (the highest intraday measure) down to the tick (the lowest intraday measure). Table 3.3 indicates the number of bars per day on the most commonly used intraday time frames. Like a daily bar, a candlestick viewed on any intraday time frame (except tick) represents the open, high, low, and close. Those price points are relative to that time frame. For example, the open of an hourly bar is the first price of that hour. The

TABLE 3.3 Intraday Time Frames

Time Frame	Number of Bars per Day
60-Minute (Hourly)	7
30-Minute	13
15-Minute	26
10-Minute	39
5-Minute	78
1-Minute	390
Tick	Reflects each movement in price

high and low are the highest and lowest points achieved during that hour. The close is the last price of that hour.

An upward price swing of six bars on a daily chart would be an upward trend of 42 bars (6 × 7) on the hourly chart—an intermediate-length trend on that time frame. It would be an upward trend of 156 bars (6 × 26) on the 15-minute chart—a long-term trend on that lower intraday time frame. Again, each chart reflects the same distance traveled in points/percentage; but the label we'd put on that trend's duration is different for each of the time frames because of the number of bars included in the price move.

Using this concept—that a swing move on one time frame equals a trend on a lower time frame—consider the following:

- The end of an upswing (the swing high) on one time frame is the reversal of an intermediate- or long-term uptrend on lower time frames.
- The end of a pullback (the swing low) during an uptrend on one time frame is the reversal after a correction on lower time frames.

Figure 3.22 shows a two-chart layout of Merrimack Pharmaceuticals, Inc. (MACK) with the daily chart on the left and the hourly chart on the right. The dotted lines on the daily chart identify a short-term upward swing followed by a pullback against the trend. On the hourly chart, there are several bars in a day. Therefore, the same upward swing between the dotted lines looks like an intermediate-term uptrend on that time frame. The pullback on the daily chart looks like a correction of the uptrend to a trader viewing the hourly chart.

As mentioned previously, it is not possible to draw a short-term trendline when there are not two pivots for connecting the line on the daily chart. However, it may be possible to draw a trendline representing that price

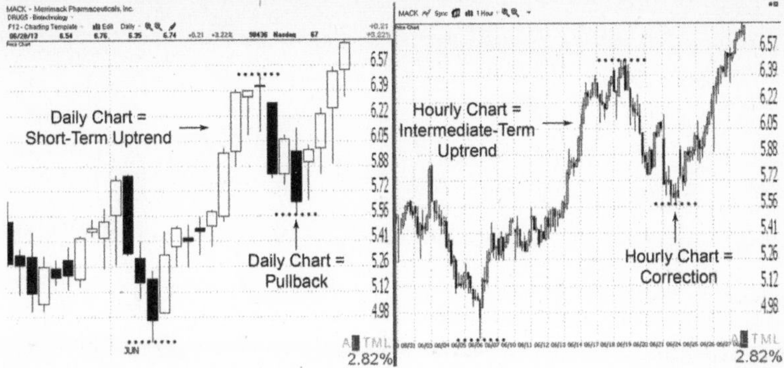

FIGURE 3.22 Daily Price Swings Look Like Intermediate-Term Trends on the Hourly Chart
Source: TC2000® chart courtesy of Worden Brothers, Inc.

move on an intraday chart. Figure 3.23 shows a two-chart layout of Body Central Corp. (BODY) with the daily chart on the left and the hourly chart on the right. The dotted lines on each chart represent the five-day upward swing—a short-term uptrend on the daily chart but an intermediate-term uptrend on the hourly chart. Note that there were pullbacks on the hourly chart, creating the price pivots needed to draw an upward-sloping support trendline. The trendline can be extended upward periodically as long as the trend is in force. When price starts to pull back (or move sideways) on the daily chart, the hourly trendline will be broken.

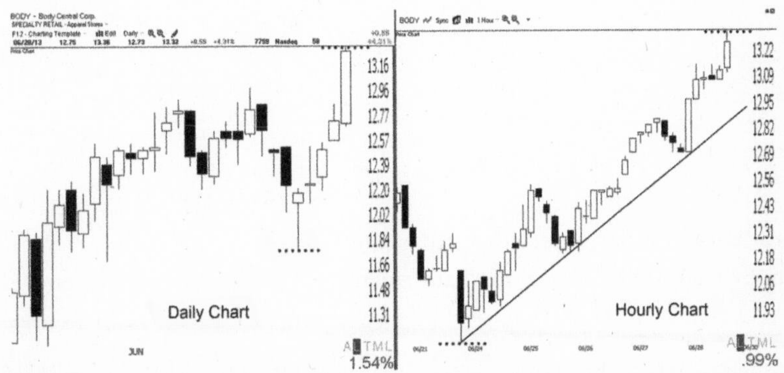

FIGURE 3.23 A Swing Up on the Daily Chart May Be Monitored on a Lower Time Frame
Source: TC2000® chart courtesy of Worden Brothers, Inc.

CHAPTER 4

Trend Interruptions

As illustrated in Chapter 3, a trend does not develop in a straight line. A typical intermediate- or long-term trend is strung together by shorter moves within it. Thus, a trend may be punctuated with one to several recognizable events within its lifespan that serve to interrupt its movement for a period of time. Those events become part of the chart landscape, thereby influencing your analysis, and they may offer opportunities to position yourself for potential price moves.

Unfortunately, there is not a standard set of labels that I am aware of used to classify the various trend interruptions that occur. For instance, when reference is made to consolidation, a trader may be referring to a very brief sideways move (e.g., a couple of days). Another trader may use that term to refer to several days of sideways movement; and yet another refers to several weeks or more of sideways movement as consolidation. While those are all forms of consolidation, following are some important differences between the events:

- The duration of the consolidation.
- The magnitude of the interruption.
- Its role in a trend's development.
- The screening method used to find the formation if utilizing it for trading setups.
- The techniques used to manage trades that are impacted by, or based on, the formation.

TABLE 4.1 **Trend Interruptions**	
Minor Interruptions	**Larger Interruptions**
Pause	Correction
Base	Consolidation
Pullback (Uptrend)	
Bounce (Downtrend)	

In order to help aspiring traders recognize the interruptions that may occur within trends, I have categorized and labeled them as indicated in Table 4.1. I distinguish them as either minor or larger trend interruptions based on their duration, magnitude, and the role they play in the development of an intermediate- or long-term trend. In this chapter, we'll take a close look at these technical occurrences so you can learn to easily identify them and implement them into your trading strategies.

The trend interruptions listed in Table 4.1 are common occurrences and can be observed in trends that occur on all time frames. You'll see these technical events referenced many times throughout the rest of this text. Understanding them, and learning to spot them as they occur in real time, will improve your chart analysis, trade selection, and trade management skills. The emergence of a trend interruption may impact an open position; or it might create an opportunity to initiate a new trade.

What contributes to the occurrence of these events? Recall from Chapter 3 the discussion of how trends tend to get exhausted. For instance, after a few to several days of directional movement, a short-term trend tends to get overbought (upward swing) or oversold (downward swing) on a *short-term basis*. That's when a minor interruption of the intermediate-term trend may occur. It usually doesn't take much to alleviate the overextended condition—often just a minor setback or brief period of sideways movement—after which the intermediate-term trend may resume.

After several weeks to a few months of trending up or down, price tends to get overbought or oversold, respectively, on an *intermediate-term basis*. It often takes a more significant countertrend move or a longer period of consolidation to alleviate that overextended condition. That's when a larger interruption of the major trend may occur.

Minor Trend Interruptions

Minor disruptions of a trend are very common. A minor interruption may take the form of a quick pause, a small base (period of minor consolidation), or a move against the trend. These events occur during intermediate-length trends, allowing the trend to take a rest before continuing on. They are healthy for the trend's development. The fact that the market is able to consolidate the gains, and then move again extending the prevailing trend, is a testament to the trend's strength.

These events tend to occur between price swings and are meaningful to short-term traders. They may impact a swing trader's decision making for open positions, or create opportunities to take new trades. For instance, rather than chasing an upward swing by entering when price may already be quite overbought (a common mistake novices make), a swing trader may choose to wait for a better opportunity when the uptrend stalls. He may monitor the price action to see if price pulls back or consolidates for a few to several days. This allows for a safer entry with a relatively close initial protective stop offering a better reward-to-risk opportunity.

In the context of the major (long-term) trend, minor interruptions don't usually have a significant impact on the trend's progress. However, they may provide opportunities relative to core positions, which are trades held for longer-term investment. For instance, a minor trend interruption may offer an opportunity to do one of the following for a core position:

- Initiate a new position to get aboard a trend that appears to still have plenty of room to run.
- Add shares to an existing position. It is a common practice for investors to ease into core trades by nibbling their way in. That is, opening a trade with a relatively small position and, as the trend shows more promise of continuing, adding more shares to increase the total position size. This may be referred to as "scaling in" to a trade.
- Add back shares to a core position that were previously sold (long) or covered (short). Experienced traders may employ a swing-trading-around-a core-position technique. For instance, a trader exits part of a core position (e.g., one-quarter to half of the shares) during a short-term directional move to lock in some profits. He then watches for an opportunity to add back shares to that position during a countertrend move bringing the position back to full size. This is a technique I favor—I refer to it as "Lock and Reload" (lock in profits and reload shares).

Note: The concept of a "minor" interruption is relative to a stock or market's current volatility. For instance, on the chart of a volatile stock, what may appear visually to be a minor interruption can result in a significant percentage move.

Pauses (Consolidation Days)

A short-term uptrend consists of a couple to several bars. A typical upswing includes primarily white (bullish) candlesticks, which shows leadership by the bulls during that period. Some of the bullish candles within an upward price swing may have bodies of about average length (numbered 6 in Figure 4.1). There may also be one or more candles with a noticeably longer body (numbered 1, 2, and 5), which is referred to as a long candle.

In contrast to an average-sized or long candle body, a consolidation day does not exhibit strong leadership by either the bulls or the bears. Rather, it represents more of a standoff between the two sides. The body of a consolidation day (bars 3 and 4 in Figure 4.1) is significantly smaller than the body/bodies of the bars that preceded it. It is often a narrow range bar, which may be either black or white. A bar's range is the distance from the low to the high of the bar, whereas the body is the boxed area between the opening and closing prices. *Note:* A small-bodied candle (bars 3 and 4 in Figure 4.1) is referred to as a Spinning Top in candlestick language.

A consolidation day may have a small body but a long upper and/or lower shadow (bar 4 in Figure 4.2); or it may have no body at all (bars 5 and 6) because the opening and closing prices are the same, or nearly so, resembling

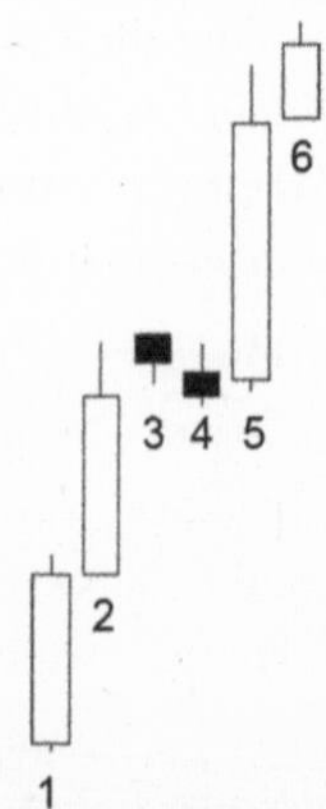

FIGURE 4.1 A Two-Bar Pause after an Upward Price Swing

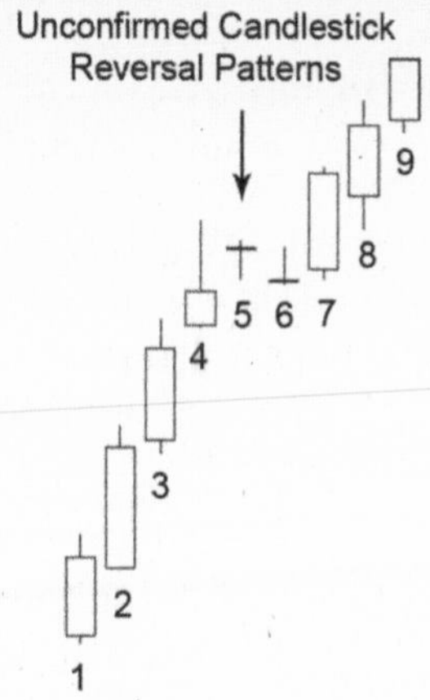

FIGURE 4.2 Candlestick Reversal Patterns Formed after an Upward Swing

a cross. This is a candlestick pattern called a Doji. Note that in these examples, the emphasis is on the size of the candlestick bodies.

Figure 4.2 is an example of candlestick reversal patterns that were not confirmed. The bar numbered 4 is a bearish Shooting Star, followed by two Doji patterns (5 and 6). These are bearish signs after an upward price swing. However, rather than pulling back or experiencing more consolidation, price pushed upward again, invalidating those patterns. Many of the candlestick patterns provide only short-term signals. Thus, if price doesn't follow through relatively soon after its appearance—in this case, it would have been to the downside—the candle reversal signal is unconfirmed and no longer valid.

I refer to these instances where consolidation days form after a price swing as a pause. Remember, it may not take long for a price swing to get overbought or oversold—often it occurs after only a few bars, and sometimes a single long candle will encourage some profit taking. And it may not take much to alleviate that short-term, overextended condition allowing for another move to occur. In some cases, just a day or two of very minor consolidation is enough to ease that condition and allow an extended price swing to develop.

It may help to think of a pause as being like a minor speed bump in the road—it only slows the trend temporarily. The following summarizes my basic criteria for a pause after a short-term upward swing:

- There is a distinctive shift in the size of the candlestick bodies for a very brief period; usually a day or two, but three days at most. If price consolidates longer than that, I refer to it as a base, which is described in the next segment of this chapter.

- Price stops making markedly higher closes, instead closing unchanged or nearly so during the consolidation day(s). Price may even close a bit lower into the prior bar's body, but it should not be a significant decline or I'd refer to it as a pullback, which is also described later in this chapter.
- Another swing up follows the consolidation day(s).

Depending on how the pause forms, it may not leave a price pivot on the chart. In other instances, a pivot will form. Both examples are illustrated in Figure 4.3. The pivot may not be as prominent as others you'll see on a chart, but it is enough to at least provide some new support below. Note that the body of the black candle labeled pivot is not as small as the other examples. However, it illustrates an exception I consider to still qualify as a pause—the bar's body was closer to average size versus a very small body, but it still clearly had the effect of slowing the trend while not pulling back much.

When price pauses, it sort of hangs in mid-air, but does not decline much, if at all. At most it is a very minor dip for that stock or index. Price will typically remain above, in some cases quite far above, the short-term moving averages (e.g., 10- and 20-period) as illustrated in Figure 4.4. The selling by swing traders locking in their profits is absorbed by bullish traders,

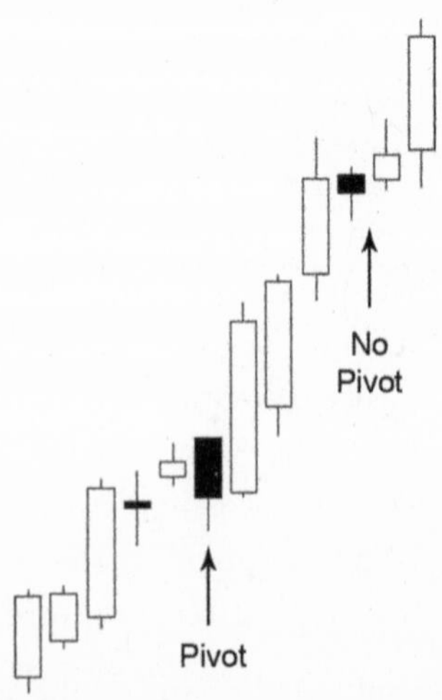

FIGURE 4.3 Brief Pauses

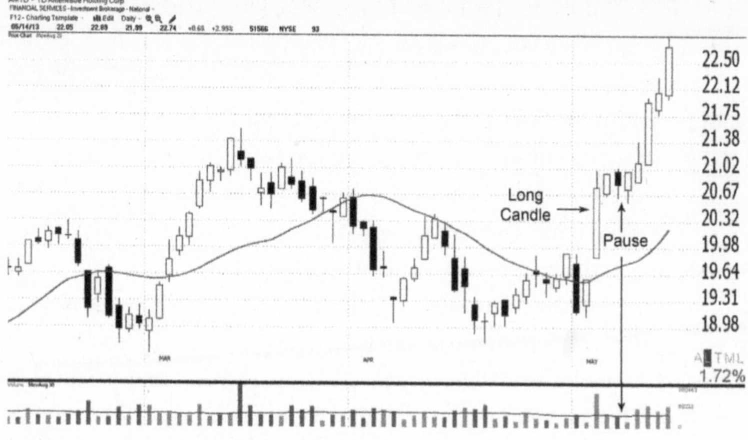

FIGURE 4.4 A Brief Pause Separating Upward Price Swings
Source: TC2000® chart courtesy of Worden Brothers, Inc.

which keeps a deeper pullback, or longer period of sideways movement, from occurring.

Figure 4.4 shows a daily chart of TD Ameritrade Holding Corp. (AMTD). A swing up from May 2 to 6, 2013, consisted of three bullish candles, one of which was a long candle. The body of a long candle is typically at least twice the length of that of an average-sized body for that stock. In my experience, it is not unusual for price to pause immediately (or soon after) the formation of a long candle in order to consolidate the gains from that strong trending day. In fact, the diminished size of the body that followed the long candle showed slowing of the upswing, followed by a brief pause.

Note in this example how volume declined during the consolidation days, supporting the idea that this might turn out to be just a pause. That won't always be the case, though. Although price does not decline much if at all during a pause, there may be a significant amount of trading activity; so there will be instances where volume is above average during the consolidation day(s). Also note that there was a minor pivot left behind where price had paused. I continue to point out where a pivot formed because it creates some new support below price. This is important for trade selection and stop loss order management for swing trading. For instance, a swing trader holding a long position may raise a stop up under a new, higher pivot that forms in order to protect the gains accrued during the upswing while also allowing the profits to run.

When price pauses, it may look like a pullback is starting, especially if the body of the pause bar(s) is a black candle (Figure 4.3) and/or it closes within the prior bar's body. Thus, some swing traders will quickly close their positions, not wanting to hold through a potential pullback. Other traders will hold the position, or only take partial profits, waiting to see what comes next. At the right edge of the chart, which is where we must make our trade management decisions, you can't know for sure that it will be just a brief pause. Although the formation of a small-bodied bar after a price swing indicates indecision, or decreased momentum, it does not necessarily mean price will pull back. But many swing traders will not risk their profits and close the trade at the first sign of perceived weakness for a price swing. If the broad market is trending up strongly, I often elect to take only partial profits on a swing trade and let the profits run on the remaining shares while monitoring the stop to protect the remaining gains accrued in the trade.

These are very minor trend interruptions. When you look back at the chart, with the benefit of hindsight, you'll see that the consolidation bar(s) was just part of a long price swing; or in some instances, it can be characterized as back-to-back price swings with a minor interruption between them (Figure 4.4).

I refer to these minor interruptions as pauses because that's precisely what they are. Price stalls just long enough to catch its breath, and then moves forward again. Although pauses occur relatively frequently, it is unlikely that you will read about this type of price action in many technical analysis books. However, I became aware of them when I began swing trading many years ago. Upon that discovery, I adjusted my trading techniques to accommodate them. That is, rather than always exiting a swing trade when price paused, fearing a pullback would follow, I learned to pay attention to the broad market environment, and that it was sometimes preferable to scale out of a trade in increments. Taking partial profits serves three purposes:

1. It allows a trader to fulfill the desire to "ring the cash register" by locking in some of the profits.
2. It reduces the amount of capital exposed to a potential pullback.
3. It fulfills the trader mantra of "letting the profits run" with a partial position.

The examples shown above were of the daily chart. Pauses occur on other time frames as well. On an intraday chart, the consolidation is relative to that time frame—it may be for a bar or two (e.g., two 15-minute bars). On a weekly chart, a pause may occur for a couple of weekly bars.

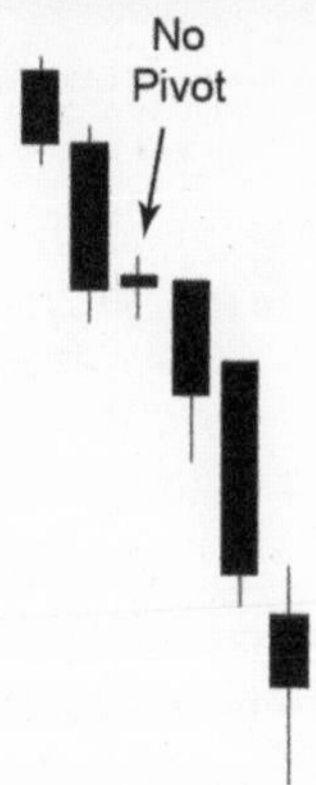

FIGURE 4.5 A One-Bar Pause during a Downward Price Swing

Pauses in a Downtrend A short-term downtrend typically consists of primarily black (bearish) candles, some of which may have bodies of about average length and others may have longer bodies. After a swing down, price may pause, forming a small-bodied bar or a Doji for a day or two. The same criteria identified above for a pause after an upward swing applies, but reverse the scenario for a downtrend.

A brief pause may occur during, or between, downward price swings. The pause may just be part of one continuous price swing as illustrated in Figure 4.5. Recall that some short-term moves will last as long as a couple of weeks (but seldom longer than three). Oftentimes in these cases, price will not form a new pivot when pausing. In other cases, the pause may form in a way that has the appearance of separating two price swings (Figure 4.6), and a minor pivot may form.

These are fine distinctions, and I'll admit to being a detail-oriented, perfectionist type! But beside that, it can make the difference in how I manage a swing trade and I know you want those details. I have many tips to share with you, but rather than veering off on a trading tip tangent here, I've provided some instruction in later chapters. The first part of this book is intended to define and illustrate the key components of trend development.

When price pauses during a downtrend, especially if the pause includes a bullish candle (Figure 4.6), some swing traders will cover their short positions fearing that a bounce may be starting. Others will hold the position, or only take partial profits, waiting to see what comes next. At the right edge of the chart, you can't know for sure that it will be just a brief pause, or if it may erupt into a short-covering rally. In this case, instead of continuing to move up price declined again.

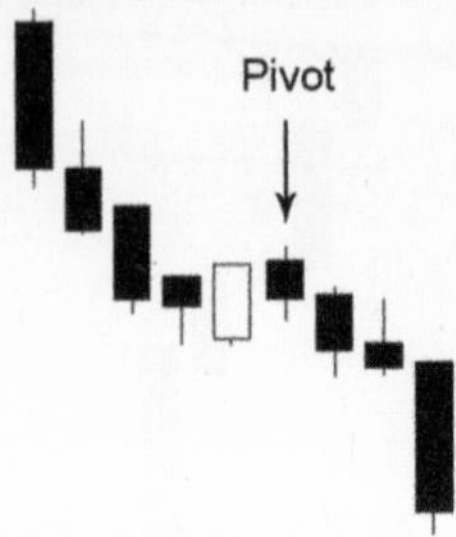

FIGURE 4.6 A Brief Pause between Downward Swings

Stocks can fall very quickly. Panic may set in, causing price to cascade. Figure 4.7 shows a daily chart of Education Realty Trust (EDR) during May and June 2013. Price formed a one-day pause (a Dragonfly Doji). After another push down, price paused again, forming a Gravestone Doji, which was confirmed the following day by a Bullish Engulfing pattern. Although that white engulfing candle was not a small-bodied bar, it was immediately followed by another push down. Hence, it behaved like a pause. The result was a failed candlestick signal. Soon after, another pause occurred including back-to-back bullish Hammers; but price dropped again, leaving another unconfirmed candlestick signal.

This example shows a series of unconfirmed or failed bullish candlestick patterns. It can be treacherous trying to catch a falling knife! A trader who had a short position during the decline fared well. However, for a trader

FIGURE 4.7 Candlestick Signals during a Downtrend
Source: TC2000® chart courtesy of Worden Brothers, Inc.

who took a long position based on one of the unconfirmed candlestick patterns, or the failed engulfing pattern, it was a different story.

Candlestick Charting I did not show the above examples of unconfirmed or failed candlestick patterns to discourage their use, nor to give the impression that candle reversal patterns are not good for signals. Note the key word I used is *unconfirmed*. Two of the three patterns in Figure 4.7 were not confirmed, while one failed to follow through with more upside movement. In later examples, you'll see plenty of successful candlestick signals.

Candlestick reversal signals can be quite helpful and I utilize them often. Following are some things to keep in mind:

- Just like anything else in charting, candlestick signals do not work 100 percent of the time.
- Candlestick signals should not be used in isolation. Their effectiveness can be enhanced significantly by analyzing their signals in the context of the surrounding chart landscape. Utilize candlesticks in context with the tenets of Western technical analysis.
- Waiting for confirmation of the candlestick signal can help avoid getting on the wrong side of a price move.
- Always be aware of the tone of the broad market, as it may influence the effectiveness of certain patterns at certain times. Look at a daily chart of the Dow from late May to late June 2013, while the stock shown in Figure 4.7 was falling, and you'll see the market was experiencing a correction during that time. You'll learn more about the influence of the broad market in Part 2.

Unless there is strong support below which price is testing, it is best to avoid going long when price is falling like a knife, even if a candlestick pattern forms. I don't recall the source, but I've never forgotten the falling knife rules (and who says traders have no sense of humor?):

1. Stand aside as the knife is falling.
2. Let it hit the ground and stick.
3. When the knife stops quivering, it is okay to pick it up.

Candlesticks make it very easy to discern when the bulls or bears are in control, or when neither is showing dominance, which is why I can't imagine ever going back to analyzing price movements using a standard bar chart. If you are not yet familiar with candlesticks, I've written a book on the subject called *Getting Started in Candlestick Charting* (John Wiley & Sons, 2008). It is an inexpensive paperback written in layman's terms. It provides everything you need in order to understand the candlestick lines and the most commonly formed patterns. There are other fine publications in the marketplace to choose from as well for more extensive study.

Bases (Minor Consolidation)

When price moves sideways for more than a couple of days, I refer to it as a *base* or *basing*. A small base forms in an uptrend when price stops rising temporarily and primarily moves sideways. It represents a temporary period of relative calm, during which neither the bulls nor bears are able to exert enough pressure to break price out of the base. The interruption of the trend is often followed by another upward move. Thus, when I see these formations, and the broad market environment is favorable for trading them, I think of them as little launching pads.

Let me just save myself a few e-mail messages by pointing out that I suggested previously a pause includes a bar or two of consolidation, but not more than three. Although I try to be as clear and concise as possible, sometimes I'll refer to three bars of consolidation as a pause and sometimes as a base. It's really splitting hairs in those cases, so I don't want to put a hard and fast rule on it. However, beyond three bars of sideways movement I term a base (or a period of minor consolidation) rather than a pause.

The shallow base provides a setup for a potential trade. For example, a swing trader may go long if price breaks out above the top of the base, or a trader holding a core position may add shares upon the breakout to increase the size of the position. In certain cases, a swing trader may even take a more assertive (earlier) entry by opening a long position while price is still consolidating in anticipation of a breakout move. Such an entry may pose a bit more risk, but the payoff may also be greater and it allows a stop to be placed fairly close to the entry price. To mitigate that risk, I suggest only taking the more assertive entry when the broad market is quite favorable for an upside break. For instance, during the early-to-mid stage of an up leg in a bull market versus when the intermediate-term uptrend is overbought and vulnerable to a correction.

Figure 4.8 shows two periods of basing action on a chart. The consolidation may be quite tight (labeled base 2). That is, it is shallow with little to no white space within the base. Some formations will have a bit of depth where there is some white space within the consolidation area (base 1).

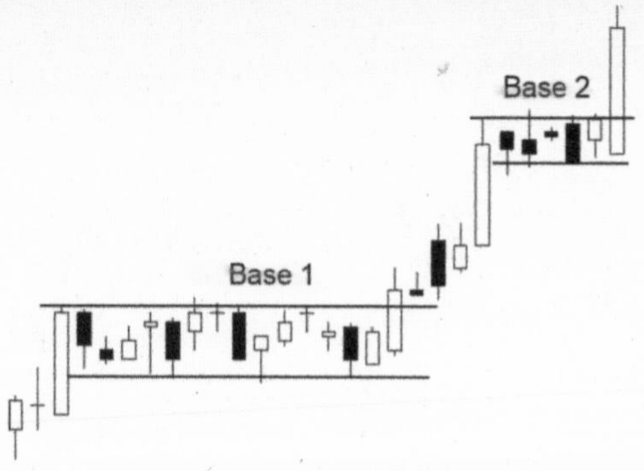

FIGURE 4.8 Bases Formed during an Uptrend

The consolidation may last from a few days (base 2) to a couple of weeks or so (base 1), but not much longer than that. Longer bases do occur, of course, but when price bases for more than about three weeks, I typically consider it to be a larger trend interruption rather than a minor event.

Note: A small base should not be confused with a larger trading range, which has more depth to it and often lasts significantly longer. Long bases and trading ranges are discussed later in this chapter.

Bases in a Downtrend Basing action may also interrupt a downtrend. It occurs when price stops falling and temporarily moves sideways. The price setup may offer an opportunity to initiate (or add to) a short position. Just as in an uptrend, the base may have a bit of depth or it may be quite shallow. It may last only a few days, or it may continue on for a couple of weeks or so. The stock often continues its decline after the period of consolidation, as illustrated on the daily chart of Chico's FAS, Inc. (CHS) in Figure 4.9.

Pullbacks in an Uptrend

A brief pause in an uptrend declines little if at all. A period of minor consolidation is a sideways move. A pullback, which may also be called a dip, is a countertrend move. A pullback turns back against the trend, retracing a portion of the prior upswing. A pullback is a short-term decline within an intermediate-term uptrend, as illustrated on the daily chart of Triumph Group, Inc. (TGI) in Figure 4.10. As price turns back up after pulling back, that pivoting action leaves a level of support below price (the rising bottoms in Figure 4.10). Price may pull back from one to several times during an intermediate-term uptrend.

FIGURE 4.9 Bases Formed during a Downtrend
Source: TC2000® chart courtesy of Worden Brothers, Inc.

Pullbacks are common occurrences within an uptrend. They form primarily because of swing traders taking profits on short-term moves—the selling pressure causes price to dip. The decline alleviates the prior short-term overbought condition and is often followed by another swing up in the direction of the prevailing trend as bullish traders employ buy-the-dip strategies.

Following are some examples of who may look upon a pullback as an opportunity:

- A trader or investor who has been sitting on the sidelines and is watching for an opportunity to get aboard the trend.
- A trader who has been participating in the trend, but had exited a swing trade to recognize the profits and is now looking for another entry opportunity at a lower price.
- An investor holding a core position who is looking for an opportunity to add shares to an existing position to increase its size.

The following may occur when price pulls back (see Figure 4.10):

- Price may retrace from about one-third to two-thirds of the prior upward swing. There will be instances, though, where price retraces the entire prior upswing.
- The decline may stop at/near an area of support below, such as a prior price pivot or a short-term moving average (e.g., the 20-period). A deeper pullback may reach the 50-period moving average.

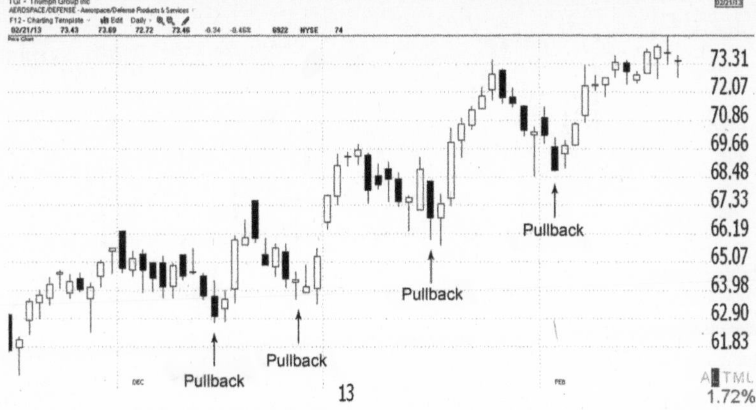

FIGURE 4.10 Pullbacks Formed during an Uptrend
Source: TC2000® chart courtesy of Worden Brothers, Inc.

- Volume may taper off during the pullback. This is usually indicative of profit taking by short-term traders rather than a major selloff where volume may be heavier. However, the lack of such a volume pattern won't keep me from entering a trade after price has stopped declining. I've observed plenty of instances where there is fairly strong volume during the dip as traders get shaken out. And as indicated above, there are often many traders waiting for a pullback entry opportunity so there may be heavy trading activity.

A pullback within an uptrend is a price setup. It creates the potential for a swing trade, or an opportunity to add shares to a core long position. A trader may require a specific entry trigger to go long—an indication that price is done falling. For instance, a break above the prior bar's high, or a break above a prominent resistance level that is visible on an intraday time frame. Remember, a pullback on the daily chart is an intermediate- to long-term downtrend on intraday charts. Thus, when price turns up out of a pullback on the daily chart, it is a trend reversal occurring on the lower time frames.

Bounces in a Downtrend During a downtrend, price may turn up against the trend and retrace a portion or, in some cases, all of the prior down swing. It is a short-term rise within an intermediate-term downtrend and is often followed by another move down, as illustrated on the daily chart of Valero Energy Corp. (VLO) in Figure 4.11. I often refer to this minor reversal as a bounce. It may also be referred to as a rally, a relief rally, or a short-covering

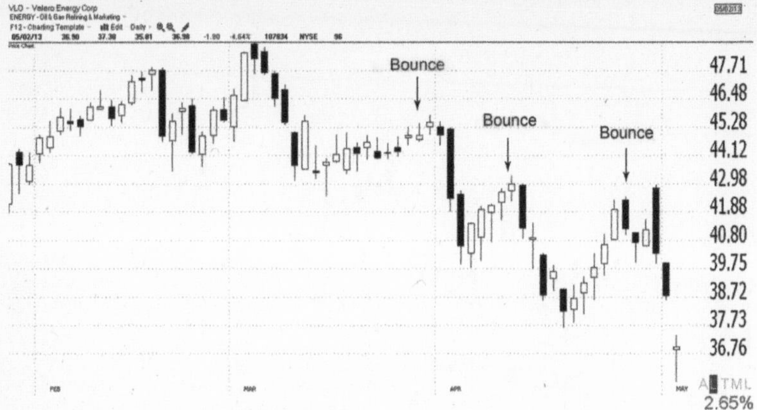

FIGURE 4.11 Bounces Occurred during a Downtrend
Source: TC2000® chart courtesy of Worden Brothers, Inc.

rally. As price turns back down after bouncing, that pivot action leaves a level of resistance above price (the declining peaks in Figure 4.11).

After a downward swing, traders may cover part, or all, of their short positions fueling a bounce. Some bottom fishers may enter long positions, adding to the buying pressure. But rather than continuing to move up, price rolls back over, extending the prevailing trend. Price may bounce from one to several times during an intermediate-term downtrend. A bounce is a price setup that may offer an opportunity to initiate a short position, or to add shares to an existing short position.

Flags and Pennants

Chartists who study classic Western chart patterns will learn about continuation formations called flags and pennants. They are minor interruptions of the trend. A flag looks like a small rectangle, and a pennant looks like a small triangle. The distinguishing factor that identifies these patterns as flags or pennants is that they are preceded by a sharp upward move (bullish flag or pennant) or a sharp decline (bearish flag or pennant). That sharp move preceding the formation of the flag or pennant is referred to as a pole.

In some technical analysis books, it will be stated that these patterns slope against the trend. In other books, it may be suggested that price moves sideways rather than leaning against the trend. By my

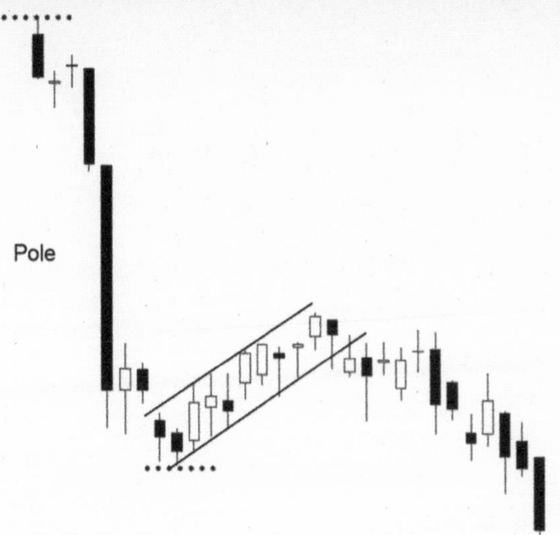

FIGURE 4.12 Bearish Flag

characterization, a flag or pennant may do either. Thus, basically it is a pullback or a bounce if it tilts against the up or down trend, respectively, or a base if it moves sideways. In other words, these patterns fit into the categories mentioned previously, but they include a distinctive factor—a pole—that identifies them specifically as flags or pennants. The horizontal dotted lines in Figures 4.12 and 4.13 identify the pole for each of those patterns.

Figure 4.12 shows a bearish flag. In this case, the flag tilts against the downtrend. The short, upward-sloping line drawn on the chart clearly identifies the flag's lower boundary. Thus, a breakdown through that line may be used as a sell signal for shorting the pattern; or a trader may wait for price to break below the swing low at the bottom of the pole. The entry chosen may depend on the intended duration of trade (e.g., a swing versus a core trade), and/or whether the trader chooses a more assertive entry versus one that is more conservative. In the case of selling short, the entry method chosen may have an impact on the trader's ability to borrow the needed shares.

Figure 4.13 illustrates a bullish pennant. In this example, it was possible to draw a short, downward-sloping resistance line to make it easy to identify the breakout point for an entry signal to go long. Alternatively, a more conservative trader may wait for price to break above the peak at the top of the pole.

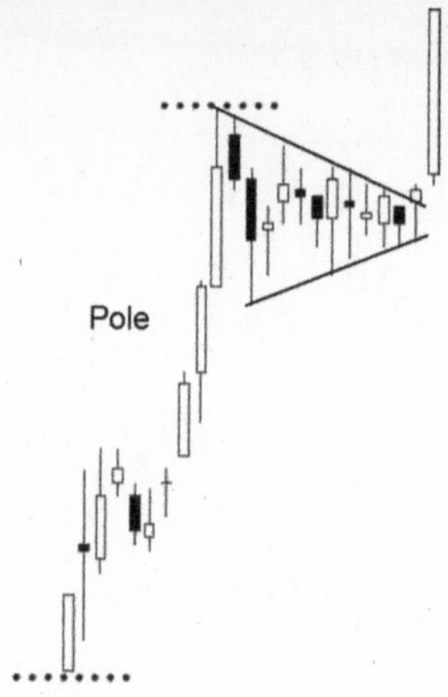

FIGURE 4.13 Bullish Pennant

A Bit on Statistics

Fortunately, it is not necessary to have a background in statistics to become a skilled chartist; however, it is helpful to understand the basic concepts of averages and probability. With this understanding, it should make perfect sense why pullbacks and periods of minor consolidation form within trends. In addition, these concepts play an important role when it is time to look for good trading opportunities and execute trades.

Reversion to the Mean *Mean reversion* is a statistical concept suggesting that a value eventually moves back toward the average, or mean. Let's apply this concept to price. As a general rule, price does not deviate too far from the average, and when it does it becomes vulnerable to a change in direction. Swing trading has become a very popular trading style. Swing traders pay close attention to price action and will take profits after a directional move. Their actions often force price back toward the average.

I pay attention to the proximity of the current price to the 20-period simple moving average (SMA). When price moves away from that strong average, I refer to it as "catching air." This is not an official technical term, but it does create a mental picture that makes it easy to understand. When price catches air it may become exhausted, or overextended (overbought or oversold), on a short-term basis and the probability increases that price will change direction, at least temporarily, rather than continuing to move farther away from the average.

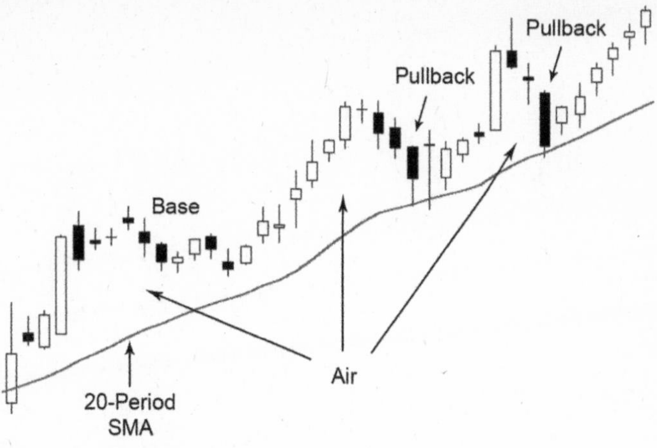

FIGURE 4.14 Reversion to the Mean

As illustrated in Figure 4.14, the overextended condition can be alleviated by either of the following:

- Price moves primarily sideways (a base), allowing the average to catch up with it (or nearly so).
- Price turns back toward the average (a pullback in an uptrend or a bounce in a downtrend).

This tendency for price to move back toward the average is an example of reversion to the mean.

My use of the 20-period SMA for this purpose was inspired by John Bollinger in his book *Bollinger on Bollinger Bands* (McGraw-Hill, 2002). I highly recommend reading (or re-reading) Mr. Bollinger's book. He uses the 20-period SMA as the central point for the Bollinger Bands. The bands are plotted at a certain distance (e.g., two standard deviations) from the 20-period SMA. The bands have a tendency to contain most of the price movement (see Figure 4.15). Price may move to the upper or lower band, or beyond it in some cases, but has a tendency to gravitate back toward the 20-period SMA centered between the bands.

Don't expect absolutes in technical analysis. There will always be exceptions to the rules. For example, when price makes a strong move up or a sharp decline, it may move much farther away from the average than you'd expect. And don't expect price to always stop right at the 20-period SMA. This is just a guideline.

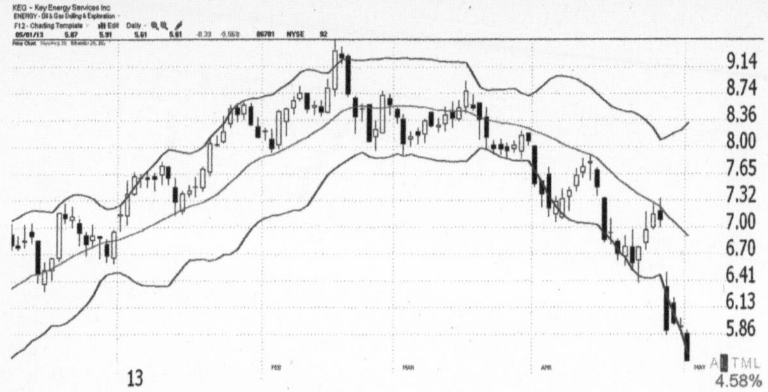

FIGURE 4.15 Bollinger Bands
Source: TC2000® chart courtesy of Worden Brothers, Inc.

The key here is that price needs to stabilize after a price swing. The 20-period SMA tends to be a good gauge to draw attention to price moving away from the average and then dipping back or moving sideways to consolidate those gains. Price may turn again before reaching the moving average, or it may overshoot it before changing direction. And if the stock is trending quite smoothly, you may find that the 10-period SMA is a better gauge for that particular trend for that stock.

Without the minor interruptions that occur within a trend, price would move too quickly to extreme, unsustainable levels. They also provide traders opportunities to get aboard a trending stock at a lower-risk area rather than chasing after a stock that is on the move and entering a position where price is vulnerable to a setback. Read that sentence again. If you grasp the importance of it, you'll benefit greatly when it comes time to selecting and executing trades, especially for short-term traders whose hold time is limited.

Probability Probability refers to the likelihood, but not the certainty, of something happening or being true. Probability provides a gauge for determining risk and reward. Whether you are aware of it or not, you are constantly making decisions based on the probability of a certain outcome. A simple example is that of driving a car. For the average, experienced driver in America, the probability of being in a traffic accident on any given day is fairly low. Therefore, drivers are willing to take the small risk in exchange for the benefits that the privilege of driving provides. However, if the likelihood of being in an accident were high, people would think twice about getting in their cars every day.

Trading successfully is not a matter of chance. Traders test out price setups and strategies to determine the probability of taking successful trades. Those who wish to have longevity in this business must learn to trade in a manner that puts the odds of winning on their side. Rather than throwing caution to the wind and taking excessive risk, successful traders study price action, volume, the impact of volatility, and so on to learn what has a high or low chance of occurring. They make their trade selection, risk management, and trade execution decisions accordingly. For example, knowing about the concept of reversion to the mean should influence a swing trader's decisions.

If a swing trader holds a long position in a stock and does not wish to hold the position through a potential pullback, he should be on the alert for signs of weakness suggesting it may be time to exit the position. However, there is the chance that, rather than turning against the trend, price may just pause briefly. Therefore, he may choose to take partial profits, allowing the remainder of his profits to run should price push forward again rather than retracing the prior move. This is a calculated risk the trader takes; and he also makes sure to protect the remaining capital still invested.

If a trader is looking for an opportunity to enter a position, but the stock has caught air, chances are good that price will turn back or move sideways soon rather than continuing to move away from the average. Thus, he may monitor the price action watching for a better entry opportunity.

■ Larger Trend Interruptions

Unlike the minor trend interruptions described previously, the larger interruptions discussed in this segment are more significant in their magnitude and/or duration. These events interrupt the major trend—they are the interruptions that *separate* the intermediate-length moves that occur in the direction of the major trend.

Moving Averages

Before delving into discussion of the more significant trend interruptions, it is appropriate to provide more information on moving averages. Moving averages are trending indicators. As such, they serve important roles in trend analysis. The 20-period is a short-term moving average that was introduced in Chapter 2 for its role in helping determine trend direction. It was brought up again in this chapter in the discussion of reversion to the mean. Additionally, sometimes price will find support at this moving average during a minor pullback within an uptrend (or resistance during a bounce in a downtrend).

Other commonly used moving averages are the 50-, 100-, and 200-period. Those longer moving averages lag farther behind price. Once an uptrend has been under way for a long enough period of time, those moving averages will be rising and stacked one above the other as illustrated in Figure 4.16. During a prolonged decline, they'll eventually all cross to the downside and reverse the stacking order.

You may be wondering why these particular lengths—the 50-, 100- and 200-period—are so widely used on the daily chart. They are approximately equivalent to the 10-, 20- and 40-*week* moving averages, respectively (e.g., 5 trading days in a week × 40 = 200). Those moving averages are frequently used by chartists who monitor weekly charts (e.g., the big-money managers). Thus, by monitoring the 50-, 100-, and 200-period moving averages on the daily chart, you're keeping an eye on those weekly lines without having to change the time frame.

Price may find support or resistance when it tests those moving averages. During a minor correction of a trend, price may find support (correction of uptrend) or resistance (correction of a downtrend) at the 50-period SMA. During a deeper correction, monitor how price responds when it tests the 100- and 200-period SMAs.

Note: The 50- and 200-period moving averages are more commonly referenced than the 100-day. However, the 100-day approximates the 20-week, which is closely watched on that time frame, so it should not be disregarded simply because it doesn't receive as much discussion as the others.

Corrections

A correction occurs in an uptrending market when price retraces a significant portion of the prior intermediate-term upward move. Thus, it may also be referred to as a retracement. You may also hear it referred to as a reaction. After a sufficient correction, price gets oversold and is often followed by another move in the direction of the major trend.

Price often retraces by a certain amount. A minimum retracement is usually about one-third of the prior trend. A retracement of about one-half of the prior trend is common. A maximum retracement is about two-thirds of the prior trend. If price retraces beyond two-thirds, it is less likely that the major trend will resume and a more significant reversal may be under way (such an event occurred on the charts of the major market averages in 2011).

The following may occur during a correction of an uptrend (reverse the direction for a correction of a downtrend):

- Price closes below one or more short-term moving averages, such as the 20-period, that it had previously remained above.
- Price may reverse direction enough to test, or break, intermediate- and longer-term moving averages, such as the 50-, 100-, and 200-period.
- The faster 10-period SMA may cross below the slower 20-period SMA.
- A prominent, intermediate-length up trendline is often broken.
- Price may retrace to a well-known Fibonacci level, such as 38, 50, or 62 percent.
- A protective stop loss order on an open core position may be triggered; in some cases, even a loose stop that is used for a trend-following strategy.
- As price turns back up after a correction, it leaves a prominent and important support level below.

Figure 4.16 shows a daily chart of Safeway, Inc. (SWY). I chose this example to emphasize the difference between the minor trend interruptions described previously and a more significant interruption of the trend.

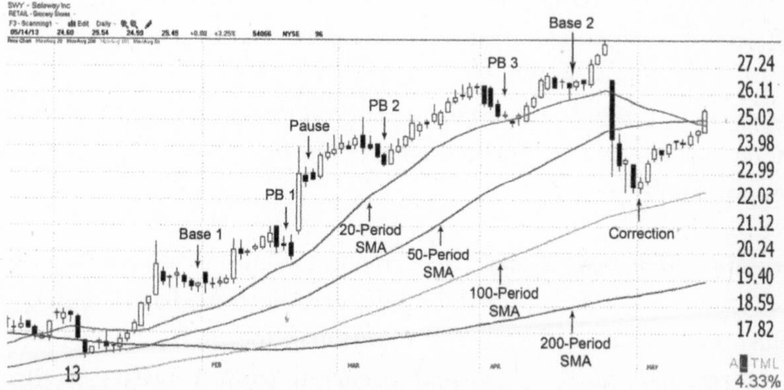

FIGURE 4.16 A Correction Compared to Minor Trend Interruptions
Source: TC2000® chart courtesy of Worden Brothers, Inc.

The commentary below corresponds to the labels in Figure 4.16 (PB = pullback):

- Base 1—After an upward swing that started in mid-January 2013, price moved primarily sideways for two weeks.
- PB 1—Price broke out above the base on February 7, starting another upward move, which was followed by a minor dip in mid-February.
- Pause—The next swing up was a long candle, followed by a couple of consolidation days.
- PB 2—There was more upside movement as the intermediate-term uptrend evolved. Price then pulled back for four days in early March.
- PB 3—After nearly three more weeks of trending higher, price pulled back again during the first week of April.
- Base 2—After another upward swing, a small base formed in mid-April.
- Correction—The next interruption was the sharp decline from April 25 to 30. Even though the correction only lasted a few days, don't let its brevity fool you. It was a decline of just over 20 percent.

Note how, during the minor interruptions, price held above the 20-period SMA (except for one day during PB 3 where price closed marginally below it). During the deeper correction, both the 20- and 50-period SMAs were broken.

A correction doesn't mean the long-term trend is over. It just means price had run far enough in the direction of the major trend for traders to consider it overbought (uptrend) or oversold (downtrend) on an intermediate-term basis and it was due to have a setback. Once the correction occurs, the stock often gets overextended in that direction and it may be a good time to look for a re-entry opportunity.

Note: There is significant discussion later in this book regarding monitoring intermediate-term trends and corrections for market analysis and trading opportunities.

Correction of a Downtrend A correction occurs in a downtrend when price retraces a significant portion of the prior intermediate-length decline as illustrated on the daily chart of Caterpillar, Inc. (CAT) in Figure 4.17. An intermediate-term downtrend occurred from February 4 through April 19, 2013. A nearly three-week correction followed, retracing just over 50 percent of the prior downtrend and stopping at the 100-period SMA.

FIGURE 4.17 A Correction of an Intermediate-Term Downtrend
Source: TC2000® chart courtesy of Worden Brothers, Inc.

This example shows why I suggested not neglecting to monitor that moving average. As price turned back down after the correction, it left a prominent and important resistance level above.

Note: During a major downtrend, a correction may also be referred to as a "bear market rally."

Fibonacci Numbers This is a good time to bring up Fibonacci, which refers to a centuries-old number sequence that was discovered by Leonardo Fibonacci, a 13th-century mathematician. Fibonacci numbers are a method of measuring price retracements that have gained popularity over the years, especially since the advent of mainstream charting programs. Many charting platforms include a Fibonacci grid that can be overlaid on the price chart, making it easy to measure the degree of a retracement (see Figure 4.18).

Traders use Fibonacci numbers to gauge the potential depth of a correction. Common Fibonacci retracement levels are approximately 38, 50, and 62 percent of the previous up or down trend. The 38 and 62 percent retracements correspond fairly closely to the one-third and two-thirds retracements mentioned previously; and obviously the 50 percent corresponds to the one-half retracement.

Unlike price pivots, which create support/resistance levels that are *visible* on the chart to all traders viewing it, the Fibonacci levels are not visible on a given chart. Like moving averages, which must be designated by the user to be plotted over the price bars, a Fibonacci grid must be activated to see its lines. Thus, only traders who plot a Fibonacci grid over the price bars will see the precise retracement levels.

Not all chartists will use this tool. However, plenty of them do and they make note of those retracement levels. Fibonacci numbers are not magical. They work relatively well because traders use them. Many traders will take action as price encounters the retracement lines just as they would when price approaches a certain moving average, or a ceiling or floor created from price pivots.

In my opinion, by themselves, Fibonacci retracements do not constitute a trading system. They are simply another technical analysis tool that can be utilized effectively in conjunction with other tools and techniques. They are also prone to some subjectivity. For instance, one chartist may start the grid at a different location than another chartist would.

Plotting a Fibonacci Grid Recall from Chapter 3 the discussion of closing highs and closing lows at the turning points of trends being used to measure the percentage move during that period. That does not apply to drawing Fibonacci lines, at least not the way I learned to do so. I draw the Fibonacci grid as follows:

- Retracement of an Uptrend—Start the grid at the lowest point (bottom of the lowest shadow) of the trend and drag it up to the highest point (top of the highest shadow) of the uptrend. On the chart of Vermillion, Inc. (VRML) in Figure 4.18, the dotted lines at bottom and top of the intermediate-term uptrend show the start and end points, respectively.
- Retracement of a Downtrend—Start the grid at the highest point (top of the highest shadow) of the trend and drag it down to the lowest point (bottom of the lowest shadow) of the downtrend.

On the chart of VRML in Figure 4.18, the stock has so far retraced 50 percent of the prior uptrend. It may not appear visually to be the case if just looking at the price decline itself; however, the Fibonacci grid reveals the depth of the retracement. This sort of visual illusion occurs because the price scale is set for logarithmic, where the distance between each horizontal gridline on the chart is an equal *percentage* rather than an equal price, or value, change. In TC2000 (version 7), the percentage is displayed in red below the price column. For VRML, if price moves the distance of one gridline, it has moved 12.04 percent.

Normally there is not a significant difference in the appearance of the chart between arithmetic and logarithmic scaling. I use logarithmic for most

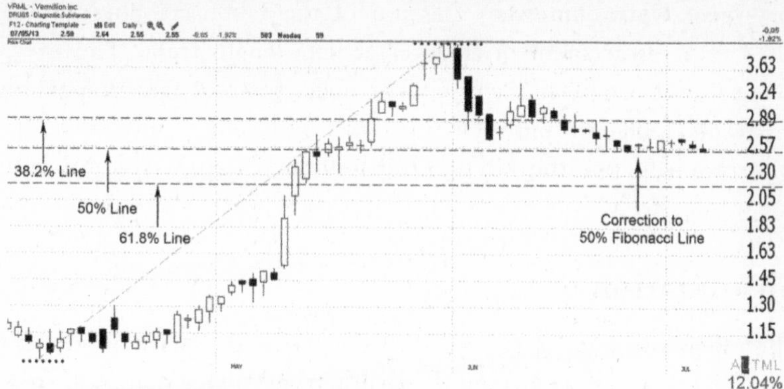

FIGURE 4.18 Logarithmic Scale: 50 Percent Retracement
Source: TC2000® chart courtesy of Worden Brothers, Inc.

of my chart analysis, but periodically shift to arithmetic for certain tasks. When looking at a Fibonacci retracement grid after price has made a swift move, though, this visual illusion may occur.

Figure 4.19 shows the chart of VRML again, but this time with the scaling set to arithmetic, which displays price movement as equal increments (in points) between each horizontal gridline. Changing the scale did not change the actual percentage of the decline—it was still 50 percent regardless of the scaling. However, the depth of the retracement was clearer when viewing the arithmetic scale because of the preceding swift move up.

FIGURE 4.19 Arithmetic Scale: 50 Percent Retracement
Source: TC2000® chart courtesy of Worden Brothers, Inc.

Short-Term Retracements The use of the Fibonacci lines above was applied to a retracement of an intermediate-length trend. However, this concept may also apply in the case where price retraces a portion of a short-term trend. During a pullback (uptrend) or bounce (downtrend), price may retrace from one-third to two-thirds of the prior upward or downward swing, respectively.

Consolidation

Rather than retracing a significant portion of the prior intermediate-term trend and then resuming the major trend, price may stop trending and move primarily sideways in a whipsaw type of motion. For a period of time, price swings back and forth but makes essentially no progress in the direction of the major trend. During this period there is basically equilibrium between the forces of supply and demand—neither the bulls nor the bears can exert enough pressure to break price out of the channel.

Periods of sideways movement are referred to as consolidation. You will see various other terms used to describe these trendless phases, such as: congestion, trading range, horizontal channel, or rectangle. Here again is an example of a technical event that may be referred to by many labels.

This type of consolidation is more pronounced than the minor basing action referenced previously. Consolidation can interrupt the major trend for weeks or months (and in some cases a year or more). There will be instances where the consolidation consists of tight price action (see Figure 4.22) instead of notable swings back and forth; however, the base continues on significantly longer than the minor basing action illustrated earlier.

Consolidation phases represent periods of indecision and are often characterized by low volatility. They develop when the major trend stalls for a prolonged period of time. Their presence creates support and resistance levels, sometimes major ones. Price will likely encounter those areas again; for instance, during a future correction, or even later when the major trend reverses course (from a bull to a bear market, or vice versa).

The following may occur during a period of consolidation:

- Two or more peaks may form at, or near, the same price level, forming a ceiling above price. Two or more bottoms may form at, or near, the same price level, creating a floor below price. Those ceilings and floors define the upper and lower boundaries of the trading range (Figures 4.22 and 4.23).

- If the channel lines are converging rather than parallel, price may be trapped in a triangle (Figure 4.20).
- The 20-period SMA will stop trending and flatten out or move sideways in a rolling motion (Figures 4.21 through 4.23). If viewing two short-term moving averages (e.g., 10- and 20-period), they may cross over each other (intertwine) one or more times during the period of consolidation.
- Bollinger Bands, using a setting of 20-period and two standard deviations, will usually begin to tighten around price after a couple of weeks of consolidation on a daily chart (Figure 4.21). This is referred to as a Bollinger squeeze.
- Volume may taper off noticeably during the consolidation phase (Figure 4.20). This will not always be the case, but is not uncommon. Plotting a 30-period simple moving average over the volume bars makes it easy to see when volume is above or below average.
- The swings back and forth may be deep enough to trigger a protective stop loss order. For example, the distance from the top of the trading range to the bottom in Figure 4.22 was almost 13 percent.

Two or three nearly parallel peaks (uptrend) or bottoms (downtrend) are often interpreted as double or triple tops or bottoms, respectively.

FIGURE 4.20 An Ascending Triangle Formed during an Uptrend
Source: TC2000® chart courtesy of Worden Brothers, Inc.

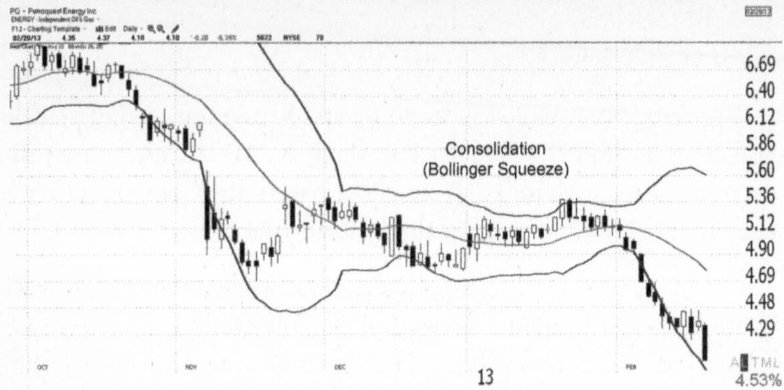

FIGURE 4.21 **A Trading Range Formed during a Downtrend**
Source: TC2000® chart courtesy of Worden Brothers, Inc.

However, a reversal pattern is not validated until it is confirmed by price breaking down (top reversal pattern) or breaking out (bottom reversal pattern) beyond a specific barrier. Many such patterns are never confirmed and instead turn out to be just periods of consolidation.

Following are several examples of consolidation that formed resulting in an interruption of the long-term trend:

When price moves sideways making fairly even swings up and down, a trading range is formed (Figures 4.22 and 4.23). In some cases, each price swing is shallower than the preceding swing. The result is a triangle (sometimes referred to as a coil) with price tightening as it moves into the pattern's apex. A triangle may have two converging trendlines, referred to as a symmetrical triangle. A triangle may have a flat top and rising bottom trendline, which is referred to as an ascending triangle (Figure 4.20); or a flat bottom and a declining top trendline, which is referred to as a descending triangle.

Trading ranges and triangles are considered to be continuation patterns, but significantly larger ones than the flags and pennants mentioned previously. Price often resumes the prior trend after the period of consolidation. There will be times, though, when price reverses direction instead. Remember that while they are forming at the right edge of the chart, you can't know for sure if it is a consolidation pattern that is forming or a top reversal pattern (uptrend) or bottom reversal pattern (downtrend). For instance, while it was still forming, the ascending triangle in Figure 4.20 may have appeared

FIGURE 4.22 A Trading Range and a Long Base Formed during an Uptrend
Source: TC2000® chart courtesy of Worden Brothers, Inc.

to many chartists to be a bearish double top setting up. The outcome is not certain until price either breaks out of the consolidation pattern and moves again in the direction of the trend, or confirms the reversal pattern.

Frequently during periods of consolidation, price will swing back and forth between the boundaries. During the trading range that formed in Figure 4.22, there were distinctive short-term price swings within the consolidation area with some white space separating the swings. Hence, while that period was a horizontal phase, there was minor price movement between its boundaries. You'll also observe periods of consolidation where price does not whip back and forth much; the swings are very shallow (a tighter trading range). Sometimes it will be quite tightly compacted with little to no white space at all—a shallow base that is long enough to interrupt the major trend for several weeks, as illustrated at the right edge of the chart in Figure 4.22.

Correction Turned into Consolidation

What starts out as a correction may evolve into a period of consolidation as illustrated on the daily chart of Kansas City Southern (KSU) in Figure 4.23. From mid-September to early October 2012, price declined almost 12 percent, retracing a portion of the intermediate-term uptrend. On the next move up, price found resistance at the peak that marked the top of the prior intermediate-term up leg. Price moved back and forth in a relatively wide trading range, later gapping above its ceiling and resuming the major trend.

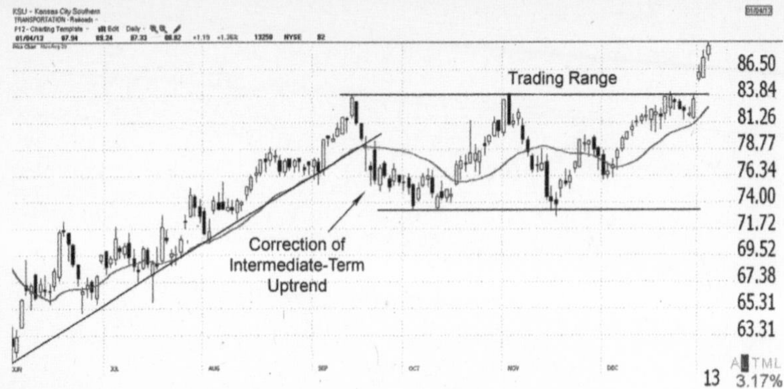

FIGURE 4.23 A Correction Turned into a Trading Range
Source: TC2000® chart courtesy of Worden Brothers, Inc.

Trend Reversals

When the term *trend reversal* is used, what does that mean? Technically, a trend reversal is not under way until price has retraced at least two-thirds of the prior trend. There will be instances where that occurs; and instances where an entire prior trend is reversed. However, it should not be assumed that is the intended meaning when the term is used.

Chartists frequently use the terms "reversal" and "trend reversal" loosely to refer to a temporary shift in the direction of price from up to down, or from down to up. But that does not suggest how far price moves when it changes direction. The question then becomes: Are they referring to just a brief change in the direction of the trend (e.g., a pullback), a deeper correction of a trend, or a reversal of the entire trend?

There will also be times when the trend stops moving up or down and shifts to sideways movement. In those cases, it is a change in direction (from up or down to sideways) rather than a trend reversal. These are syntax issues, but they may cause confusion, especially for newcomers to the marketplace. Make sure you understand the context in which the term reversal is being used. I periodically use reversal or trend reversal generically to mean a shift from up to down, or vice versa. However, I nearly always provide more information, like designating it as a pullback (minor) or a correction (deeper).

Here's an example where a newcomer could get confused. I once read in a technical analysis book that a trend reversal occurs "when prices are held at a resistance level." It seemed to suggest that price must test an already established resistance level and turn down from it to constitute a reversal. However, what about a stock that is moving to new, continually higher highs? The stock is at an all-time high, so there is no resistance overhead in that case. When price eventually stops rising and turns down, say correcting the prior intermediate-term uptrend, could we not say price reversed direction?

Although price often does change direction, at least temporarily, when a visible support or resistance area is tested, that is not the only factor contributing to reversals. It is not necessary for price to test prior resistance (uptrend) or support (downtrend) to reverse direction; it may do so for one of the following reasons:

- For an individual stock, the broad market (or the stock's sector or industry group) turned up or down, pulling that stock with it.
- The stock or market became overbought (uptrend) or oversold (downtrend) and traders took profits they had accrued during the prior move. Their cumulative actions caused a reversal.
- News was released that caused a stock, or the market, to reverse direction.

Profiting from Trend Interruptions

There are good reasons why I've devoted valuable page space to recognizing various types of trend interruptions. First, these events become part of the chart landscape. They occur within trends, and analyzing trends is the crux of technical analysis. Hence, in order to master chart reading, you must understand how trends evolve and the implications of the movements and formations that occur within them.

Of course, one of the primary reasons for this instruction is so that you can profit from the interruptions that occur. For instance, since the inception of the current bull market that began in March 2009, there have been many opportunities to go long on breakouts from bullish bases and flags, or after pullbacks, within the upward movements during the major trend. Those setups (minor trend interruptions) have been plentiful at times during this bull market. There have also been several corrections, which allowed traders to get aboard the trend after prices had declined more significantly. There are boundless opportunities for swing trading, as well as for initiating core positions and letting the profits run with the trend.

CHAPTER 5

Early Trend Reversal Warnings

A trend remains in motion until there are clear signs that it has changed direction. While we cannot predict precisely when a change in a trend's direction will occur, a trend can be monitored in order to identify the turning points, and often relatively quickly. There are technical tools and techniques at our disposal to help chartists spot potential trend reversals.

When an intermediate- or long-term trend changes direction, it seldom occurs without some type of forewarning. An exception for individual stocks is when news is released that has an impact significant enough to reverse the trend. However, in some cases the news is an earnings release and traders have the opportunity to exit, or hedge their position, prior to such an announcement if their trading rules dictate (as mine do).

There are often warning signs that a trend may be weakening *prior to* the actual shift in direction. You just need to know what to look for, and that is the focus of this chapter. There are also some signals that may occur later, *after* a trend change may already be under way, which are covered in Chapter 6.

Don't fight the trend, but neither should you be caught off guard if a change in the trend direction occurs. Learning to spot the early warnings listed in Table 5.1 allows traders to be proactive in their decision making. In addition to defining and illustrating these early warnings, at the end of the chapter I include some tips on how to respond to them.

TABLE 5.1 Early Warnings of Potential Trend Reversal	
Uptrend	**Downtrend**
Bearish Climax Move	Bullish Climax Move
Bearish Divergence	Bullish Divergence
Failure to Break Prior Peak	Failure to Break Prior Bottom
Change of Slope—Rising Trendline	Change of Slope—Declining Trendline
Break of Tight Rising Trendline	Break of Tight Declining Trendline
Approaching a Strong Ceiling	Approaching a Strong Floor
Bearish Candlestick Reversal Pattern	Bullish Candlestick Reversal Patterns

There are two primary reasons for monitoring a trend for signs of weakness, either on the chart of a stock you own or are interested in owning, and on the chart of a major market average, which may impact your overall trading activities:

1. In the event of a reversal, it is important to protect the gains that have accrued in an open position(s) during the trend.
2. To prepare to initiate a new position(s) in the direction of a trend that emerges out of a reversal.

The concepts addressed in this chapter and in Chapter 6 are applicable to trends that occur on the charts of stocks and indices. There are some other tools specifically for monitoring trends of the broad market that are not applicable to the chart of an individual stock. Those will be covered in a later chapter. For now, let's focus on the signs that are applicable to trends in general.

Reference to a reversal of the trend should not be construed to mean an entire trend would be erased. It refers to a trend changing direction from up to down, or vice versa. The duration and magnitude of the move following a reversal may vary. Additionally, price may shift from up or down to sideways, which is also a change in direction.

The warnings listed in Table 5.1 may occur at the end of an intermediate-term trend. Hence, I watch for them on a daily chart. And since the last leg of a bull or bear market is typically an intermediate-length move within the major trend, you may observe that one or more of these warnings appears at the end of a long-term trend. However, often the final top or bottom of a bull or bear market, respectively, is tested one or more times before a reversal begins in earnest. Therefore, these events may occur as part of a larger topping or bottoming process, respectively.

If monitoring the long-term trend on a weekly chart, you may see these trend-ending warnings appear on that time frame. In fact, I regularly take a glance at the weekly chart of the stocks I trade, and the indices I monitor, to get a bigger picture perspective.

When using weekly charts, it is important to realize that there may be differences in the way the bars look from one charting platform to the next. The discrepancies are usually not substantial, but may make the difference in, say, how a weekly candlestick appears or where to connect a trendline.

The reason for the difference is that a weekly chart in some charting platforms (e.g., TC2000 version 7) is actually a rolling five-day chart. Hence, if you were to look at the weekly chart on Wednesday, the most recent bar would reflect data from the prior Tuesday's close to today (Wednesday to Wednesday). On Thursday, it would show Thursday to Thursday. That is, a day drops off and a new day is added because it is a rolling five-day chart.

In other platforms (e.g., MetaStock and eSignal), it is a true weekly bar. If you are able to look at the weekly bar intraweek on a Wednesday, the bar will not be a complete week yet, so it reflects just Monday's, Tuesday's, and Wednesday's data. By the close of Friday, you'd see the whole week's data. Some platforms may allow users to see the intraweek bar, while others may not provide it until the close of the week.

Some of the warnings listed in Table 5.1 cannot be applied to short-term trends. Many short-term trends would not last long enough to generate the criteria needed for those warnings. However, there are specific warning signals that may occur prior to a short-term trend changing direction. Some swing-ending warnings are included at the end of Chapter 6.

■ Climax Move

After a long or strong up or down trend, a climax move is strong enough that it has the potential to alter the direction of the trend. Climax moves signal potential exhaustion by buyers (uptrend) or sellers (downtrend). A climax move that occurs at the end of an uptrend may also be referred to as a blowoff top. A climax move at the end of a downtrend may also be referred to as a selling climax or capitulation. The initial move following a climax event may be fast and sharp.

The events described below are strong enough to abruptly end an intermediate-term trend. A long-term trend may take weeks, or sometimes months, to truly reverse direction, especially on the chart of a major market average. Thus, a shift in the direction of a long-term trend may be more of a topping or bottoming process (e.g., from up to sideways to down or vice versa) than attributed to a single event, such as a climax move. However, periodically a major trend reversal will occur from such an event; or a climax move may mark the start of a longer topping or bottoming process.

Key Reversal

A key reversal is a climax move. A negative (bearish) key reversal occurs when price gaps up open to a new high in an overbought stock or market. Price reverses direction and closes near, or below, the prior bar's close accompanied by heavy volume. A negative key reversal formed on the daily chart of Applied Materials, Inc. (AMAT) on February 17, 2012 (Figure 5.1).

A positive (bullish) key reversal occurs when price gaps down open to a new low in an oversold stock or market. Price reverses direction and closes near, or above, the prior bar's close accompanied by heavy volume. A positive key reversal formed on the daily chart of Mellanox Technologies, Ltd. (MLNX) on January 24, 2013 (Figure 5.2).

A key reversal bar should gap open strongly in the direction of the trend. It is followed by an abrupt intraday reversal, which completely erases the opening gap and creates a bar that astute chartists will recognize as an obvious change in sentiment. The key reversal bar has a long body. The longer the bar and the heavier the volume, the more significant is the signal. True

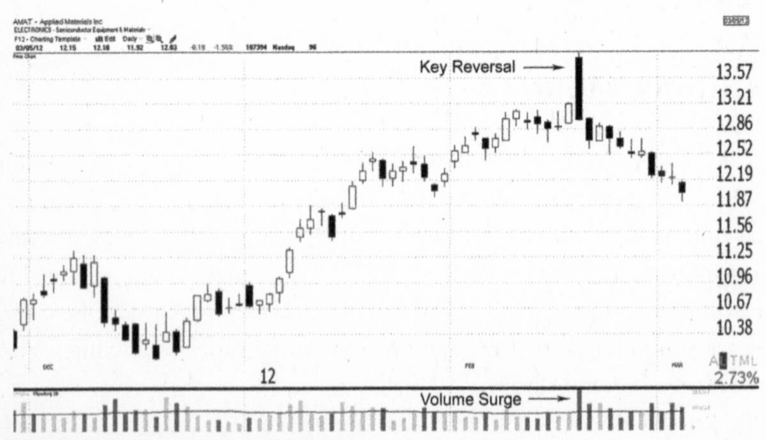

FIGURE 5.1 Negative Key Reversal
Source: TC2000® chart courtesy of Worden Brothers, Inc.

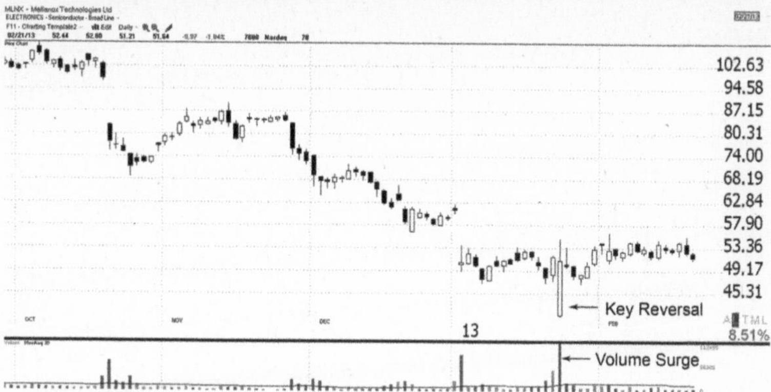

FIGURE 5.2 Positive Key Reversal
Source: TC2000® chart courtesy of Worden Brothers, Inc.

key reversals form infrequently; but when they do occur, they often mark the start of a trend reversal.

Price need not completely engulf the prior bar's range (from high to low) in order to meet the criteria of a key reversal; however, in some cases it will do so and create an outside day and strengthen the signal. *Note:* A key reversal may meet the criteria of a candlestick reversal pattern—a Dark Cloud Cover, Piercing pattern, or Engulfing pattern.

Exhaustion Gap

An exhaustion gap is another type of climax move. It occurs when price is trending and leaps forward with a last gasp of buying pressure in an uptrend (Figure 5.3) or selling pressure in a downtrend (Figure 5.4) and leaves a void on the chart. That final push quickly fades as price reverses back into the gap in the following days and fills it. These gaps are accompanied by heavy volume.

If the opening of an exhaustion gap in an uptrend does not provide support when tested, and price closes decisively below it, that is a bearish sign. If the opening of an exhaustion gap in a downtrend does not provide resistance when tested, and price closes decisively above it, that is a bullish sign.

A gap in an up or down trend is only a *potential* exhaustion gap because, at the right edge of the chart, you won't know for sure yet if it will turn out to be an exhaustion gap or a continuation gap. However, when a gap accompanied by strong volume occurs after price has been trending for at least an

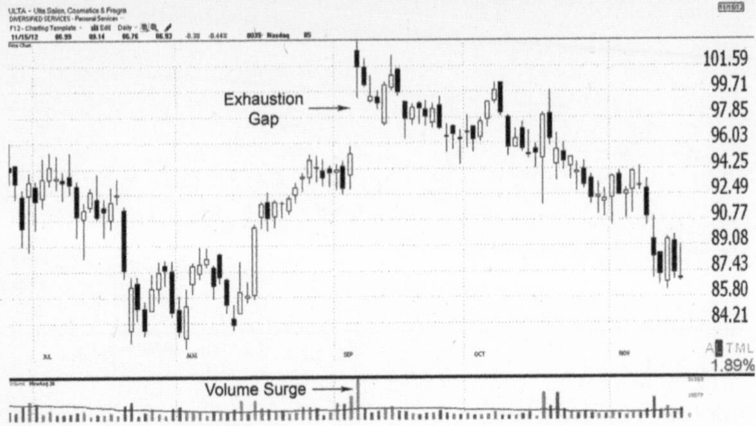

FIGURE 5.3 Bearish Exhaustion Gap
Source: TC2000® chart courtesy of Worden Brothers, Inc.

intermediate-length period of time, or after a swift trend, I err on the side of it being an exhaustion gap and take steps to protect my profits.

If price gaps up to/near, but not above, a strong ceiling (resistance) or down to/near, but not below, a strong floor (support), I also err on the side of it being an exhaustion gap. Price often reverses direction when major support or resistance is tested. Thus, a gap to a significant ceiling or floor is often followed by an immediate reversal.

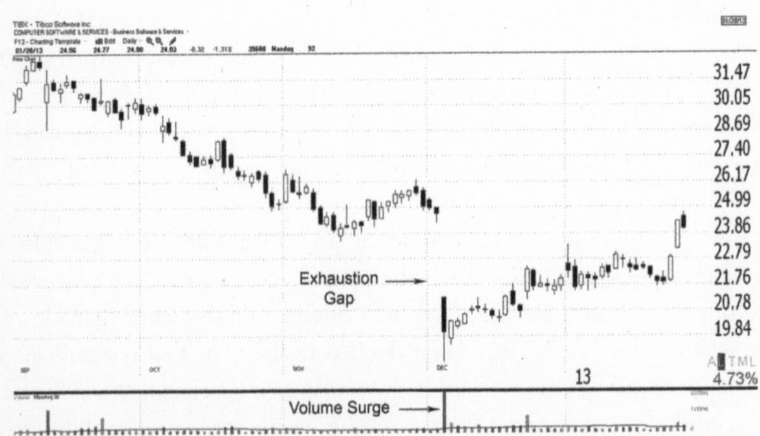

FIGURE 5.4 Bullish Exhaustion Gap
Source: TC2000® chart courtesy of Worden Brothers, Inc.

Divergence

Divergence is a technique used by chartists to determine if a trend is losing momentum, which is one of the earliest warnings of a potential trend change. A divergence occurs when an indicator loses momentum before it is apparent in the price action. Thus, it is said to be *leading*, because it occurs before a trend actually changes direction.

It is important for chartists to become proficient at recognizing when a divergence occurs. Various indicators can be used for this purpose. Oscillators, such as Wilder's Relative Strength Index (RSI) or the Stochastic oscillator, are often used. I typically use the Moving Average Convergence Divergence (MACD) with a standard 12-26-9 exponential setting plotted as a histogram as shown in Figures 5.5 and 5.6. I also use On-Balance Volume (OBV) for divergence analysis. *Note:* The RSI is an oscillator and should not be confused with Relative Strength (RS).

In order to understand the concept of divergence, a chartist must recognize when there is confirmation. Confirmation is present in an uptrend when price rises to a new swing high for the cycle, and an indicator that measures the upside momentum of price also makes a corresponding new high. In a downtrend, the price level declines to a new swing low for the cycle and the indicator makes a corresponding new low.

A negative (bearish) divergence occurs when price forms a higher peak during an uptrend (from P1 to P2 in Figure 5.5) while the corresponding peak of the indicator either flattens out or turns down (from A to B on the MACD histogram in the middle panel). For rising stocks, think of peak-peak. That is, compare the prominent *peaks* in price to the *corresponding peaks* of the indicator.

The negative divergence on the chart of Citigroup (C) in Figure 5.5 provided an early warning of a potential reversal of the uptrend that had formed during August to October 2012. After the divergence, the trend changed direction; first from up to sideways forming a shallow double top, and then down into a correction.

In this example, the RSI is plotted in the lower panel for another viewpoint. Note how the peaks in the RSI were rising, confirming the intermediate-term uptrend until the point labeled A. The indicator then turned down during the formation of higher peaks in price, creating a negative divergence between price and the RSI. The *trend of the RSI peaks* (labeled A through C) was down even while price was still rising. Thus, if you are not sure if a divergence is present by looking at the two most recent peaks in

FIGURE 5.5 A Negative Divergence between Price and the Indicators Preceded a Correction

Source: TC2000® chart courtesy of Worden Brothers, Inc.

price compared to the indicator, look at the overall trend of the indicator's peaks as a guide.

A positive (bullish) divergence occurs when price forms a lower bottom during a downtrend (from B1 to B2 in Figure 5.6), while the corresponding bottom of the indicator either flattens out or turns up (from A to B on the MACD histogram). For declining stocks, think of bottom-bottom. That is, compare the prominent *bottoms* in price to the *corresponding bottoms* of the indicator. If it is not clear whether a divergence is present, look at the overall trend of the indicator's bottoms as a guide.

Divergence Lines

Some novices struggle with spotting divergences at first. They may find it helpful to draw lines on the chart as illustrated in Figures 5.5 and 5.6. The trendline drawing feature may be used for this purpose. However, divergence lines should not be confused with trendlines. If a stock is in an uptrend, the primary trendline is drawn below the stock's rising *bottoms*. To check for divergence in an uptrend, the *peaks* are compared to the peaks in the indicator.

If your charting platform does not allow lines to be drawn in the indicator panels, you could print the chart and draw the lines manually if needed.

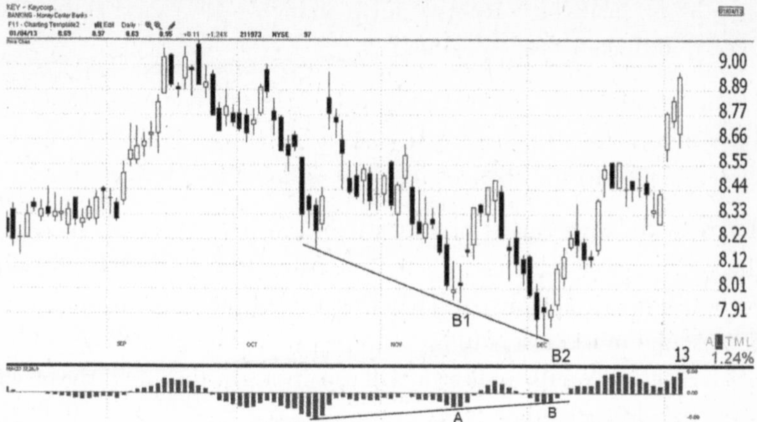

FIGURE 5.6 A Positive Divergence between Price and the MACD Histogram Preceded the Reversal
Source: TC2000® chart courtesy of Worden Brothers, Inc.

Alternatively, save paper by using the pointer feature included in most charting platforms. The pointer is a vertical line that runs the length of the chart and indicator panels. Use it to line up the peaks or bottoms in price with the corresponding peaks or bottoms in the indicator panel below. Once you become proficient at determining if a divergence is present, just a quick glance at the chart is usually all that is needed.

Guidelines for Divergence Analysis

Divergence is referenced in many technical analysis texts, but there may not be a tremendous amount of details included, which might leave some novices wondering if they are completing the task correctly. Thus, I hope the instruction and illustrations above, along with the following guidelines, will help you to quickly master this task:

- The purpose of checking for a divergence is to determine if the trend is weakening—it is a trend-ending signal. Look for divergence only when price is trending up (negative divergence) or down (positive divergence).
- Look for divergence during intermediate- or long-term trends. Use the daily chart for intermediate-term trends. For major trends, check the weekly chart periodically. It can take several weeks, and sometimes

months, for peaks or bottoms to form on the weekly chart; so this doesn't need to be a daily task.

- Do not check for divergence while price is in a prolonged period of sideways movement. If price has been consolidating for a while, the trend direction has already changed from up or down to sideways.
- To check for divergence, first locate the *prominent* price pivot closest to the right edge of the chart. Look back from there to find the prominent pivot that formed prior to it. Then look for the pivots in the indicator that correspond most closely to those price pivots. The pivots formed on the price chart and on the indicator will usually occur the same day, or within a few days of each other.
- There must be a pivot present to check for divergence. For example, don't check for a negative divergence while price is still forming higher highs from one bar to the next. Wait for price to pivot and then check for divergence.
- If the trend fails to change direction after the appearance of a divergence, and the trend then continues onward, there is no longer a divergence. Wait for price to form another pivot before checking for divergence again.
- Sometimes there are two or more divergences that occur during the trend before it actually changes direction.
- If price forms a double top (uptrend) or double bottom (downtrend) and the corresponding pivots in the indicator have already changed direction, it shows a loss of momentum so it is considered to be a divergence.
- The presence of a divergence does not suggest how significant a reversal may be should one follow. The duration and magnitude may vary; or it may be followed by a shift to a period of sideways movement.
- A divergence is relatively precise in the following way: If a reversal does occur, it typically starts fairly soon after the divergence signal (usually within one to a few days).
- A divergence is stronger if it occurs from an overbought (negative divergence) or oversold (positive divergence) level on the indicator. For example, if the highest peak used to check for a negative divergence on the RSI or Stochastics formed above that indicator's overbought line.

In my opinion, a divergence is not always a precise timing tool; nor is it an automatic signal to enter or exit a trade. It is an early warning that a change in the direction of the trend may occur. Divergences can fail during a strong trend, so their signals should be confirmed by price.

■ Failure to Break a Prior Peak or Bottom

Recall from discussion in Chapter 2 that while in an uptrend, price will form a series of rising peaks; and in a downtrend, price will form a series of declining bottoms. A simple yet effective way to spot a potential trend change fairly early is by monitoring the price peaks and bottoms as the trend evolves.

In order for an uptrend to continue to rise, price must eventually close above each peak (swing high) that is formed as price pulls back or consolidates within the trend. That is, it must break up through each near-term resistance level during a subsequent rally.

Price must close decisively above the prior peak rather than just a marginally higher close. Sometimes price will break the prior peak by a bit but then roll over (Figure 5.7). The word decisive is subjective. Many traders use a percentage rule. That is, they require price close a certain percentage (e.g., from 1 to 3 percent, or less for day trades) beyond a barrier when determining breakouts and breakdowns. Other traders may require a lesser amount. *Note:* Without a decisive close above the prior peak (followed by price moving higher), it may be a double top forming, which suggests the trend may be weakening rather than continuing its ascent.

The dotted lines on the daily chart of C & J Energy Services, Inc. (CJES) in Figure 5.8 show each peak being surpassed on a subsequent move up until mid-March 2013 when price failed to break above the prior peak. The upper

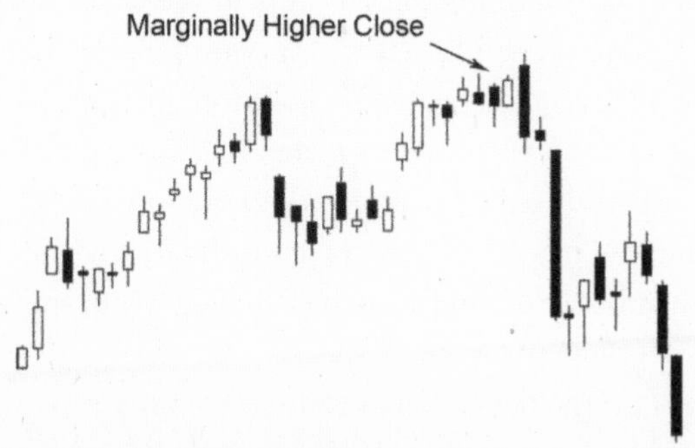

FIGURE 5.7 Price Failed to Close above the Prior Peak by a Sufficient Amount

FIGURE 5.8 Price Failed to Close above the Prior Peak
Source: TC2000® chart courtesy of Worden Brothers, Inc.

shadow tested that peak, but price did not *close above* it. When price fails to move above the prior peak, it suggests the trend is losing momentum.

A nuance to point out on the CJES chart: When the first of the double tops formed in February, note the bullish candle that marked that top. It was significantly longer than normal, and was accompanied by heavy volume. This is another example of a climax-type move, but only because it occurred after price had been trending for a prolonged period of time. If a long, high volume candle were to form at the beginning of an uptrend, for instance, it would obviously tell a very different story.

Also note in this example that, prior to failing to break the prior peak, the strong intermediate-term up trendline was broken. Failing to surpass the prior peak is a fairly early signal that a trend change may occur; however, early warnings don't necessarily mean nailing the very top, or the very bottom, of a trend. In this case, the decline off the February top was deep enough to break the trendline, and possibly trigger a protective sell stop for some long positions.

Now let's look at a downtrend. In order for the trend to continue its descent, price must eventually close decisively below each bottom (swing low) that is formed as price bounces or consolidates within the trend. In other words, it must break down through each near-term support level during a subsequent decline.

The dotted lines on the daily chart of Anika Therapeutics, Inc. (ANIK) in Figure 5.9 show how each bottom was broken on a subsequent move down. In late December 2012, price failed to move below the prior bottom, setting

FIGURE 5.9 Price Failed to Close Below the Prior Bottom
Source: TC2000® chart courtesy of Worden Brothers, Inc.

up a potential double bottom and serving as a warning that the downtrend may be weakening. A trend reversal began soon after.

Traders continually attempt to determine when price has put in the final top in an uptrend, or the final bottom in a downtrend. If the trend continues beyond the last prominent price pivot, then it was not the top (or bottom) after all and traders will again be on the watch for the potential topping (or bottoming) of the trend.

Note: If you prefer to monitor the long-term trend on the weekly chart, watch for the above instances to occur on that time frame.

Failure to surpass a prior peak (uptrend) or bottom (downtrend) is how double tops and bottoms form, respectively. Another test and failure of that high or low may result in the formation of a triple top or bottom, respectively. Those are only *potential* reversal patterns and must be confirmed. That means price must close below the lowest point between the peaks (topping pattern) or above the highest point between the bottoms (bottoming pattern). Remember, many unconfirmed reversal patterns turn out to be periods of consolidation and are eventually followed by resumption rather than reversal of the trend.

■ Change in Trendline Slope

Trendlines are not static; they should be monitored regularly. As a trend evolves, there will be times when new price action requires you to adjust the slope and/or length of a trendline; or to draw a new trendline. If you are

FIGURE 5.10 A Change in the Slope of the Up Trendline
Source: TC2000® chart courtesy of Worden Brothers, Inc.

forced to draw a steeper trendline because of an acceleration of the trend, be on the alert for a correction.

If the uptrend accelerates rapidly, the slope of the trendline will become much steeper (Figure 5.10). When that occurs, the trendline is likely to be broken soon because a steep ascent cannot be sustained for very long. The uptrend may not reverse completely, but it is likely to at least retrace part of that steep ascent or move sideways to consolidate the gains from the uptrend.

In a declining stock or market, acceleration may occur to the downside (Figure 5.11). In some cases, this may be an indication of capitulation. Capitulation is a phenomenon where investors still holding long positions finally give up and are willing to sell a declining stock at almost any price in order to exit their positions and end the financial and emotional pain. True capitulation will be accompanied by heavy volume and a sharp decline. This occurred on the charts of many stocks as the market declined into the March 2009 bear market low. Once the panic selling is over, the stock (or market) is vulnerable to a short covering rally and may also draw in bottom seekers opening long positions.

On the daily chart of Synaptics, Inc. (SYNA) in Figure 5.11, the trendline numbered 1 was started at the top of the intermediate-term downtrend. However, there are only two touches on the line; and as the downtrend continued, it was clearly too far away to represent the actual slope of the trend. Line 2 was drawn as the trend got steeper. As price accelerated further, line 3 was drawn across three peaks, identifying the

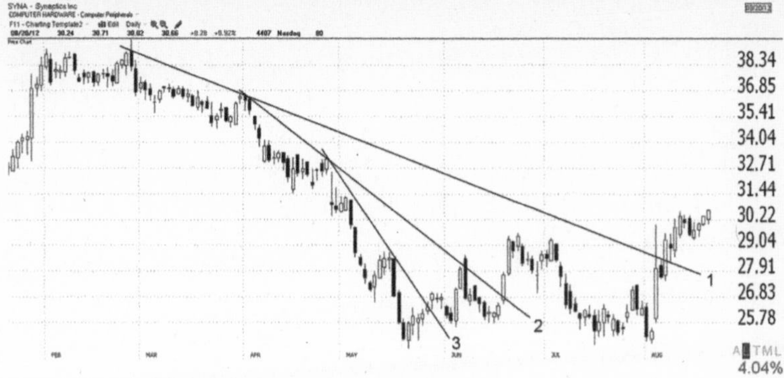

FIGURE 5.11 A Change in the Slope of the Down Trendline
Source: TC2000® chart courtesy of Worden Brothers, Inc.

new slope. When the decline stopped and price changed direction from down to sideways from late May through July 2012, all three lines were eventually broken.

Break of a Tight Trendline

Whereas a change in the trendline's *slope* can send an early warning, I typically consider a trendline *break* to be a later warning that the trend may be changing direction. That's because the trendline often lies a distance away from the price action. However, there may be times, because of the way the price movement occurs within the trend, that there is a relatively tight trendline. When a tight line is broken, it can occur quickly enough to be treated as an early warning.

In many instances, the tight line will be due to an acceleration of the trend as shown in Figure 5.10. In that example, both the slope change and the breaking of the trendline were early warnings. There will also be instances, though, where that is not the case. That is, it may not be that the trendline slope changed resulting in a tight line, but rather how the price action occurred within the trend as illustrated in Figure 5.12.

On the daily chart of Lasalle Hotel Properties (LHO) in Figure 5.12, price first failed to push above the January 2013 peak, flashing an early warning that the trend was losing momentum. Additionally, as the trendline had been extended upward at the right edge of the chart, price was literally

FIGURE 5.12 A Tight Up Trendline Was Broken
Source: TC2000® chart courtesy of Worden Brothers, Inc.

walking up the line. Therefore, the trendline was broken very quickly when price turned down, providing another early warning that the trend may be ending.

Approaching a Strong Ceiling or Floor

Support and resistance are clearly crucial components of trend analysis. Here we'll look at how a strong ceiling (resistance) or floor (support) can warn of a potential reversal. Even if there are no other signs a trend is weakening, if price is approaching a major ceiling or floor, the trend's movement may be halted there. I see it as trouble on the horizon; that's why I consider it an early warning of a potential reversal.

When an uptrending stock or index tests a strong ceiling (dotted line in Figure 5.13), the trend is very vulnerable to a reversal. When this occurs on the chart of a major market average, it has implications for many stocks (more details will be provided in Part II).

Eventually, even a very strong ceiling can be broken; otherwise, how could a stock or index in a bull market move to a new high? However, since we can't know until after the fact when that will occur, be aware that many experienced traders will use a strong ceiling as a target to exit their long positions, or at least take partial profits. Additionally, bearish traders may initiate short positions at/near that barrier. As illustrated in Figure 5.13, the selling pressure forced price to retreat from the ceiling.

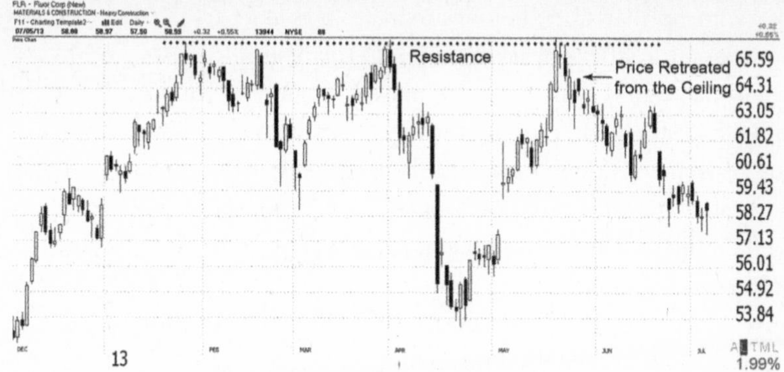

FIGURE 5.13 The Trend Reversed Direction after Testing a Strong Ceiling
Source: TC2000® chart courtesy of Worden Brothers, Inc.

In a downtrend, when price approaches a strong floor (dotted line in Figure 5.14) many traders holding short positions will cover them. Additionally, traders who are looking for an opportunity to go long may initiate positions at/near the support area. The buying pressure may push price up from the floor.

Eventually, even a very strong floor can be broken; otherwise how could a stock or index in a bear market move to a new low? A break of strong support on the chart of an individual stock often occurs when the broad market declines, causing most stocks to fall; or if money rotates out of a sector or

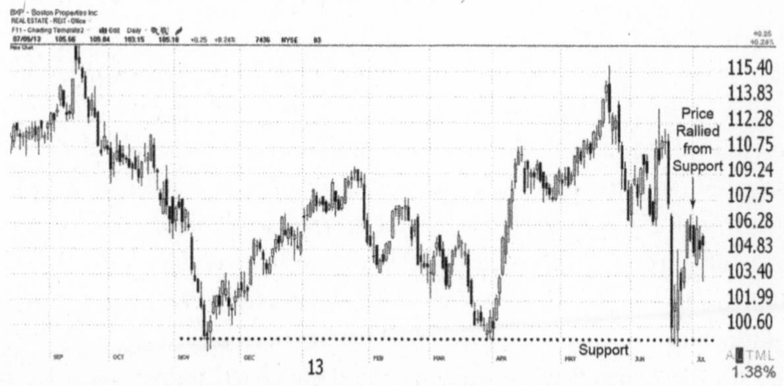

FIGURE 5.14 Price Bounced after Declining to a Strong Floor
Source: TC2000® chart courtesy of Worden Brothers, Inc.

industry group that stock belongs to as traders start taking profits. News is also a reason for stocks breaking support (or resistance).

The broad market environment may have a strong influence on whether an individual stock will push up through a ceiling, or decline below a floor. If strong resistance is to be broken, it is most likely to occur in a bull market; likewise strong support may be broken in a bear market. It won't necessarily happen on the first attempt, though; price may still retreat from that barrier for a time before punching through it.

I use a major ceiling (long position) or floor (short position) like those illustrated above as my target for exiting a trade. Even if it is a core position, I'll typically take at least partial profits when price approaches such a strong barrier. I don't wait until price retreats from the barrier to exit. I don't even wait for price to get right up against it. Instead, I sell as price *approaches* that barrier—near it but not right at the barrier. I know from experience that price may not quite reach it before reversing direction.

Check the Next Higher Time Frame

Chartists should periodically check the time frame one level higher than the one they are trading on. Just because there is no strong ceiling or floor visible on the chart you are viewing (e.g., daily), that does not mean there is not one that can be seen on the next higher time frame (e.g., weekly). Experienced traders analyze more than one time frame. They will be aware of a past ceiling or floor on the weekly chart and may respond when price approaches it again.

Until the time when price is actually successful at breaking through a strong ceiling or floor, you cannot be certain on which attempt it will do so. Thus, when a stock is approaching strong resistance or support on the weekly chart, it should serve as a warning to be alert for a change in the direction of the trend you are monitoring on the daily chart.

In Figure 5.15, a daily chart of Mercury General Corp. (MCY) is shown on the left and the weekly chart on the right. The intermediate-term uptrend on the daily chart that began around mid-March 2013 came up against very strong resistance (dotted line) that stretched back to 2010. That ceiling was the trigger for the start of the correction. The presence of, and the importance of that resistance area (having been tested multiple times), would not be realized when viewing the daily chart; unless the price bars were so tightly compressed that a few years of data appeared in the daily chart window.

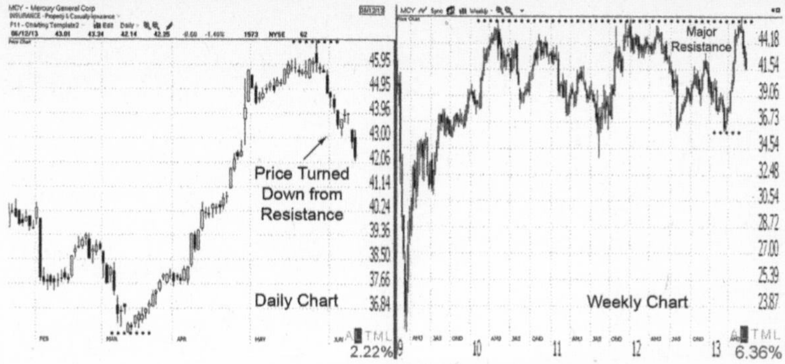

FIGURE 5.15 Price Turned Down from a Major Ceiling that Was Visible on the Weekly Chart
Source: TC2000® chart courtesy of Worden Brothers, Inc.

Figure 5.16 shows a two-chart layout of Bancolombia (CIB), with the daily chart on the left and the weekly chart on the right. The stock is in an intermediate-term downtrend on the daily chart and it may appear as if there is nothing to stop its fall. However, looking at the weekly chart, it is obvious that this stock has been trapped in a trading range for a few years and is approaching the floor of that channel again.

Other Support and Resistance

In Figures 5.13 through 5.16, the ceilings and floors were created from past price pivots. There may also be instances where other perceived support-resistance levels may stop a trend's movement. Of course, it is not actually the support-resistance level itself that causes price to change direction, but rather the cumulative effect of traders taking some action when price is at/near that level.

During corrections of the major trend, I pay close attention to strong moving averages (e.g., 50-, 100- and 200-period) and Fibonacci numbers as they may contribute to stopping an intermediate-term retracement. For example, during the October to November 2012 market correction, the S&P 500 index stopped falling right at the 62 percent retracement line of the prior intermediate-term uptrend. Even though that line was not visible to all traders like the ceilings illustrated above, it was clearly meaningful to many traders monitoring Fibonacci levels.

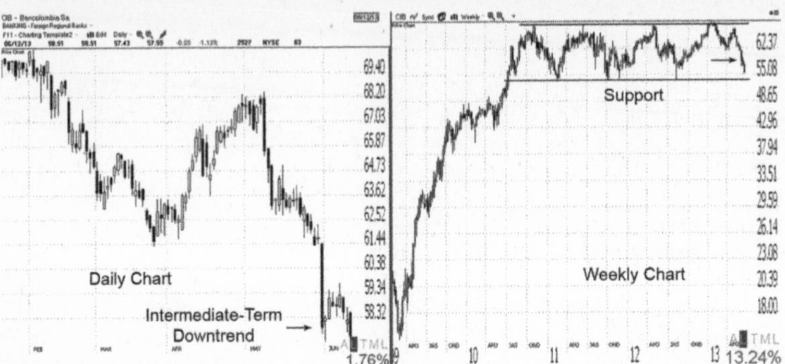

FIGURE 5.16 Price Is Approaching the Floor of a Trading Range that Is Visible on the Weekly Chart
Source: TC2000® chart courtesy of Worden Brothers, Inc.

Candlestick Reversal Patterns

As a general rule, candlestick reversal patterns provide fairly short-term signals, so they are a tremendous tool for swing trading. I consider them to provide swing-ending warnings. However, there will be many instances where a strong candlestick reversal pattern marks the end of an intermediate-term trend. Hence, I include them in the early trend reversal warnings as well.

The daily chart of LifeLock, Inc. (LOCK) in Figure 5.17 illustrates how candlestick reversal patterns may form within and at the ends of intermediate-term trends:

- The November to December 2012 correction ended with a bullish Hammer.
- A bearish Dragonfly Doji formed on January 2, 2013, after an upward price swing. It was followed by a period of minor consolidation.
- After another upward swing, a Hanging Man was followed by a Bearish Engulfing pattern (February 4 and 5, respectively) leading into a minor pullback/consolidation.
- After the next swing up, a bearish Hanging Man formed on February 21 and was followed by minor consolidation.
- At the end of the next upswing, a bearish Shooting Star formed on March 5, marking what would ultimately become the top of the intermediate-term uptrend.

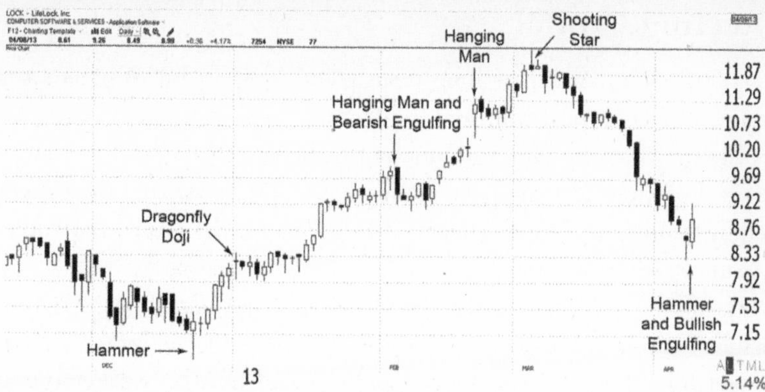

FIGURE 5.17 Candlestick Reversal Patterns Marked the Ends of the Trends
Source: TC2000® chart courtesy of Worden Brothers, Inc.

- After a decline of almost 28 percent during March and April 2013, the correction ended with back-to-back bullish candlestick reversal patterns—a Hammer and a Bullish Engulfing pattern. That reversal was followed by another intermediate-term uptrend (not shown).

I mentioned earlier the usefulness of candlesticks for identifying when a price swing may be weakening. This example demonstrates how candlestick signals frequently form after short-term price swings, and are often followed by brief interruptions of the trend. It also shows how such patterns may also mark the tops and bottoms of intermediate-term trends. Often there is also a Western technical warning(s) to support the presence of a candlestick signal at the end of an intermediate-term trend, such as a divergence, or price testing a strong support or resistance level.

Responding to Early Warnings

Recall that the primary reasons for monitoring a trend are to protect the gains that have built up in an open position, and/or to initiate a new position in the opposite direction if a trend reversal occurs. In many instances, an early warning allows a trader to take some action before price has reversed significantly. Following are some suggestions, which may also be applicable in regard to the later trend reversal warnings you'll learn about in Chapter 6.

Protecting Capital

During an intermediate- or long-term trend, quite a lot of profits can be built up in a core position, and/or from swing trading activities. Don't make the mistake of giving too much of those profits back when that trend reverses direction. Always make protecting your capital, and the gains generated by that capital, your highest priority. After all, it's not what you make that matters, but what you keep.

None of the warnings discussed above is a *guarantee* that a significant reversal of the trend will occur. However, it should encourage traders to stay alert for additional warnings that the trend may be weakening. Additionally, a trader may choose to take some defensive action, especially if there is more than one warning already present (a convergence of signals). How you react to one or more warnings of a potential reversal may depend on the following:

1. Your risk tolerance.
2. The intended duration of the trade.
3. The rules and guidelines of the specific strategy being employed.
4. The current broad market environment.

If you have been taking swing trades within the longer trend, signs of weakness may encourage you to move on to another, fresher swing trading opportunity. If you hold a core position when signs of a weakening trend arise, following are some options to consider.

Close the Position Close the entire position to lock in the gains and avoid a potential reversal. The downside of this option is that the warning sign(s) may be shrugged off as the trend continues to move forward.

In some cases, your trade will have already been stopped out if price is significantly off its high (long position) or low (short position) by the time a warning occurs. Even though the warnings described in this chapter are early warnings, in some instances price may have moved enough on a percentage basis to trigger a protective stop loss order.

If you choose to close the position or it is stopped out, but you are interested in trading the stock again, keep it on your radar. Monitor it for a reentry opportunity in the future. I keep watchlists of my favorite stocks, and certain groups of stocks (e.g., cloud computing, solar, and so on), and check their charts regularly. I may also maintain alerts in my trading platform for certain stocks to make sure I don't miss an opportunity. Taking steps like these keeps your "woulda-coulda-shoulda" pile from getting too big!

Take Partial Profits Exit part of the position (e.g., from one-third to two-thirds of the shares) in order to lock in some of the profits and reduce the amount of capital exposed to a potential sharp reversal if price follows through on the warning(s). Closely monitor the protective stop on the remainder of the position. If price continues to move against the trade, a trader may choose to close the position (or it gets stopped out), preserving the remaining gains acquired during the trend.

If the trend continues onward instead of reversing direction, you'll benefit from the additional movement with a partial position. There may even be an opportunity to add back the shares previously sold in order to bring the core position back up to full size.

If using hard stop loss orders for protecting capital instead of audible alerts, make sure when you reduce or increase the size of a position that you adjust the protective stop to match the number of shares you currently hold. For example, if you had 1,000 shares of stock and sold 500, but the sell stop was still set for 1,000 shares, if triggered it would sell your remaining 500 and also sell short 500 shares. Policies may vary from one broker to the next. Make sure you understand the order execution policies of your broker to avoid such surprises. Incidentally, the majority of the things I caution you about were learned from personal experience!

Tighten the Protective Stop Don't exit any shares, but instead tighten the protective stop. While this may be fine in the face of a single warning, such as a divergence, it may not be the best option in a case where there are multiple warning signs. If more than one warning occurs, it is a more ominous sign. In those instances, it may be wiser to at least take partial profits.

Stop and Reverse Even multiple warnings do not necessarily warrant entering a position in the opposite direction—for instance, closing a long position and selling short. There may be times, though, when a particular scenario supports doing so. Make sure the criteria are met for a high-probability short position, and require that a price trigger occurs, before simply exiting a long position and going short, or vice versa.

The Trend Is Your Friend until it Ends When you see one or more warnings that the trend may be weakening, you don't have to just leave it in the hands of your stop loss order to get you out, unless doing so is specifically called for in your strategy (e.g., a trend-following system using a stop as the exit strategy). You may choose to take a proactive stance to protect your precious and hard-earned capital.

The above practices fall under the category of money management. Unfortunately, many aspiring traders overlook prudent money management practices, which is one of the primary reasons why so many newcomers fail in this business. Managing risk is the most important element for long-term success.

Initiating a New Position

Let's say there is a stock you have been watching for a chance to go long, and it is currently experiencing a correction. You may notice signs that the downward move is weakening, encouraging you to watch closely for price to bottom out and turn back up, thereby offering that opportunity you seek to go long. I recommend maintaining an alert on that stock's symbol in your broker's platform rather than just keeping an eye on it. I know from experience that it is easy to get distracted by other tasks and miss the opportunity. Remember the "woulda-coulda-shoulda" pile I mentioned earlier?

Another example would be that of a trader who holds a long position in a stock. He may choose to close that position when the uptrend ends and initiate a new position for that same stock in the opposite direction (sell it short) if the trend reverses. This is the stop and reverse technique mentioned previously.

One more example: I monitor trends on the charts of sectors and industry groups, or a specific stock or exchanged traded fund (ETF) that acts as a proxy for that group if there is no index chart. This allows me to monitor where the money is flowing in the marketplace (e.g., watching for sector rotation) in order to participate in opportunities in certain groups of stocks.

Warnings versus Buy–Sell Triggers

I want to be very clear that the discussion in this chapter was about *warnings* of a potential trend change, but that does not mean they are necessarily *triggers to enter or exit a trade*. Rather, it draws the chartist's attention to potential weakness of the trend. A trader should clearly define what constitutes an entry and exit trigger when developing a strategy.

Observing an event doesn't necessarily mean pushing a button to buy or sell. For instance, when a double top appears to be forming (it is still unconfirmed), that may not be a trigger to automatically close a core long position; especially if it is a shallow pattern, and the broad market environment is supporting more upside movement. However, it may encourage a trader to take partial profits.

What looks like a double top forming may turn out to be consolidation; so as long as the stop hasn't triggered on the core trade, you may choose to maintain at least a partial position. Additionally, the appearance of a potential double top does not warrant automatically selling the stock short. The setup should be analyzed for its likelihood of success, and there should be a specific price trigger to encourage a short entry.

There may be instances when a trader does buy or sell based on a warning. For instance, he may exit a long position when price is approaching a major ceiling above. That resistance area serves as a warning, but it is also his *target* for exiting the trade. It is a designated sell trigger as defined by his strategy. Or a trader may exit a long position if price breaks a trendline because that is what his strategy calls for doing. Just make sure to spell out in your strategies the difference between something occurring that requires monitoring versus something that requires executing an order.

CHAPTER 6

Later Trend Reversal Warnings

Astute chartists watch for early warnings of an impending trend reversal, but they also recognize signs that may come later because an early warning won't always present itself. Listed in Table 6.1 are some signs that may be evident after an intermediate- or long-term trend has already begun to change direction. These later warnings are the focus of this chapter.

Some of the earlier warnings outlined in Chapter 5 come before a trend reversal even begins. For instance, when price is approaching a strong ceiling (uptrend) or floor (downtrend), or a trend accelerates, requiring a steeper trendline be drawn, the trend has not yet begun to reverse direction; but it may do so fairly soon.

Other early warnings may occur as the shift in trend direction is taking place. For example, if price is unable to surpass the prior peak, the uptrend may be setting up for a reversal. The key point of the early warnings is that they typically occur either before the trend has changed direction, or before it is significantly off its high (reversal of an uptrend) or up from its low (reversal of a downtrend).

TABLE 6.1 **Later Warnings of Potential Trend Reversal**

Uptrend	Downtrend
Breakdown through Support	Breakout above Resistance
Break of Up (Support) Trendline	Break of Down (Resistance) Trendline
Breakdown below a Strong Moving Average	Breakout above a Strong Moving Average
Change in Direction of Peaks	Change in Direction of Bottoms

The later warnings listed in Table 6.1 tend to occur as price is already breaking down (uptrend) or breaking out (downtrend), or after a change in trend direction is already under way. In some cases, by the time one or more of those warnings occurs, price will already be considerably off the trend's high or low. In other cases, though, it is still relatively early in the trend reversal when the warning(s) occurs.

You may be wondering, "If the trend is already reversing direction, isn't it too late?" The answer is, "No, at least not in many of the cases." There may be much more movement to follow in the direction of the reversal, especially if it is out of a correction and moving again in the direction of the major trend. Recall from Chapter 3 the discussion of how intermediate-term trends that serve to extend the major trend often last significantly longer than the corrective moves. Thus, if you are monitoring a correction looking for an opportunity to initiate a trade in the direction of the major trend, there may still be plenty of upside movement remaining for a long position in a bull market, or plenty of downside movement for a short position in a bear market.

If it is fairly late into the reversal when a warning occurs, an open position may have already been stopped out. Those traders who are disciplined in using mental stops or audible alerts may have already exited as well. But if not, they should take steps to protect their remaining profits and avoid allowing much or all of those gains to be lost; or worse, allowing a positive trade to turn negative.

Traders may benefit greatly from monitoring the intermediate-term trends of the broad market, but longer-term investors would be wise to do so as well. Just imagine if most typical investors knew enough about market trends to react to trend reversal warnings back in 2000 before the Nasdaq declined almost 78 percent; or in late 2007 to early 2008 before that devastating bear market accelerated. Even if they were only monitoring the major trend by periodically checking the weekly chart for trend reversal warnings, trillions of dollars of wealth may have been preserved rather than lost to those bear markets. Using protective stop loss orders would have also helped avoid such devastating losses.

As stated previously, warnings that a trend reversal may occur can also be used to generate new trading opportunities. For traders who are looking for a chance to enter a long position after a downtrend has ended, or to go short after an uptrend has ended, these later warnings provide useful signals. Rather than trying to nail the very top or bottom of a trend, which is not easy to do consistently, in many cases these signs provide more evidence that the trend may be turning. Traders who recognize them can then look for an entry opportunity to get aboard a new trend with a core position; or swing traders may take one or more trades within the new trend.

Here again, imagine if most typical investors knew how to monitor trends for opportunities, and would spend enough time to at least monitor the weekly chart. They may have participated in significantly more of the uptrends during some of the strong bull markets we've experienced in recent decades. Conversely, many investors feel so burned and fearful after a bear market that they hesitate to re-enter the market when the bull returns. They often miss a sizable portion of the next bull market by sitting on the sidelines for too long.

The instruction in this segment is applicable to the potential reversal of an intermediate- or long-term trend. I suggest using the daily chart for analyzing intermediate-term trends. If using a weekly chart to monitor a long-term trend, the warnings described in this chapter may also be observed on that time frame. They may not be applicable to many short-term trends, though, because a price swing may not last long enough to meet the criteria. Some suggestions for monitoring swing trades are included at the end of this chapter.

Be aware that when the word "reversal" is used, it means a change in direction from up to down, or vice versa, but it does not suggest how long it may last or how significant that reversal may eventually be. For instance, price may reverse direction, correcting the prior trend, but we don't know if it will retrace one-third to two-thirds of the prior trend, or erase the entire prior trend and keep going. There will also be instances where a trend reversal appears to be starting, but it turns into a period of consolidation. In other words, you cannot know in advance precisely what price action will follow a warning(s); however, you can make decisions on how to respond to such warnings.

It is the fact that we cannot know how significant a reversal may be that should encourage taking action to protect trading capital. For instance, once an intermediate-term trend has been in force for several weeks to a few months it tends to get overbought (uptrend) or oversold (downtrend) and becomes vulnerable to a correction. A trader may wish to avoid holding an open position through what may turn out to be a significant interruption of the trend. Hence, he may choose to take some defensive action when one or more signs of weakness occur. Refer to the suggestions for responding to trend reversal warnings included at the end of Chapter 5. They are applicable to the discussion in this chapter as well.

Break of Support or Resistance

In order for an uptrend to remain in force, price must eventually surpass each new, higher peak that forms during the trend. In addition, price should find some support when it pulls back. Thus, when price has been trending up but then closes below support, it is an indication that the uptrend may be changing direction.

Figure 6.1 shows a daily chart of Coronado Biosciences, Inc. (CNDO). Price continually formed higher peaks during the intermediate-term uptrend from January to late April 2013. Price pulled back from that final top and found temporary support at the prior pullback's low (horizontal line). A few days later, price plunged down through that level and the 50-period SMA (labeled Breakdown 1).

Prior to that breakdown, there was a negative divergence between price and the RSI (an early warning). The RSI peak labeled *A* formed above the indicator's overbought line. The lower peak labeled *B* formed while the corresponding peak in price was still rising. This example emphasizes the difference between an early warning, which came as the final top of this intermediate-term uptrend formed, and the later warning, which came as the trend began to break down.

After breaking through support (Breakdown 1), note how price attempted to rally back up, forming a potential double bottom below the 50-period SMA.

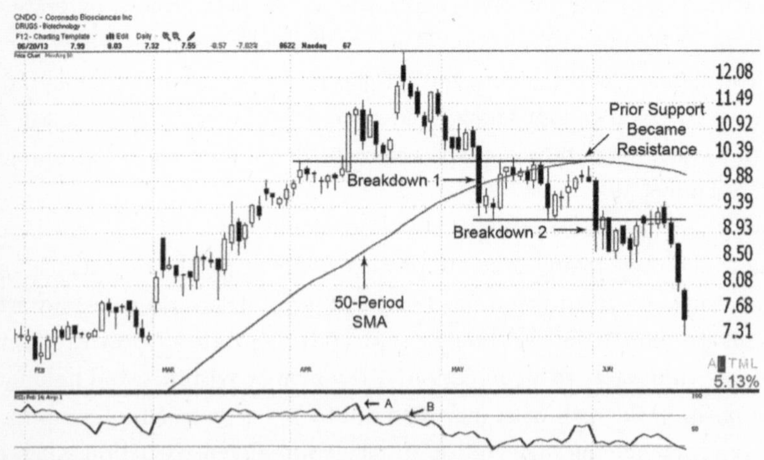

FIGURE 6.1 Price Broke Down below Support
Source: TC2000® chart courtesy of Worden Brothers, Inc.

FIGURE 6.2 The Trend Changed Direction from Down to Sideways to Up
Source: TC2000® chart courtesy of Worden Brothers, Inc.

Price found resistance near the prior breakdown level and the 50-period SMA (prior support became new resistance above price) leaving the bottoming pattern unconfirmed. Price turned down again breaking support at the failed double bottom lows (Breakdown 2), continuing the downtrend. This case illustrates how a bottoming pattern may be consolidation and why it must be confirmed.

Now let's look at a downtrend. In order for the trend to move lower, price must not only surpass each new lower bottom that forms, but it should also find some resistance during the bounces. Therefore, when price has been trending down but then closes above resistance, it is a sign that the downtrend may be reversing direction.

On the daily chart of CSX Corp. (CSX) in Figure 6.2, price was in an intermediate-term downtrend from late August to mid-November 2012. As the November low formed, there was a positive divergence (early warning) between the prominent bottoms in price and the corresponding bottoms on the MACD histogram (labeled A and B). Price did not decline all the way back down to the November bottom and break it. Instead, it moved primarily sideways for the next few weeks forming a ceiling above (horizontal line). In early January 2013, price broke out above that ceiling as well as the 50-period SMA.

Once decisively broken, support and resistance levels tend to reverse roles. Where market participants were once selling at resistance, there will be buyers as price tests that area from the other side as support, and vice versa. In Figure 6.2, soon after the breakout in January, price pulled right back to that prior resistance level and found support there, offering a good opportunity to enter a long position in what was proving to be a new uptrend. This emphasizes my earlier point that, in addition to being utilized for protecting the capital invested and the profits that have built up in open positions, trend reversal warnings may also identify opportunities for initiating new positions in the direction of the emerging trend.

■ Break of a Strong Trendline

In Chapter 5, some examples were shown of tight trendlines being broken, providing an early warning that the trend may be changing direction. Now we'll look at situations where price is further off the high (reversal of an uptrend) or low (reversal of a downtrend) when the trendline is broken.

Break of an Up Trendline

When monitoring an uptrend, maintain an intermediate-length upward-sloping trendline below and connecting the prominent rising bottoms. If monitoring the long-term trend on a weekly chart, maintain a long-term trendline on that time frame.

Figure 6.3 shows an intermediate-term uptrend on the daily chart of Parker Hannifin Corp. (PH). In early March 2013, price tested the February

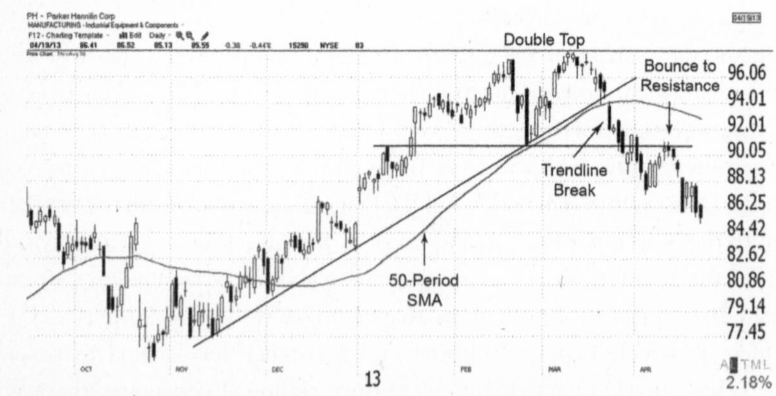

FIGURE 6.3 The Intermediate-Term Trendline Was Broken
Source: TC2000® chart courtesy of Worden Brothers, Inc.

high but did not close decisively above it, which created a potential double top. On March 21, price gapped below the strong up trendline and the 50-period SMA. A few days later price closed below the bottom between the two peaks, confirming the double top and extending the correction that was under way.

From April 4 to 9, price bounced back up to the breakdown level of the double top, where prior support became new resistance above. I hope you are noticing how often support and resistance reverse roles. This is a crucial concept to understand. In this case, it provided two opportunities:

1. Those who held long positions during the intermediate-term uptrend, but had not exited or had their trades stopped out as price broke down, had an opportunity to close the position when price bounced before more downside movement occurred. In doing so, they preserved the remaining gains accrued during the prior uptrend.
2. Those interested in selling the stock short had an opportunity to do so just below a strong resistance area with a good reward-to-risk ratio for at least a swing trade; and where it was more likely there were shares available to borrow since price had been ticking up during the bounce.

Break of a Down Trendline

When monitoring a downtrend, maintain an intermediate-length downward-sloping trendline above and connecting the prominent declining peaks. A close above the declining resistance trendline is required to proclaim it a valid break.

Look again at the chart of CSX in Figure 6.2 and note that the intermediate-length down trendline had been broken prior to the formation of the consolidation during December 2012. Price was not that far off the November low when the line was broken. Between the broken trendline, and then the breakout above the narrow trading range (horizontal trendline), it was a pretty good indication that a new uptrend was starting.

The break of a strong trendline does not necessarily mean a significant trend reversal is imminent. Sometimes the trendline is broken during a deep pullback (up trendline) or strong bounce (down trendline) and the stock resumes the prevailing trend shortly after; or it may be broken during the formation of a shallow base. However, I'll say again that we cannot know, at the right edge of the chart where we must make our trading decisions, how far price may reverse direction once a trendline is broken.

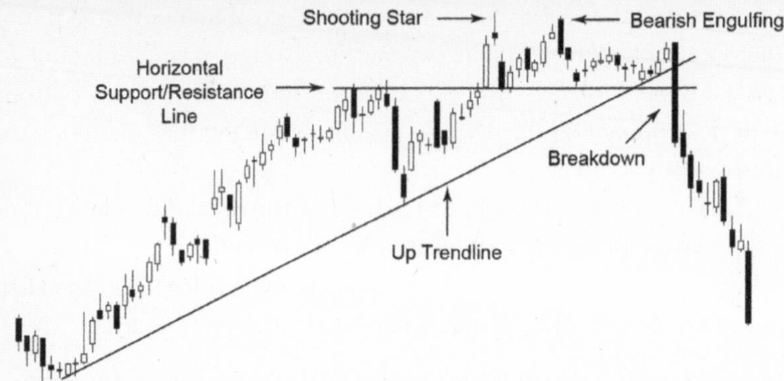

FIGURE 6.4 The Sloped and Horizontal Support Lines Were Both Broken
Source: TC2000® chart courtesy of Worden Brothers, Inc.

Horizontal Support and Resistance Lines

In addition to sloped trendlines, I maintain horizontal lines on the charts that I monitor in order to identify prominent support and resistance levels. If a sloped trendline and a horizontal line are both broken, either simultaneously (Figure 6.4) or in relatively close proximity, for me that is a sterner warning than when only the sloped line is broken; especially if it is a very significant horizontal line (e.g., a long line or one that has been tested several times).

A few times throughout this book, I suggest that the initial break of a trend may be sharp and fast. Figure 6.4 is an example. Note the very long bearish candle on the breakdown day. Plenty of damage was done to the uptrend with that single candle. Price continued down for the next several days with only brief pauses along the way.

When trying to exit during a swift break, or if a stop order is triggered, the order may suffer quite a lot of slippage. Now you see why I watch for those earlier warnings. In Figure 6.4, prior to the breakdown, a bearish Shooting Star formed at the top of the intermediate-term uptrend. Several days later, price tested but did not close above that peak. Therefore, price failed to surpass the prior peak and also left a Bearish Engulfing pattern behind (early warnings).

■ Break of a Strong Moving Average

During a trend, price may have a tendency to remain above (uptrend) or below (downtrend) a certain moving average. For example, during a strong uptrend in which the stock or index experiences only minor interruptions, price may remain above the 20-period simple moving average (SMA) for a prolonged period of time. If the pullbacks are deeper, price may remain above the 50-period SMA.

The 20- and 50-period settings are fairly robust and they may offer support (uptrend) or resistance (downtrend) when tested. I primarily use the simple setting for the moving averages for this purpose. However, there may be instances where a stock tends to test the exponential line, and I will utilize the exponential setting in those cases.

The 20-period SMA can be broken relatively quickly; however, it takes a more significant move to break the 50-period SMA. By that time, a correction may be under way. A minor correction may only reach the 50-period SMA, but a deeper correction will break it.

Breakdown below a Strong Moving Average

When a stock or index in an uptrend closes below a strong moving average that it has remained above during the trend, especially if that moving average had previously provided support when tested, it is a signal that the uptrend may be changing direction.

Figure 6.5 shows a daily chart of Hasbro, Inc. (HAS). Price remained above the 20-period SMA for the entire intermediate-term uptrend. Hence, a break of that moving average would have me watching closely for more signs of weakness for the uptrend. Those signs came very soon in the form of the sloped trendline and the horizontal support line being broken.

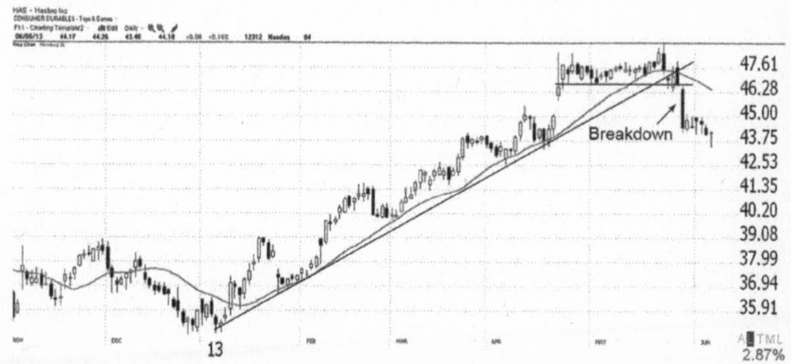

FIGURE 6.5 Price Closed below the 20-Period SMA after Remaining above It for a Prolonged Period

Source: TC2000® chart courtesy of Worden Brothers, Inc.

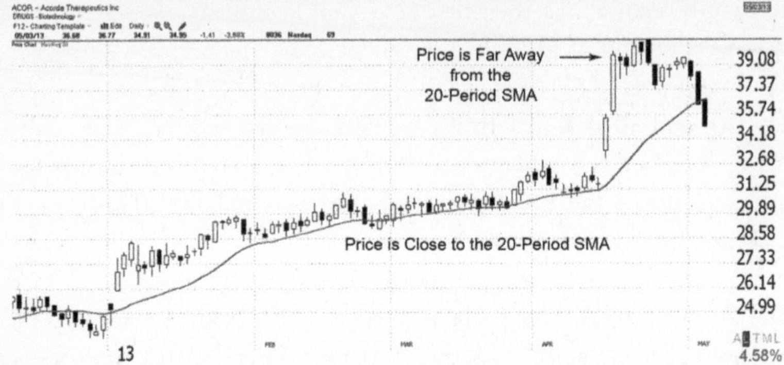

FIGURE 6.6 Price Remained Close to the 20-Period SMA for a Few Months Followed by a Swift Move up from the Moving Average
Source: TC2000® chart courtesy of Worden Brothers, Inc.

A close below (uptrend) or above (downtrend) the 20-period SMA is not always followed by a significant trend reversal. For instance, sometimes the 20-period SMA is broken during a pullback but the stock rebounds shortly after. And if price moves sideways, the 20-period SMA will flatten out so price may close above and below it during that period.

In some cases, price will be relatively far off the trend's top (uptrend) or bottom (downtrend) when a strong moving average is broken. In other cases, it will not take a significant move to break it. It depends on the price action that *preceded* the topping or bottoming of the trend, respectively. For instance, during a strong or extended swing, price can get fairly far away from even the short-term moving averages. In those cases, it may take a while for price to break the 20-period SMA as illustrated in Figure 6.6.

Conversely, price may trend closely to the 20-period SMA (or even hug it) for stretches of time. For example, during an uptrend there may be times when price works its way up relatively slowly with only brief pauses or very minor interruptions. This scenario is illustrated in Figure 6.6 as well. The 20-period SMA will follow the price action closely during that time. In those cases, the moving average would be broken very quickly if a trend reversal started, serving as an early warning. However, because price is close to the 20-period SMA, it may break the moving average as it makes a very minor movement giving a false signal of a breakdown. Thus, watch for more evidence of a solid breakdown (e.g., the break of a trendline or horizontal support line) when price is so close to the moving average.

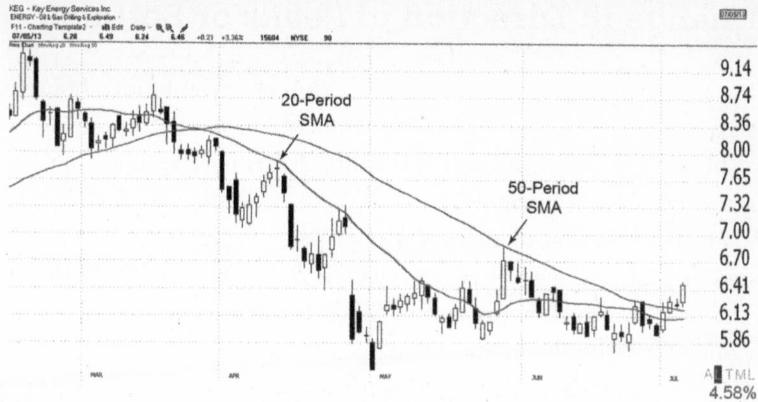

FIGURE 6.7 Price Closed above the 20-Period SMA after Being below it for a Prolonged Period
Source: TC2000® chart courtesy of Worden Brothers, Inc.

Breakout above a Strong Moving Average

During a downtrend, watch for a close above a moving average that price has remained below during the decline. Figure 6.7 shows a daily chart of Key Energy Services, Inc. (KEG). Each bounce during the downtrend found resistance at the 20-period SMA until May 2013 when price closed above that moving average for the first time in a few months.

As price shifted from down to sideways during May to June, note how the 20-period SMA flattened out. At the right edge of the chart, the 50-period SMA had caught up with price and offered resistance above for a few weeks. At the time of this writing, price had very recently closed above it.

If you are wondering why I have not referenced the 100- and 200-period SMAs, it is because usually by the time price reaches those levels a reversal is already well under way. In fact, I'd be monitoring those moving averages to see if price finds support (bull market correction) or resistance (bear market rally) there that stops a reversal that is under way.

In summary: In the early stages of a trend reversal, watch for short-term moving averages to be broken as a warning of a potential reversal. Once the change has occurred and price is trending the other direction, watch for longer-term moving averages that had been farther away to provide potential support or resistance.

■ Change in Direction of Peaks or Bottoms

During an uptrend, when the price peaks stop rising and move sideways, it signals a loss of momentum. It may be a double or triple top setting up, or it may be a period of consolidation forming. A stronger reversal sign occurs when the price peaks begin declining.

When the direction of the prominent price peaks shifts downward, it is a sign the uptrend may be reversing direction (Figure 6.8). Once a new, prominent lower peak is present, a down trendline can be started above and connecting the declining peaks. When I refer to a prominent price pivot, I mean one where there is a clear support or resistance level created by the pivoting action (or formed from minor consolidation). There will be many very minor pivots that form within trends that I do not consider to be prominent. They won't stand out on the charts like the prominent price pivots do.

After a downtrend, if the prominent bottoms begin rising (also illustrated in Figure 6.8), the trend may be in transition from down to up. Once a new, prominent higher bottom is present, an up trendline can be started below and connecting the rising bottoms.

When the peaks begin declining after an uptrend, it may form a head-and-shoulders top, which is a classic bearish reversal pattern (Figure 6.9). After a downtrend, the rising bottoms may form a bullish head-and-shoulders bottom reversal pattern.

A head-and-shoulders pattern is not confirmed until its "neckline" is broken. By then, in some cases a reversal may be well under way; especially

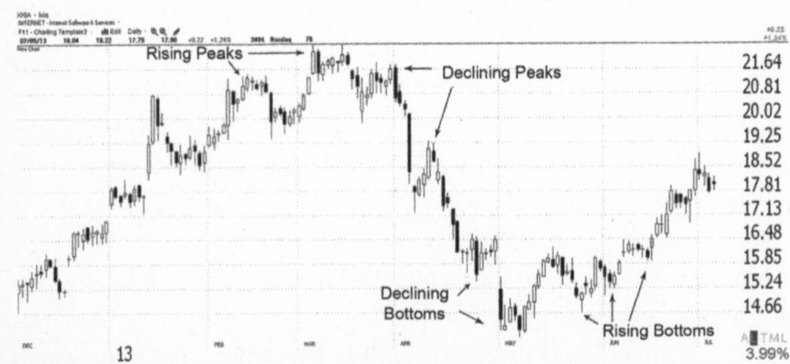

FIGURE 6.8 Peaks and Bottoms Helped Identify Trend Reversals
Source: TC2000® chart courtesy of Worden Brothers, Inc.

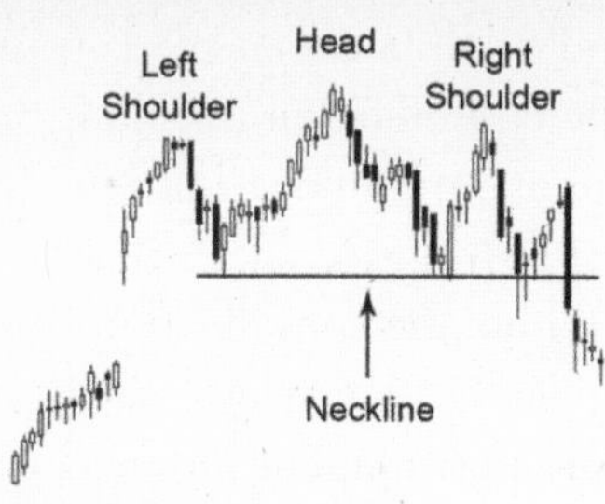

FIGURE 6.9 Head-and-Shoulders Top

if it is a downward-sloping neckline for a head-and-shoulders top, or an upward-sloping neckline for a head-and-shoulders bottom.

If a trader is focusing on trading the pattern itself, he may choose to wait for confirmation of a neckline break before entering a trade. However, if a chartist is looking for earlier trend change warnings, he should notice a change in the direction of the peaks even if he doesn't realize it is a head-and-shoulders pattern forming.

Shift to a Period of Consolidation

There will be instances when it appears that a trend reversal may be starting, but it turns out to be a period of consolidation. For example, if the peaks in an uptrend start declining but the bottoms are still rising (Figure 6.10), price may be forming a symmetrical triangle. In a downtrend, a symmetrical triangle may be present when the bottoms begin rising but the peaks are still declining. Although price may reverse direction after consolidating in a symmetrical triangle, these are continuation patterns—they often break in the direction of the prior trend.

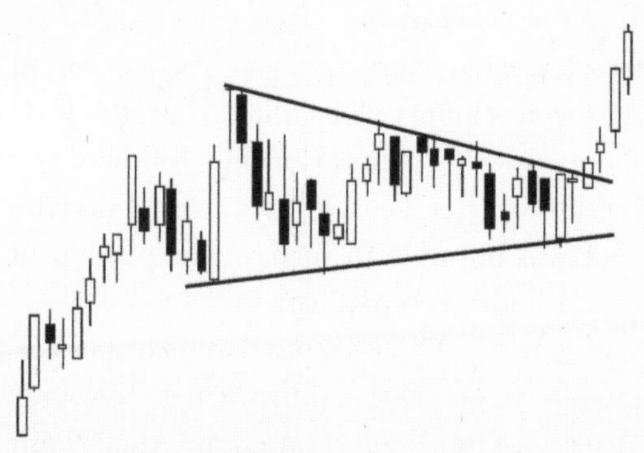

FIGURE 6.10 Symmetrical Triangle

If the swings back and forth between the consolidation boundaries are deep enough, and/or the consolidation lasts long enough, it may break an intermediate-length support trendline (uptrend) or resistance trendline (downtrend). The nearest moving averages will also catch up with price and may flatten or whipsaw within the consolidation.

When price is consolidating, the swings may be deep enough to trigger a protective stop on a core position. For instance, if using a volatility-based trailing stop that adjusts automatically to price movement, it may be tightened enough to be triggered.

A trader may choose to exit a core position (or take partial profits) due to a warning, such as a trendline being broken; or the trailing stop may be triggered. If it ultimately proves to be a period of consolidation, and he is still interested in owning the stock, the price action can be monitored for a breakout. A new position can be established as a trend emerges again; or if the trader still holds a partial position having taken some profits, the shares that were exited may be added back to bring the position up to full size again.

■ Multiple Warnings

Multiple technical warnings may occur, suggesting a higher likelihood of a change in trend direction than a single warning. There may be more than one early warning, or more than one later sign, or a combination of multiple early and later warnings (a convergence of technical signals).

Figure 6.11 shows a daily chart of Ingram Micro, Inc. (IM). There were several signs suggesting the intermediate-term uptrend may be shifting sideways or in danger of turning down. The following discussion corresponds to the warnings labeled in the chart and indicator windows:

1. Climax Move—On February 14, 2013, price gapped up with heavy volume, creating a potential exhaustion gap. The gap was filled several days later and did provide support when filled. Thus, this gap by itself was not of great concern. However, other warnings followed.
2. Failure to Break the Prior Peak—Price turned up after filling the gap and tested, but was not able to surpass, the prior peak. That set up a potential bearish double top pattern.
3. Negative Divergence—When testing that prior peak, a negative divergence occurred between price and the MACD histogram.
4. Trendline Break—After being raised up tightly under price, the intermediate-term up trendline was decisively broken on April 2.

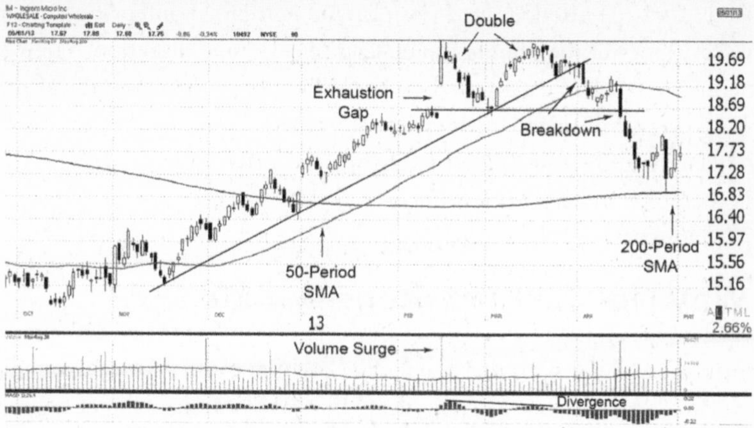

FIGURE 6.11 Multiple Trend Reversal Warnings
Source: TC2000® chart courtesy of Worden Brothers, Inc.

5. Moving Average Break—The following day, price closed below the 50-period SMA.
6. Declining Peaks—The peaks shifted from rising to declining.
7. Break of Horizontal Support—The line where price had previously filled the gap was broken on April 12.

Note that numbers 1 through 4 above were all early warnings that were outlined in Chapter 5. Numbers 5 through 7 occurred after the shift from uptrend to downtrend was already in progress.

Earlier in this chapter I indicated that a longer moving average, such as the 200-period, should be watched for potential support or resistance once a trend reversal is under way. In Figure 6.11, price declined nearly 15 percent to the 200-period SMA during the reversal (retracement) of the prior uptrend. The long-term uptrend resumed (not shown) after the successful test of that strong moving average.

Even with several negatives weighing against a trend, there will be instances where price defies them and moves higher (uptrend) or lower (downtrend). However, the probability is high that price will change direction, at least temporarily. And that's precisely what occurred in Figure 6.11. This exemplifies why I often take partial profits on a core position upon the emergence of early warnings and maintain a defensive posture on the remainder of the shares. In some instances, I may even prepare to enter a short position due to the preponderance of warnings.

If a trader had exited his long position in Figure 6.11 and price had moved above resistance at the double top instead of reversing direction, a new position could have been established on the other side of that barrier. If part of the long position was closed in order to capture some profits, shares could have been repurchased (added back) on the other side of that barrier to bring the position back up to full size.

■ Why Not Just Let Stops Get Me Out?

As you reviewed the signs that warn of a potential trend reversal, you may be wondering, "Why bother learning these things? My stops will get me out if a trend changes direction." It is important to learn these concepts in order to become a skilled chartist. The warnings outlined in Chapters 5 and 6 reveal important information about how trends start, progress, and finally end.

And while it is true that a stop loss order will eventually get you out of a trade, that choice is not without its challenges. First and foremost, if you will simply set a protective stop and let it be your exit strategy, it is imperative that you implement the stop with discipline. Novices have a tendency to make costly decisions with stop orders, such as the following:

- Failing to place a stop loss order because they intend to watch the price action and close the position if the trend breaks (referred to as a mental stop). I could write pages on the havoc this decision can wreak, both financially and emotionally. Many traders intend to exit the trade, but end up watching their gains disappear; or even worse, allow a winning trade to turn into a loser.
- Traders have been known to place a stop loss order, but cancel it when they notice that price is approaching the order. The trader does not want to acknowledge that the market has moved against him, and he believes he can recover the profits that have been lost (or salvage the trade if it has gone negative). This often ends badly.
- Placing the stop loss order very far away from price to allow the stock plenty of room to avoid getting stopped out unnecessarily. When the stop is triggered, a significant amount of the profits that had built up in the trade are lost. In some cases, all the profits are erased and the trade has turned into a loss.

If using stops for an exit strategy, I strongly advise placing sensible stop loss orders and obeying them. Unless a trader has absolutely proven he'll pull the trigger to exit when required, he should place the order rather than using a mental stop or an alert.

Disciplined traders may choose to use mental stops or alerts (also referred to as alarms). I regularly use audible alerts in lieu of stop loss orders to avoid much of the price manipulation (running of the stops) that can occur in the marketplace. I also use alerts to avoid having stops triggered by morning gaps that may quickly reverse direction after the opening bell. However, like so many newcomers, when I first began trading I endured some painful experiences with large losses. I had to shift to using stop loss orders. Once I gained enough experience and discipline in my trading activities, I was able to go back to utilizing alerts.

Many of the stop loss orders I do set are volatility-based trailing stops; I especially like them for core positions. I recommend looking into this method of stop loss management. The stop is automatically adjusted as price moves in the direction of the trend, by an amount based on that particular stock's current volatility rather than some arbitrary percentage. If price ticks down (long position) or up (short position), the stop locks in to protect the capital and the gains that have built up in the position.

If used effectively, trailing stops can be a great tool for traders, especially for investors who may primarily hold core positions. Even though I use them, I still monitor the trends of my open positions; and for me, it is still imperative to monitor the trends of the market averages. In spite of using trailing stops, I still tend to periodically take partial profits on core positions. It is not unusual for me to swing trade around a core position, the technique I referred to earlier as Lock and Reload. Thus, I monitor trades for such opportunities.

Even when using stops, the following concepts support spending time monitoring the trend:

- When a trend begins to break, often the first move down off the top (or up from the bottom) is very sharp and fast. A stop loss order may suffer quite a lot of slippage (sometimes severe slippage) before it is executed. Taking partial profits reduces the amount of capital exposed to that type of swift move.

- Failing to monitor the trend may leave a trader unprepared to participate in an emerging trend in the opposite direction when it occurs.

- Failing to monitor the trend of the broad market would mean not spotting the opportunities that suggest it makes sense to increase the overall financial exposure (or decrease it), or change strategies, based on the market environment. You'll learn more about this in Part II.

In my opinion, the focus should be on managing risk and improving profitability rather than how to do less work. For those who wish to be active traders and/or take control of their own long-term investments, and if they wish to produce above-average returns, let alone superior returns, doing so requires a commitment of time and effort.

Market participants may achieve above-average returns either by managing their own funds with prudent risk management and an edge that allows them to excel; or they may turn their money over to a trusted and proven individual who can produce good returns for them by managing their money wisely.

If you choose to do it yourself, you'll need to commit to the process. And if you intend to trade for a living, this becomes your job. It must be treated like a business. I do not know of any venture where the business activities can be put on autopilot and expect it to survive, let alone thrive. But fortunately, this is also a mentally stimulating business with a lot of potential for wealth creation. Those who are successful get paid for their time and effort.

Mechanical Systems versus Discretionary Trading Strategies

Traders using trend-following methods stay with the trend until forced to exit. Some traders will use automated (mechanical) systems, and may have no interest in monitoring the trend for warnings. Others will use discretionary methods and may gain an important edge in the marketplace by monitoring the trends.

If you do not wish to monitor trends regularly and execute trades using discretionary techniques, look into implementing a mechanical system where the entry and exit signals are computer generated. But keep in mind that executing such a system still requires plenty of work—first to develop the system and test it, and then the ongoing task of implementing the system and monitoring it to ensure it maintains its efficacy.

You'll need to have the discipline to implement the system consistently, as it is intended, and not override the signals it generates. For instance, if the system suggests that you may need to endure a potentially significant drawdown of your account equity in order to achieve the gains indicated through testing, you must be able to work through the anxiety you may feel when such drawdown occurs. Assume that it will occur at some time rather than hoping the drawdown won't happen to you.

Here's an example of how a trader may fail with a mechanical system even though it has proven to be very profitable in testing. Let's say the system testing suggests it may endure drawdown of up to 30 percent of account equity if certain conditions were to arise (e.g., the trend-following system gets whipped around in a choppy market). At some point, the trader's account declines by 25 percent. That is less than the maximum drawdown of 30 percent. However, the trader gets frustrated or despondent and decides to *not* allow the system to take the next trade that is indicated. He has now overridden his tested system. Inevitably, soon after doing so, the conditions bearing against the system change and he is not invested in the market when the system shifts back to a positive mode. He misses the opportunity to recover the drawdown, and to go on to enjoy the gains the system showed were possible.

Some of the most successful traders in the world use mechanical systems, so please do not misread what I'm saying. *I am not criticizing mechanical systems.* In fact, many traders would argue they are superior to discretionary trading methods. It is not my intention to try to influence you to use one or the other. But not everyone feels able to, or desires to, trade a mechanical system for a variety of reasons.

First, one must develop the mechanical system. Many newcomers wouldn't know where to start. It requires that you be able to specifically define the parameters of your system in order to generate the needed buy and sell signals. Next, you'll need to back-test your theory against a sufficient amount of data, and then forward trade it to prove it is viable. It may need some tweaking and optimizing, retesting, and then putting it back to work again in real time.

You must be able to code the strategy, or hire someone skilled at doing so, in order to test it and receive the trade execution signals. There are software platforms that can help with this process, such as MetaStock and TradeStation. These are sophisticated programs, so it is important to put in the time and effort to become proficient in their use. Alternatively, you may be able to purchase a mechanical system. Master traders with very successful mechanical systems may not be willing to share them, though, at any price. There are a number of "black box" systems available for purchase, but they have their pros and cons to be sure.

You must also be extremely disciplined with implementing the system, and have the risk tolerance and emotional control to withstand up to the maximum drawdown the system may experience (refer to the example above of a trader who overrode the system).

If you feel you may be well suited to employ a mechanical system, your work becomes that of designing, testing, and implementing the automated system. You should still continue on with this book, because you'll develop an important foundation of technical analysis, and the content may help you generate ideas for your trading system.

If a mechanical system sounds suited to you, I suggest reading the book *Trend Following* by Michael Covel. I also recommend reading *Trade Your Way to Financial Freedom* by Van Tharp to get you focused on the importance of risk management. In fact, I suggest reading both books even if you intend to trade a discretionary system because, in my opinion, they are excellent resources that include important information and insights for all traders.

If you don't believe a mechanical system is well suited to you, and you prefer to implement discretionary techniques as I currently do, you'll still need to develop a strategy with rules and guidelines to follow, and put it to work successfully in the marketplace. In order to do so, you'll need a strong knowledge base of technical analysis. This book will help you with that development. Trend analysis is the crux of technical analysis, so you're on your way. A discretionary strategy will also experience periods of drawdown; how much will depend on a trader's knowledge, how effectively he employs his capital, and how well he controls risk.

Whether you opt for a mechanical system or discretionary trading methods, there is work to be done. The tasks may vary, but rest assured there are tasks that need doing; and there are things to be learned for either method. Wall Street is seldom kind to the unprepared individual!

■ Swing Trading Tips

The discussion of the various trend change signals included in this chapter and in Chapter 5 was geared primarily toward intermediate- and long-term trends. Swing traders benefit from short-term price moves. However, that does not mean these chapters are not helpful to them. Quite the contrary—short-term traders can benefit greatly from this information.

One of the tasks I consider most important for my swing trading activities is that of analyzing trends. I continually monitor the intermediate-term trend, regardless of whether I'm executing short-term trades or managing core positions. Let's explore this further.

Price Swings Form within Intermediate-Term Trends

Remember, many intermediate-length trends are actually strung together by a few to several short-term price swings. A swing trader may "work a trend." That is, he may recognize an opportunity for a swing trade early in the development of a new intermediate-term trend. Rather than just taking that one swing trade and moving on, he may take a few to several trades in that stock as long as the intermediate-term trend is still in force. Thus, it is in his interest to be alert for signs of a potential reversal of that trend.

If a trader sees signs that a trend he has been extracting profits from is getting exhausted, he may choose to look for a fresh opportunity elsewhere, at least for a while. He can always keep that stock on his radar and come back to it, for instance, to trade it on the long side again after a correction. Unless, of course, the trader is also skilled at trading the short side, in which case he may attempt to benefit on the downside for a while when the uptrend reverses direction.

Swings Are Trends on Lower Time Frames

As stated previously, a short-term trend may not last long enough to meet the criteria of some of the warning signs covered in Chapters 5 and 6. However, recall from discussion in Chapter 3 that a price *swing* on one time frame is a *trend* on a lower time frame due to the number of bars included each day for the intraday time frames. Thus, a swing trader may monitor a trend on an intraday time frame to assist with the management of a trade he chose based on a setup selected from the daily chart.

If price makes a swing up for a period of five days, that is an intermediate-term uptrend on the hourly chart and a long-term uptrend on lower time frames. Since there is a trend present on the lower time frame, a swing trader may monitor that trend for warning signs, which would suggest that the price swing on the daily chart is losing momentum or starting to change direction.

Figure 6.12 shows a two-chart layout of National Penn Bancshares, Inc. (NPBC) with the daily chart on the left and the hourly chart on the right. Let's say a swing trader held a long position as price made a strong swing up during June to July 2013. He wanted to avoid giving back a significant amount of those profits during a potential pullback. That short-term swing up on the daily chart was an intermediate-term uptrend on the hourly chart because there are seven hourly bars in one trading day.

The trader may have chosen to monitor the trend on the lower time frame for warnings of a potential reversal. Signs of a reversal of the trend on the

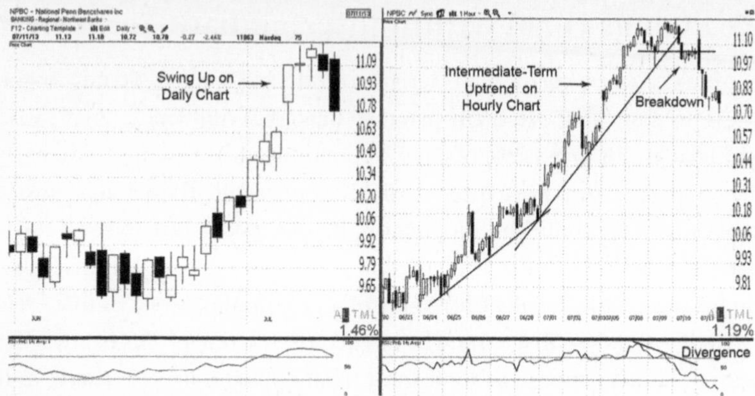

FIGURE 6.12 Trend Reversal Warnings on the Hourly Chart
Source: TC2000® chart courtesy of Worden Brothers, Inc.

hourly chart would suggest that price may soon pull back on the daily chart (early warning) or may already be starting to pull back (later warning). Note the following on the hourly chart in Figure 6.12:

- The uptrend accelerated, resulting in a steeper trendline being drawn.
- Price failed to close decisively above the prior peak and broke the up trendline.
- There was a negative divergence between price and the RSI.
- Price formed a slightly lower peak. In fact, a head-and-shoulders top marked the end of the uptrend.
- Price broke down below the horizontal support line. By that time, a pullback had started on the daily chart.

Swing-Ending Warnings

I may periodically check an intraday chart for trend-ending warnings on the lower time frame as described above. However, when I choose a price setup from the daily chart for a swing trade, the daily chart is the main time frame. Therefore, I would watch for the following on the daily time frame, which I refer to as swing-ending warnings:

- Support and Resistance—When a price swing is approaching a level that is perceived to be resistance (up swing) or support (down swing), such as one or more price pivots or a strong moving average, swing traders consider that level to be a target. Price may retreat from such a barrier.

- Loss of Momentum—The body size of the candlesticks is a barometer for short-term momentum. After the formation of average-to-long bodies for a few to several days, I take notice if the body size decreases significantly. It may turn out to be just a brief pause, or it may be the prelude to a reversal.
- Candlestick Reversal Patterns—As illustrated in several examples in this book, a candlestick pattern often marks the end of a price swing.
- Morning Gaps—A morning gap occurs when price gaps open but then reverses direction intraday and fills the gap before the end of the trading session. If a price swing is getting extended, I'll often exit at the opening bell, or in the pre-market session if possible, if price is set to gap open. It may act like an exhaustion gap on intraday charts—the gap may end up being the start of what turns out to be a pullback (after an up swing) or bounce (after a down swing).

■ Categorizing and Quick Reference Guides

By reading and absorbing Chapters 5 and 6, you are benefitting from some of the frustration I experienced many years ago. Like most newcomers to chart analysis, when I first began my studies, I tried to soak up all the information I could from several different technical analysis books. One of them had almost 500 pages, and I read every single page twice!

I noticed as I studied the various chapters of the various books, I'd often come across a statement such as "this often precedes a reversal of the trend" or "this may suggest the trend is losing momentum." I'd see similar statements in later chapters, or in other charting books. I started to see a pattern—there were apparently several signs that may occur prior to, during, or soon after a trend reversal begins.

It was one of those "aha moments." I thought, "I sure wish all the technical warnings that may precede or accompany a trend reversal were just listed in one spot instead of having to comb through hundreds of pages to learn it all." So I started a list of trend reversal warnings and hung it on my trading wall. I added to it every time I read or re-read a charting book and learned about another warning. I also created other quick reference lists as I progressed in my studies. Doing so really helped me to learn, and retain, the information. I encourage you to do the same.

I believe this gets at the heart of why learning technical analysis is challenging for many aspiring traders. They read book after book and get a *head full of knowledge*, but they can't quite get their arms around it all to put it to work by *applying that knowledge*. Thus, I strive to categorize the concepts that I teach in a way that makes the information easer to learn, understand, and ultimately retain. One of my clients referred to me as "scary organized," so that probably has a lot to do with my compulsion to categorize things and make quick reference lists.

Chapters 5 and 6 were derived from that list of trend reversal warnings I made years ago. I've now shared it with you, along with a description and picture of every item on the list so you have the details you need to apply the information. But once you've reviewed these two chapters a couple of times, you can use the summary below as a quick reference guide. Hang it on your trading wall and refer to it until you know it so well you no longer need it.

Trend Reversal Quick Reference Guide

Early Warnings of Potential Trend Reversal

Uptrend	Downtrend
Bearish Climax Move	Bullish Climax Move
Bearish Divergence—Price vs. Indicator	Bullish Divergence—Price vs. Indicator
Failure to Break Prior Peak	Failure to Break Prior Bottom
Change of Slope—Steeper Rising Trendline	Change of Slope—Steeper Declining Trendline
Break of Tight Rising Trendline	Break of Tight Declining Trendline
Approaching a Strong Ceiling	Approaching a Strong Floor
Bearish Candlestick Reversal Pattern	Bullish Candlestick Reversal Pattern

Later Warnings of Potential Trend Reversal

Uptrend	Downtrend
Breakdown through Support	Breakout above Resistance
Break of Up (Support) Trendline	Break of Down (Resistance) Trendline
Breakdown below a Strong Moving Average	Breakout above a Strong Moving Average
Change in Direction of Peaks	Change in Direction of Bottoms

PART II

Putting Trend Analysis to Work

CHAPTER 7

The Broad Market

In addition to analyzing the charts of the stocks you trade, it is important to be aware of the trends of the broad market. Traders usually see improvement in their results when they implement monitoring of the market's movements into their routines.

One of the great things about being a technical trader is that you don't have to be an expert on all the things that may impact the market. The market is a discounting mechanism. It is continually pricing in all known information, such as economic conditions, government legislation, severe weather conditions, energy crises, and so on—everything that may affect the balance of supply and demand.

The market is always looking ahead. For instance, let's say something is anticipated to occur up to several months down the line (e.g., a specific piece of legislation). Market participants anticipate the future impact and begin pricing it in immediately rather than waiting until later when the event actually occurs. You may have heard the phrase "Buy the rumor, sell the news." The market also prices in seasonal events, such as anticipated holiday retail sales.

The market quickly prices in new information. For example, in May and June 2013, when the Federal Reserve commented about potentially decreasing (tapering) the $85 billion-a-month bond-buying program, the market responded by selling off. After years of very accommodative monetary policy, the market was not thrilled at the prospect of having the punch bowl taken away. The market was long overdue for a correction, so that news just helped it along. After such news is fully digested, the market adjusts to any initial overreaction (or underreaction).

Rumors and false information get discounted as well. In April 2013, a tweet was released from the Associated Press (AP) Twitter account suggesting President Obama had been injured in an explosion at the White House. The market began to sell off. Soon after, it was revealed the AP's account had been hacked and the information was false. The market recovered quickly.

Because of this tendency to discount information, the price movement on the chart reveals how the market anticipates and responds to all known events, whether you know about those events or not. Given that, some analysts may elect to solely focus on the charts while largely ignoring the external factors that influence the price action on those charts.

With that said, I like to know what makes things tick, so I do spend some time delving into the underlying fundamental factors that move the market. I find the background information is not only interesting (call me a geek if you wish), but I feel it adds a lot to my knowledge base. It gives me important insights, and ideas are generated from that knowledge and understanding. However, it still comes down to the analysis of the market trends, and watching for sector rotation and leadership that is revealed on charts, which provide the keys to my trading activities.

The Business Cycle

The direction of short- and intermediate-term trends of the major market averages can be influenced by rumor, news, and the sentiment of market participants. However, when evaluating the long-term trend of the market, chartists should be aware of the crucial role that fundamentals play. In this case, the word "fundamentals" is in reference to the condition of the U.S. economy.

Bull and bear markets are largely driven by the business cycle, which may also be referred to as the economic cycle. The business cycle does not provide precise timing signals; it is for big-picture analysis. Shifts in economic conditions typically occur over time rather than in an abrupt manner. *Note:* If you wish to learn more about the business cycle, I suggest starting with the book *Beating the Business Cycle* by Lakshman Achuthan and Anirvan Banerji.

The business cycle includes phases of expansion and contraction. Generally speaking, during periods where the economy is expanding, the market is bullish, and during times when the economy is contracting, the market is bearish. I say generally because the market tends to lead the economy.

The stock market is anticipatory—it often turns down before the economic conditions worsen significantly (bull market reversal), or turns up prior to dramatic improvement (bear market reversal).

A broad market decline coincides with a contraction phase. The United States experienced a severe contraction during 2007 to 2009 as evidenced by that vicious bear market. Contraction may be accompanied by an economic recession. The worst recession in decades coincided with the last contraction phase. The market is currently in an expansionary phase; however, during this cycle it has been one of slow economic growth and stubbornly high unemployment, making it difficult for the economy to experience prosperity. But as far as the stock market is concerned, it has clearly done well for the past few years. It has been helped along greatly by the extraordinary measures (monetary policy) employed by the Federal Reserve.

Although the long-term trend is primarily influenced by fundamentals, major trends can be exacerbated by the emotions of market participants (e.g., greed and fear). How else can one explain market bubbles, such as the dot-com and housing bubbles that ran to dizzying heights but then burst? And looking at the decline into the March 2009 bear market low, it was evident that severe panic had taken hold, pushing the market lower than may have been merited by the fundamentals.

■ Let the Market Be Your Guide

One of the primary tasks of many experienced traders is to continually monitor the broad market to determine the direction and strength of the trends that occur. Monitoring the broad market's movements is such an important part of my routine that Part II of this book has been devoted to its discussion. I continually do so for the reasons stated below:

- The market environment may have a significant influence on individual stocks, regardless of the respective fundamentals of the underlying companies. Most stocks tend to move in the general direction of the broad market averages. Thus, the Wall Street adage "A rising tide raises all boats" (and vice versa).
- The market environment influences the price setups and strategies I trade at any given time, and how assertively or conservatively I trade them.

I also regularly monitor the market movement because, I must admit, I'm a bit obsessed with the market! I really do enjoy doing this. It is fascinating to watch it all unfold—you'll learn a lot about market behavior through paying attention to the contributing factors, and continually monitoring the market trend.

Before determining how, what, and when you'll trade, it is important to understand how the market you'll be trading works. Learn about the organizing principles of the market—the fundamental and technical concepts that tend to hold fairly consistently over time. Understanding how the market works can give a trader an edge. That's why so much of the focus of this book is on analyzing the trends of the broad market to guide your trading.

It is okay to try to anticipate market movement; however, I discourage being dogmatic with predictions about what the market should do. Rather, just regularly assimilate data and information, and analyze the charts watching for technical signs that provide confirmation of the trend, or warnings that it may be weakening or changing direction.

If the market doesn't do what you predicted, don't insist on being right. Adjust to the market conditions. For instance, during every bull market there are a number of stubborn bearish traders who are short the market, insisting that it must turn down soon. Even as the market continues to move higher, they believe they will soon be vindicated. There's an old adage that goes something like this: "The market can remain irrational longer than a trader can remain solvent."

Monitoring the Market

What does it mean to monitor the market? To me, since I trade the stock market, it primarily refers to the following three concepts:

1. Monitor the Charts—Regularly monitor the price action on the chart of a stock index that represents the broad market, such as the Dow Jones Industrial Average or the S&P 500 Index. Periodically review other charts that reveal additional information (e.g., market sectors, bonds, commodities, and so on).
2. Monitor the Market Internals—Regularly review the internal market measures in order to gauge the strength (or weakness) of the market trend. Review other market sentiment measures for clues as well.
3. Monitor the Fundamentals—Stay up to date on news, events, and economic reports that have a tendency to impact the markets.

Monitoring the charts is the primary focus of this book, so most of the discussion will focus on that task. However, some discussion on items 2 and 3 above is also included.

The information provided in all the chapters in Part I is applicable to trends that occur on the charts of individual stocks as well as indices. In the chapters in Part II, the focus shifts to monitoring the market to guide our overall trading decisions. Thus, some new concepts will be introduced that are applicable specifically to broad market analysis rather than to the charts of individual stocks. For instance, market internals will be introduced, as well as scanning for stocks that meet certain conditions. Market internals and scans reflect the movement of many stocks, which is representative of the market as a whole, versus just one specific stock.

Monitor the Charts

A market average, or index, is a market barometer. An index may provide a measure of the overall performance of the stock market, meaning it is a major or broad market average. There are also indices that represent specific segments of the market, such as transportation and utilities. There are indices that represent currencies, commodities, the bond market, foreign markets, and more.

Many index charts reflect the movement of their components. Thus, the price scale actually reflects values rather than prices. However, the word "price" is generically used in charting and should be construed to mean the value when indexes are referenced.

Select Market Barometers to Monitor You'll need to decide which market averages you'll monitor. In the United States, traders analyze the condition of the stock market primarily by observing the charts of the following market averages. Traders often use slang words to quickly identify them (indicated in parenthesis):

- Dow Jones Industrial Average (the Dow).
- S&P 500 Index (the S&P).
- Nasdaq Composite Index (the Nasdaq, the Composite, or the Naz).
- S&P 400 Mid Cap Index (the Midcaps).
- Russell 2000 Small Cap Index (the Russell or the small caps).
- Dow Jones Transportation Average (the Transports or Trannies).

I regularly monitor all six of the indices listed above. But at a minimum, I suggest analyzing a major large cap average that represents the broad market activity. The Dow Jones Industrial Average and the S&P 500 Index both fit that role. *Note:* "Cap" refers to market capitalization, which is used to categorize companies by their size as large, medium (mid), or small.

The Dow Jones Industrial Average is a relatively narrow large cap index; narrow in that it only includes 30 component stocks. However, it is widely used as a barometer of broad market activity. I monitor the daily and intraday charts of the Dow throughout each daily trading session, and have done so since early in my trading career.

I also regularly monitor the S&P 500, which is a broader large cap index than the Dow in that it includes 500 stocks representing all the sectors of the economy. Consequently, the S&P 500 is considered to be a benchmark and is often used as a means of comparison of performance (e.g., using Relative Strength analysis). For instance, a mutual fund's performance may be compared to the performance of the S&P 500 Index over the same period of time.

The Nasdaq Composite Index is a technology-heavy index. It is not one I'd consider to be representative of the broad market. I do monitor it regularly, but I don't make my broad market decisions based upon it. That's the role of the Dow or the S&P 500 in my opinion.

For mid-cap stocks, I analyze the S&P 400 Index. For small-caps I utilize the Russell 2000 Index. It is the best known representative of the small companies; however, some traders prefer to view the S&P 600 Small Cap Index.

The Dow Jones Transportation Average represents 20 transportation and related companies. The Transports provide important information about the economy, since most everything that is consumed or incorporated into a product gets transported via ship, truck, rail, or plane. For decades, analysts have referred to the Transportation Average to confirm movements in the Dow Jones Industrial Average. Periodically, the Transports will lead the Industrials (e.g., moving to a new high first).

The charts of the Dow Jones Industrial Average and the S&P 500 Index move fairly well in tandem. The Nasdaq Composite Index will generally move in the direction of the Dow and S&P 500; however, it includes a preponderance of stocks from the technology sector, so it can get out of sync with them at times. The S&P 500 includes plenty of stocks from the financials and technology groups. Thus, while the S&P 500 tends to move in sync with the Dow, sometimes the S&P will get hit harder or get a stronger push because of the makeup of its components.

Acquire a Charting Platform If you are a newcomer to this business, you'll need to select a good charting platform in order to analyze the charts. Your broker may provide adequate charting for their accountholders. If not, or if you need a platform with more capabilities, there are many excellent choices. TC2000 (also known to long-time users as TeleChart), MetaStock, TradeStation, and eSignal are a few popular choices.

I've used TC2000 (version 7) for demonstration and illustration throughout this book. It is my primary platform and has been since the year 2000. I periodically use a different platform when I wish to see a true weekly chart versus the five-day rolling chart.

Create Watchlists I suggest creating one or more watchlists in your charting platform that contain the symbols of the indices you'll monitor regularly. Assigning the symbols to a watchlist allows for quick browsing and analysis. For example, I have one watchlist in my charting platform titled Market Review—Daily. It contains the 16 symbols listed in Table 7.1.

TABLE 7.1 Daily Market Review

	Index Name	TC2000 Symbol
1	Dow Jones Industrial Average	DJ-30
2	Dow Jones Transportation Average	DJ-20
3	Nasdaq Composite Index	COMPQX
4	Russell 2000 Index	RUT-X
5	S&P 400 Index	MID--X
6	S&P 500 Index	SP-500
7	SPDR S&P Retail ETF	XRT
8	SPDRs Select Sector Consumer Discretionary ETF	XLY
9	SPDRs Select Sector Consumer Staples ETF	XLP
10	SPDRs Select Sector Energy ETF	XLE
11	SPDRs Select Sector Financials ETF	XLF
12	SPDRs Select Sector Health Care ETF	XLV
13	SPDRs Select Sector Industrial ETF	XLI
14	SPDRs Select Sector Materials ETF	XLB
15	SPDRs Select Sector Technology ETF	XLK
16	SPDRs Select Sector Utilities ETF	XLU

Note: Some of the TC2000 symbols listed in Tables 7.1 and 7.2 include either one or two hyphens (e.g., DJ-30 and MID--X, respectively). If there are two hyphens indicated, they must both be typed in order to access that chart. Some symbols also include a zero at the end (e.g., CRY0 and DXY0), which should not be mistaken for the letter *O*.

The first six symbols in Table 7.1 are for the market averages mentioned previously, representing the large-, medium-, and small-cap stocks, as well as the Nasdaq and the Dow Transports. The other 10 symbols are the main sector SPDRs exchange-traded funds (ETFs). They are not indices, but those ETFs act as a proxy for their respective market sectors.

Regularly monitoring sector charts can help determine when money is rotating from one group to another in order to invest funds where the money is flowing. I also periodically review a list of industry group charts to determine which smaller segments of the economy are in or out of favor. In TC2000, they are included in the Morningstar Industry Groups watchlist.

The combination of symbols in Table 7.1 covers the broad market and the major sectors of the economy. By reviewing those charts each day, I am constantly in tune with the market trend and the general economic conditions. I watch the Dow throughout the daily trading session, and regularly glance at the S&P 500 during trading hours. However, I typically just do a quick analysis of the daily charts of the other symbols each day (and periodically check their weekly charts).

I have another watchlist I call Market Review—Weekly that has a much broader scope. It includes the 51 symbols listed in Table 7.2. In addition to the market averages and sector charts from Table 7.1, it includes symbols that represent specific industry groups, the bond market, commodities, currencies, and some foreign markets. It also includes some market indicators for monitoring the internals (the Advance/Decline Line and the McClellan and Zweig indicators). *Note:* The symbols SCCO or FCX can be used as a proxy for copper in lieu of MG132.

TABLE 7.2 Weekly Market Review

	Index Name	TC2000 Symbol
1	Advance/Decline Line	T2100
2	AMEX Airline Index	XAL--X
3	AMEX Biotech Index	BTK--X
4	AMEX Oil Index	XOI
5	AMEX Pharmaceutical Index	DRG--X
6	AMEX Securities Broker/Dealer Index	XBD--X
7	CBOE 10-Year Treasury Yield Index	TNX--X
8	CBOE 30-Year Treasury Yield Index	TYX--X
9	CBOE Market Volatility Index	VIX--X
10	Commodity Research Bureau (CRB) Index	CRY0 (zero)
11	Copper	MG132
12	Dow Jones Industrial Average	DJ-30

TABLE 7.2 *(continued)*

	Index Name	TC2000 Symbol
13	Dow Jones Transportation Average	DJ-20
14	Dow Jones Utility Average	DJ-15
15	Guggenheim Solar ETF	TAN
16	HOLDRs Oil Service ETF	OIH
17	iShares Barclay's 20-Year Treasury Bond Fund	TLT
18	Light Sweet Crude Oil Index	XOIL.X
19	Market Vectors Agribusiness ETF	MOO
20	McClellan Oscillator	T2106
21	McClellan Summation Index	T2118
22	Morgan Stanley Cyclical Index	CYC--X
23	Nasdaq 100 Index	NDX--X
24	Nasdaq Composite Index	COMPQX
25	NYSE Composite Index	NYSE
26	Philadelphia Gold/Silver Sector Index	XAU
27	Philadelphia Housing Sector Index	HGX--X
28	Philadelphia Marine Shipping Index	SHX.X
29	Philadelphia Semiconductor Sector Index	SOX--X
30	Russell 2000 Index	RUT-X
31	S&P Midcap 400 Index	MID--X
32	S&P 500 Index	SP-500
33	Shanghai Composite Index	SSEC-X
34	SPDR KBW Bank ETF	KBE
35	SPDR KBW Regional Banking ETF	KRE
36	SPDR S&P Retail ETF	XRT
37	SPDRs Select Sector Consumer Discretionary ETF	XLY
38	SPDRs Select Sector Consumer Staples ETF	XLP
39	SPDRs Select Sector Energy ETF	XLE
40	SPDRs Select Sector Financials ETF	XLF
41	SPDRs Select Sector Health Care ETF	XLV
42	SPDRs Select Sector Industrial ETF	XLI
43	SPDRs Select Sector Materials ETF	XLB
44	SPDRs Select Sector Technology ETF	XLK
45	SPDRs Select Sector Utilities ETF	XLU
46	Tokyo Nikkei Index	NIKI-X
47	U.S. Dollar Index	DXY0 (zero)
48	U.S. Natural Gas ETF	UNG
49	World Gold Index	XGLD
50	World Silver Index	XSLV.X
51	Zweig Breadth Thrust	T2103

I recommend looking at the charts in a more extensive list such as Table 7.2 a minimum of once per week. I try to flip through this list a few times each week since I can devote myself full time to this business. For those with limited time, though, I suggest a daily review of key market averages and sector charts in Table 7.1, and a more extensive review as often as your schedule allows. You may even choose to trim a few symbols from the longer list by removing any redundancy. For instance, XLK, the Nasdaq Composite Index, and the Nasdaq 100 Index are all technology focused. Additionally, XLU and the Dow Jones Utility Average are both utilities focused.

A Note about Symbols The symbols for charts of stocks and ETFs are universal. However, the symbols for index charts may vary from one charting platform or website to another. For instance, in TC2000 the symbol for the Dow Jones Industrial Average is DJ-30. On the popular website StockCharts.com, the symbol is $INDU.

For many indices, the core of the symbol is common to all platforms, but there may be additional lettering or characters before or after it. For instance, the symbol for the Philadelphia Housing Sector Index is HGX--X in TC2000 and is $HGX on StockCharts.com. The Philadelphia Semiconductor Sector Index is SOX--X in TC2000 and $SOX on StockCharts.com.

Create a Chart Template Now that you're ready to start looking at the charts, you'll need to decide which technical indicators to use to assist with the analysis. Your charting platform may provide users multiple chart templates. In the TC2000 (version 7) platform, users are provided access to numerous templates that they can configure to suit their charting preferences. The 12 main templates correspond to the function (F) keys on the keyboard for quick and easy access.

When I look through the watchlists comprised of the symbols from Tables 7.1 and 7.2, I use a specific chart template. My main template is shown in Figure 7.1. It is relatively simple and intended for quick browsing. It includes the following technical indicators:

- Chart Window—The 20-period SMA quickly draws my eye to the direction of the intermediate-term trend as illustrated in Chapter 2. The 50-, 100-, and 200-period simple moving averages represent the intermediate- to long-term trend, and often provide support or resistance when they are tested during market corrections.

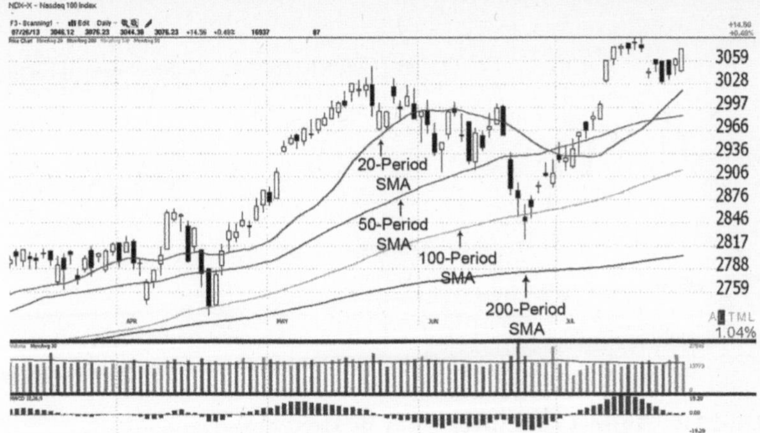

FIGURE 7.1 Logan Main Chart Template
Source: TC2000® chart courtesy of Worden Brothers, Inc.

- Middle Panel—Volume bars with a 30-period simple moving average of volume plotted over the bars. The moving average smoothes the data and allows for quickly gauging whether volume is above or below average.
- Bottom Panel—The Moving Average Convergence Divergence (MACD) with a setting of 12-26-9 exponential is plotted as a histogram. I use this indicator primarily for divergence analysis.

These are *not the only indicators I use* for chart analysis. However, I don't like having too many indicators represented in a single chart template. I find it gets too cluttered and distracts from the price action. It can also be difficult to draw precise trendlines with too many indicators in the price window. Even with just the moving averages, it can be difficult at times. Therefore, I also have a blank template with nothing in the chart window except the price bars. I often shift to that template to fine-tune my trendlines.

I can quickly switch to another template when I wish to look at other indicators, such as On-Balance Volume (OBV), Bollinger Bands, Relative Strength, or an oscillator, such as Stochastics or RSI. Alternatively, I often employ a two-chart layout when browsing through my daily and weekly market watchlists (Tables 7.1 and 7.2). I put up the main chart template on the left (labeled main template in Figure 7.2) and another to the right of it (secondary template). I use 24-inch monitors, so each chart is large enough for clarity.

FIGURE 7.2 A Two-Chart Layout May Be Used for Viewing More Technical Indicators
Source: TC2000® chart courtesy of Worden Brothers, Inc.

An index chart may not have volume to reference. In those cases, in TC2000 there will either be no volume bars at all, or they will run the full length of the indicator panel as shown in Figure 7.2 of the Philadelphia Semiconductor Index (SOX--X).

If you wish to analyze the volume pattern, there may be an ETF that mimics the index. For example, to see the volume, or to analyze the On-Balance Volume indicator, of the Semiconductor Index, view the chart of the HOLDRS Semiconductor ETF (SMH). It tracks closely to the index and provides a good gauge for the volume of the semiconductor group.

Monitor the Market Trends With your watchlists and chart template(s) ready to go, it's time to analyze the charts using the key tenets of technical analysis. Listed below are some of the technical events to observe when flipping through the charts, all of which were outlined in the chapters in Part I:

- The direction, duration, and slope of the trend. Maintain sloped trendlines on the daily chart for monitoring the intermediate-term trend, and on the weekly chart for monitoring long-term trends. Be alert for the break of a sloped trendline.
- Identify the visible support and resistance levels created by price action. Draw horizontal support/resistance lines to provide visual cues so it is

clear when price has reached those levels. Be alert for the break of an important horizontal line.

- Observe when price approaches, and how it responds to, a strong moving average, such as the 50- or 200-period.
- Pay attention to Fibonacci retracement levels during market corrections.
- Utilize candlestick lines and patterns, and Western bar patterns (e.g., a Key Reversal), to identify shifts in market sentiment.
- Be alert for the formation of classic chart patterns, such as triangles and double tops or bottoms.
- Note when minor trend interruptions occur, such as pullbacks (uptrend), bounces (downtrend), or minor basing action.
- Note when larger trend interruptions occur. When the long-term trend of the major averages and/or certain sectors of the economy experience a correction, it often provides an excellent opportunity for market participants to get aboard stocks and/or ETFs at nicely discounted prices.

Once you get some practice identifying the technical events listed above, moving through the watchlist shouldn't take too much time. I usually move pretty quickly through most of the symbols, while stopping periodically to do a more extensive evaluation when needed. For instance, if I have my eye on the banking stocks, I'll spend some additional time evaluating the charts of the KBW Bank ETFs (KBE and KRE).

I spend the most time monitoring the chart of the Dow. I keep it up on one of my screens (I use multiple monitors) throughout each trading day. I also regularly check the S&P 500 Index so I'm aware of important support/resistance levels on its chart. At all times I am aware of the trends of the broad market using the Dow and S&P 500 as my guide as follows:

- Long-term Trend—The major trend provides a big-picture outlook for the market. I periodically shift up to a weekly chart for a quick look, especially when a bull or bear market has been under way for a year or longer. Doing so reduces much of the noise of the daily chart and keeps things in perspective.
- Intermediate-term Trend—This is the primary guide for my trading activities, which is why I've dedicated all of Chapter 10 to its coverage. I use the daily chart for this analysis. Closely monitoring the intermediate-length

movements within the major trend helps determine the setups I trade, as well as the strategies employed for profiting from those setups.

- Short-term Trend—The price swings that form within the longer trend are useful for swing trading techniques; or for profit taking opportunities for core positions (e.g., swing trading around a core position). For instance, if the Dow pulls back after an upward price swing, I know a lot of individual stocks will pull back as well.

Monitor the Market Internals

In addition to analyzing the price movement plotted on the charts, many experienced chartists also monitor the strength (health) of the market's trend using a specific group of indicators. Those indicators may be called by various names, such as: market indicators, market internals, breadth indicators, or market breadth indicators. I typically refer to this whole group of indicators as market internals. Following are some commonly used internal measures:

- New Highs and New Lows
- Advancers and Decliners (and/or Advance/Decline Line)
- Up and Down Volume
- McClellan Oscillator
- Tick and TRIN (Arms Index)

If you intend to take short-term trades, you may benefit from monitoring certain market internals daily (e.g., New Highs–New Lows). Briefing.com provides the daily numbers for the New York Stock Exchange (NYSE) every hour on the hour, as illustrated in Figure 7.3, as well as for the Nasdaq Stock Exchange. This resource allows active traders to monitor the health of the market trend throughout the day, and day by day. These data can be accessed at www.briefing.com/investor/markets/market-internals.

Those who invest primarily for the long term may choose to monitor the numbers less frequently. For instance, your charting platform may provide a cumulative chart showing the *trend of those numbers* (e.g., the Advance/Decline Line) rather than focusing on the hourly numbers every day. StockCharts.com has a free NYSE New Highs–New Lows Index ($NYHL). Make sure to change it to a solid line rather than candlesticks. One way to utilize such charts is to look for divergence between the market indicator and the market average.

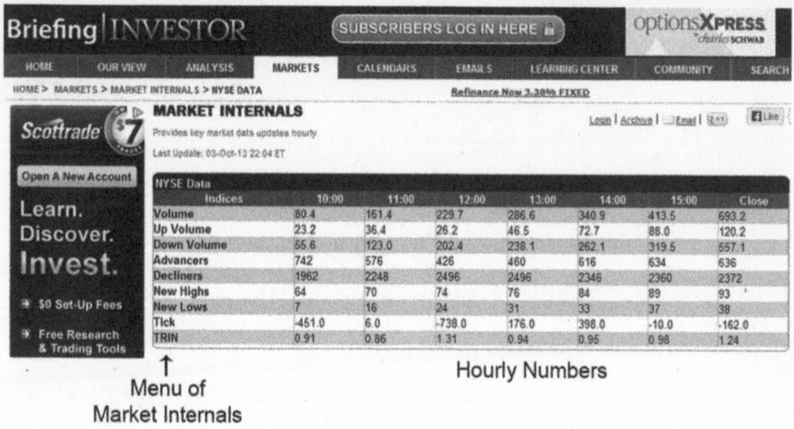

Briefing | INVESTOR
SUBSCRIBERS LOG IN HERE
optionsXPRESS charles SCHWAB

HOME | OUR VIEW | ANALYSIS | MARKETS | CALENDARS | EMAILS | LEARNING CENTER | COMMUNITY | SEARCH

HOME > MARKETS > MARKET INTERNALS > NYSE DATA
Refinance Now 3.38% FIXED

Scottrade $7
Open A New Account
Learn.
Discover.
Invest.
$0 Set-Up Fees
Free Research & Trading Tools

MARKET INTERNALS
Provides key market data updates hourly
Last Update: 03-Oct-13 22:04 ET
Login | Archive | Email | +1 | Like

NYSE Data

Indices	10:00	11:00	12:00	13:00	14:00	15:00	Close
Volume	80.4	161.4	229.7	286.6	340.9	413.5	693.2
Up Volume	23.2	36.4	26.2	46.5	72.7	88.0	120.2
Down Volume	55.6	123.0	202.4	238.1	262.1	319.5	557.1
Advancers	742	576	426	460	616	634	636
Decliners	1962	2248	2496	2496	2346	2360	2372
New Highs	64	70	74	76	84	89	93
New Lows	7	16	24	31	33	37	38
Tick	-451.0	6.0	-738.0	176.0	398.0	-10.0	-162.0
TRIN	0.91	0.86	1.31	0.94	0.95	0.98	1.24

Menu of Market Internals

Hourly Numbers

FIGURE 7.3 Market Internals Available at Briefing.com
Source: www.Briefing.com

Note: Briefing.com is a good resource for traders, but a subscription fee is required to access some of the analysis tools on the website. I don't shy away from reasonable subscription fees for resources that easily pay for themselves.

An in-depth discussion of market internals is beyond the scope of this text. However, I feel it is essential for readers to be aware of these important analysis tools, so some discussion of the internal measures was included. You don't have to monitor the market internals, but if you intend to be an active trader, doing so may give you an advantage over other market participants. In this business, we refer to that as an "edge."

Gregory L. Morris wrote a great book called *The Complete Guide to Market Breadth Indicators* (McGraw-Hill, 2006). Unfortunately, the book is no longer in print. A limited number of copies are available for purchase, but they have been selling for up to several hundred dollars. Mr. Morris is currently finishing a new book encompassing his 40 years of knowledge and experience. It is called *Investing with the Trend: A Rules-Based Approach to Money Management*. The book was slotted for release in late 2013. Based on his past publications, I anticipate it will be worth the investment many times over. Among its impressive, comprehensive table of contents is a segment on breadth-based indicators.

Create a Chart Template for Viewing Market Indicators The following symbols listed in Table 7.2 are market indicators: T2100, T2103, T2106, and T2118. I've set up one of my chart templates specifically for viewing those charts. The price scale of that template is set for arithmetic rather than logarithmic for those that require a baseline of zero (e.g., the McClellan indicators). Instead of candlesticks as the bar type, this template plots the data in the form of a line graph, since those charts are formed from a daily data point rather than having open-high-low-close prices.

Monitor the Market Fundamentals

The word "fundamentals" is used to refer to a company's fundamentals (e.g., earnings, revenues, and so on). The term is also used in the broader context of market fundamentals. For the market, that may include news, economic reports, and so on—the external forces that impact supply and demand.

I find it helpful to note how external events and news impact the short-, intermediate-, and even long-term market trend. For instance, the events that have unfolded in Europe regarding their debt issues have influenced the global markets over the past few years.

Certain economic reports, such as the monthly employment report (the jobs report) released by the Bureau of Labor Statistics, can move the market. There are a number of economic reports released on a regular basis. Some are released weekly (e.g., Initial Claims for unemployment), some are monthly (e.g., Retail Sales), and some are quarterly (e.g., Gross Domestic Product). A calendar of their release dates and times, along with some information about the reports, can be found on Briefing.com. For a more in-depth study of each report, try Evelina Tainer's book *Using Economic Indicators to Improve Investment Analysis* (John Wiley & Sons, 2006) or Bernard Baumohl's *The Secrets of Economic Indicators* (Wharton School Publishing, 2004).

Additionally, when the Federal Reserve speaks, the market listens. The Fed directs monetary policy, so the release of the Federal Open Market Committee (FOMC) minutes, and subsequent comments from the Fed Chairman (currently Ben Bernanke), can be a market mover.

I pay attention to economic reports and indicators, domestic and global events, opinions of respected executives and analysts, and so on. However, I am discerning with what I watch, read, and listen to, and how much weight I give to various sources. Otherwise, it is easy to get overwhelmed, misled, and/or distracted.

Each weekday I record a television show on CNBC, *Closing Bell*; it comes on right after the market close. If I don't get a chance to tune in to any of the stock market programs during the day, I know I'll usually get a recap of the daily events through that show. It often includes interviews with industry executives, and I find many of those to be very insightful. I also record a weekend news show that recaps the economic, political, and global events of the week. Recording the shows allows me to watch them at my leisure. I often do so keeping one eyeball on the TV and the other looking at charts. I admit I'm a multitasker!

Market Statistics

As you start learning more about the markets, you'll undoubtedly hear about various statistics, seasonal events, market relationships, and predictions. You'll hear about things like the Santa Claus rally, the January effect, the best six months, and the presidential cycle, just to name a few. Some of those concepts and market models can be very helpful.

The *Stock Trader's Almanac* (John Wiley & Sons) is a good general resource for determining what has happened in the past. It includes statistical analysis of common market events and updates are published annually. Additionally, statistics are often mentioned on popular stock market shows, such as those on CNBC, the Fox Business Network (FBN), or Bloomberg.

Keep in mind that those figures are based on averages from past data and there will almost always be exceptions, so take care to not get rigid about the statistics. I'd still recommend paying close attention to the broad market and carefully analyze charts because the market won't always follow the same track. Additionally, certain well-known market relationships may get turned upside down or inside out for periods of time.

Statistics can certainly be helpful. But also be aware as you read the information that it is not a guarantee of future market performance. For instance, if (hypothetically speaking) something occurs 70 percent of the time, there is still the other 30 percent of the time when it does not comply. Thus, information from the *Almanac* and other sources is not a replacement for ongoing analysis of the market; rather, they are good resources for learning about past market behavior and for generating ideas for trading strategies.

CHAPTER 8

Bull Markets

There have been many bull markets since trading began underneath a buttonwood tree on Wall Street over 200 years ago. A great amount of cumulative wealth can be gained during a bull market. On an individual basis, though, some investors will fare much better than others, depending on their level of knowledge, experience, risk management practices, and overall involvement in the management of their investment funds.

Bull Markets of the Past 50 Years

Listed in Table 8.1 are the ten bull markets that occurred during the past 50 years, including the current one that began in March 2009. The figures shown are for the Dow Jones Industrial Average using daily market data from TC2000 (version 7). The percentage rise indicated for each of the bull markets is measured from the closing low of the prior bear market to the bull market's closing high.

Table 8.1 illustrates my interpretation of the bull markets of the past five decades. Although there is general consensus on the start and end dates of most of the past bull markets, there is some subjectivity involved; so there may be instances where different sources list different dates for some bull markets based on their reading of the market.

The *Stock Trader's Almanac* (John Wiley & Sons, 2013, p. 131) shows a bull market during 1970 to 1971 and another during 1971 to 1973, whereas I portrayed it as one bull market from mid-1970 to 1973 (as did another source I consulted). I did so in order to stay consistent with the generally accepted requirement of a 20 percent decline before officially declaring a bear market; and the deepest decline during that 1970 to 1973 period was just over

TABLE 8.1 U.S. Bull Markets

Dates in Force	Length	Percent Rise	Closing Low	Closing High
June 26, 1962 to Feb. 9, 1966	3.6 Years	85.78%	535.70 6/26/1962	995.20 2/9/1966
Oct. 7, 1966 to Dec. 3, 1968	2.2 Years	32.37%	744.30 10/7/1966	985.20 12/3/1968
May 26, 1970 to Jan. 11, 1973	2.6 Years	66.62%	631.20 5/26/1970	1,051.70 1/11/1973
Dec. 6, 1974 to Sept. 21, 1976	1.8 Years	75.69%	577.60 12/6/1974	1,014.80 9/21/1976
Feb. 28, 1978 to April 27, 1981	3.2 Years	37.99%	742.10 2/28/1978	1,024.00 4/27/1981
Aug. 12, 1982 to Aug. 25, 1987	5 Years	250.42%	776.90 8/12/1982	2,722.42 8/25/1987
Oct. 19, 1987 to July 17, 1990	2.7 Years	72.52%	1,738.74 10/19/1987	2,999.75 7/17/1990
Oct. 11, 1990 to Jan. 14, 2000	9.3 Years	395.67%	2,365.10 10/11/1990	11,722.98 1/14/2000
Oct. 9, 2002 to Oct. 9, 2007	5 Years	94.4%	7,286.27 10/9/2002	14,164.53 10/9/2007
March 9, 2009 to Present	Almost 4.5 years to date	139.17% as of 8/2/13 close	6,547.05 3/9/2009	Still in Force

16 percent. It could be argued, though, that it was deep enough to be considered a mild bear market, or a "baby bear." There is more discussion on this topic in Chapter 11 since a decline of over 16 percent also occurred during the current bull market.

Additionally, the *Almanac* and some other sources show a bull market having occurred during 2001, whereas I consider the period from January 14, 2000, to October 9, 2002, to have been a continuous bear market; and it is often referred to as such by traders and on financial shows.

Duration of a Bull Market

According to my calculations based on Table 8.1, the average length of a bull market during the past five decades has been approximately 3.9 years. *Note:* Since it was still in force at the time of this analysis, the current bull market is not included in that average.

As Table 8.1 illustrates, during the past several decades there have been bull markets ranging from less than two years to longer than nine years.

Thus, we can't just rely on the concept of average bull market length to guide our trading. Rather, we can analyze each bull market as it evolves so we can profit from as much of the major uptrend as possible.

Fortunately for the typical investor, most bull markets are significantly longer than most bear markets. Bear markets are often relatively brief. However, the decline may be quite significant. Thus the old axiom: "The bull walks up the stairway but the bear jumps out the window."

I say it is fortunate for the typical investor because most investors have a long bias and suffer significant drawdown of their portfolios during a bear market. That is, they lose much, and sometimes all, of the gains accrued during the prior bull market. They need the longer bull market that follows a bear in order to recover those lost gains and go on to grow their investment portfolios. This challenge can be overcome, though, by becoming more knowledgeable and involved (e.g., utilizing inverse ETFs), and taking steps to protect capital.

Magnitude of a Bull Market

According to my calculations, the average rise of the bull markets during the past 50 years is over 123 percent. The most significant rise during that period was over 395 percent, and the smallest rise was just over 32 percent. *Note:* Since it was still in force at the time of this analysis, the current bull market is not included in the average rise.

■ Early Development of a Bull Market

As every bear market goes through its transition into a bull market, and vice versa, market participants attempt to make the determination of when that change has officially occurred. The discussion in this segment reveals how bull markets emerge from a bear market bottom.

Shift from Bear to Bull Market

Eventually a bear market reverses direction, and at first, it won't be obvious. At the right edge of the chart, the first leg up of a new bull market may look like just another correction within a bear market. You won't know whether it is a bear market rally or whether it is the beginning of a new bull market until there is enough evidence that a major trend reversal has occurred. It is only definitive with the benefit of hindsight.

Oftentimes after the first leg up, price declines again for a test of the bear market low. When that occurs, at the right edge of the chart, as price is declining back toward that low, you can't be certain if it will find support at/near that level; or whether the index will break down through it, resulting in a resumption of the bear market.

According to John Murphy in his book *Technical Analysis of the Financial Markets* (New York Institute of Finance, 1999, p. 29): "The most difficult task for a Dow theorist, or any trend follower for that matter, is being able to distinguish between a normal secondary correction in an existing trend and the first leg of a new trend in the opposite direction. Dow theorists often disagree as to when the market gives an actual reversal signal."

There are different schools of thought on where the line is drawn that determines whether a new bull market is truly in effect. Following are three of the factors I've heard over the years from various sources, and you may come across other determinants in your own studies:

- The index rises by 20 percent off the bear market low.
- The index closes decisively above the peak of the last bear market correction.
- The index closes decisively above the 200-day (40-week) moving average.

Each of these events may occur at different points as a new bull market emerges, and each poses challenges. For instance, by the time the index rises by 20 percent, it may be well into the new bull market in some cases (e.g., two of the past 10 bull markets gained less than 40 percent). Other times, there will still be significant upside movement to come. Recall that the average bull market of the past 50 years had a run of over 123 percent.

As for closing above the peak of the last bear market correction, or above the 200-day moving average, that can also occur during a strong bear market correction followed by a resumption of the bear market rather than a reversal into a bull market.

Figure 8.1 shows a daily chart of the Dow during the transition from the last bear market of 2007–2009 to the current bull market. All three of the factors mentioned above are identified on the chart. Because the depth of the final decline into the March 2009 low took price far below the prior correction high and the 200-period SMA, a 20 percent rise occurred much sooner than a decisive breakout above either of those barriers.

These are just guidelines for making a *determination* of whether a major trend change has occurred from a bear to a bull market—they don't need to

FIGURE 8.1 Factors Used to Identify a New Bull Market
Source: TC2000® chart courtesy of Worden Brothers, Inc.

dictate when a person chooses to *participate* in that major market reversal. There is no rule declaring that an investor must wait to enter a bull market until one or all of the above criteria are met. By monitoring the intermediate-term market trends, you may have already benefitted from one or more early up moves, even if it hasn't yet officially been declared a bull market.

The Bottoming Process It is difficult to time the precise turning point of a new bull market. Major market shifts have fundamental underpinnings related to the business cycle, so they take time to unfold—usually at least several weeks, and often several months. It also tends to take time because, from a technical standpoint, most bull markets do not start from a single bottom reversal. The reversal is more of a transitional process than a specific turning point. Therefore, it can take a few to several months before it is officially deemed a new bull market.

"A bottom is not a price, it's a process." This is one of the clever expressions of Larry Wachtel, a well-known Wall Street commentator who, sadly, passed away in 2007. It describes one of the strong, organizing principles of market behavior. By my interpretation, that insightful phrase rightly suggests that markets don't typically change direction in an abrupt manner. The shift from downtrend to uptrend is usually more gradual.

A major bottoming process involves the market putting in the final bear market low, and then testing that low one or more times before a new bull market can begin in earnest. That does not mean price has to decline all the way back to the bear market low; it may fall short of reaching it. When that occurs, it may be setting up the right shoulder of a head-and-shoulders bottom.

A typical reversal from a bear to a bull market will be from a double, triple, or head-and-shoulders bottom; or the market will bottom out and form a rectangular-type bottoming process (often referred to as base building or accumulation) or a rounding-type bottom. Any of those bottoming formations sets up a more significant zone of support below the market than would occur if the trend reversed from a single bottom.

There are those infrequent occasions, though, when a new bull market will start from a single bottom. You may hear it referred to as a *V* or spike bottom. In fact, that's precisely how the March 2009 bear market reversal occurred. In my experience, it is more common to see a *V* reversal occur on the chart of an individual stock than on the chart of a market average. For example, a single stock may make an abrupt reversal if significant news is released, whereas a market average represents many component stocks. In order to significantly change its course, market participants must be willing to trade many of the components (and/or one or more corresponding ETFs) in the new direction.

Figure 8.2 illustrates a two-chart layout of the Dow. The charts have been tightly compressed to compare the bear market reversal that occurred between 2002 and 2003 (left) to the 2009 bear market reversal (right). The 2002 to 2003 reversal occurred as a bottoming process. A bullish head-and-shoulders bottom formed between October 2002 (the actual bear market low) and March 2003 where the right shoulder constitutes a test of the October 2002 low.

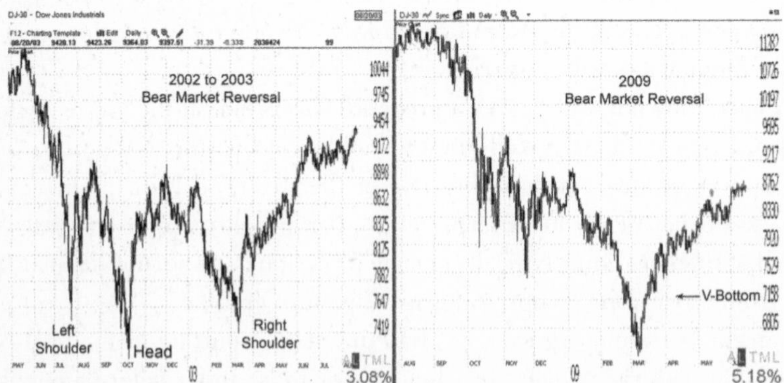

FIGURE 8.2 Comparison of the Last Two Bear Market Reversals on the Dow Jones Industrial Average

Source: TC2000® chart courtesy of Worden Brothers, Inc.

In contrast, the March 2009 bear market low was not tested. Rather than transitioning from a bear market to a bull market in a gradual manner, the Dow reversed direction in a *V* formation. Such an abrupt reversal is more the exception than the rule. I looked back across the charts of many bear market reversals over the past several decades and found only a few where this type of abrupt reversal occurred versus a more gradual bottoming-type process.

Surge off the Bottom

The first leg up of a new bull market may start with a powerful surge off the bottom—a strong push up that comes off an oversold level. For instance, in the first seven trading days off the very oversold March 2009 low, the Dow gained over 14 percent. During the first 19 trading days, it had run up over 22 percent. It was sort of like observing capitulation in reverse! A strong price surge sometimes occurs after a bull market correction as well. You'll recognize a price surge off a bottom when you see the following:

- The index makes a strong percentage rise in a relatively short period of time. For instance, the rise may be into the double digits within a couple of weeks or less.
- The move is typically accompanied by quite heavy volume.
- The push up includes a few, and sometimes several, long bullish candles.
- There may be only brief pauses during its run.

I tell you about this phenomenon not to taunt you if you miss it, but to recognize it for what it is—a major shift upward. It should also reinforce why I closely monitor the intermediate-term trends within major trends. You should snap to attention when you see it. There is likely more, and often much more, upward movement to come, especially when it marks the start of a new bull market. If you do miss out on a strong price surge off the bottom, watch for a retracement afterward (or at least a period of sideways movement) so you can get aboard for the next up leg.

Moving Averages Turn up and then Cross

As a new bull market emerges, short-term moving averages, such as the 10- and 20-period, will turn up first. It won't take long before the 10-period moving average crosses above the 20-period. However, those short-term moving averages track fairly close to price, so just because they turn up, or even cross, does not mean a trend reversal is imminent. They'll turn down and cross again if what appears to be a new bull market emerging turns out to be just another bear market correction.

Eventually, as the bull market gains ground, the intermediate- (50- and 100-period) and long-term (200-period) moving averages will also turn up and experience crossovers. For example, the 50-period will cross above the 200-period (referred to as a golden cross). In fact, price will encounter all those strong moving averages on the way up and will have to break up through the resistance they pose.

Observations Prior to the Reversal

Even though it may take time for a major reversal to occur and/or be declared as such, there are often clues prior to the start of, or during, the bottoming phase that suggests a new bull market may be forthcoming. Some of those clues may come in the form of technical warnings as discussed previously. They may occur on the daily chart if monitoring the intermediate-term trend; or on the weekly chart if monitoring the long-term trend from that vantage point.

You may also see an early technical sign on the charts of many individual stocks. For instance, prior to the reversal off the 2009 bear market low, I started noticing bottom reversal patterns and base building on the charts of many individual stocks (particularly on several commodity-related stocks). Oftentimes before a new bull market starts, a number of stocks will start developing rectangular-type bottoming patterns.

In many of the cases I observed, the On-Balance Volume (OBV) indicator began rising while price continued to move sideways. That suggested there was *accumulation under cover* occurring while price was confined within the base (Figure 8.3). The "smart money" market participants tend to begin building up core long positions prior to a major upside reversal in anticipation of the emergence of a new growth cycle. They try to hide their activities inside the base—building up their positions before the little guys (that's us!) all start moving to action and force a breakout from the base. However, they cannot hide their volume, and it shows up in OBV.

The Fundamentals There is more to be considered than just technical events when determining whether a major market shift is under way. The long-term trends are largely driven by the business cycle. That doesn't mean

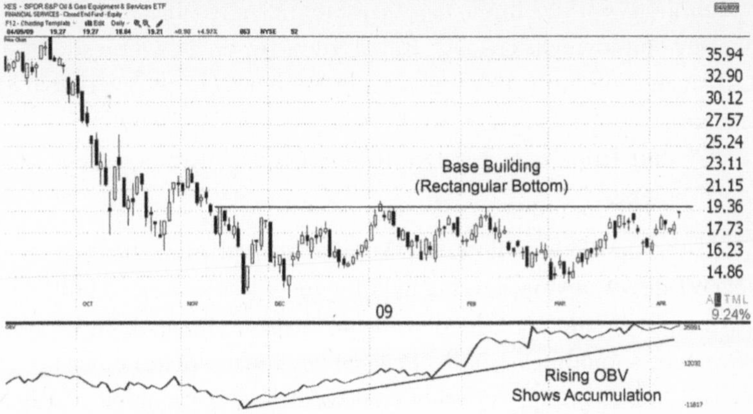

FIGURE 8.3 Rising OBV While Price Was Building a Large Base Revealed Accumulation under Cover
Source: TC2000® chart courtesy of Worden Brothers, Inc.

you have to know all the factors bearing on the market; but do be aware that it is chiefly the fundamentals that influence the major trend. Fortunately, all known information and anticipated events get priced into the charts. Hence, you don't have to be an expert on the economy to participate in the movements of the market.

Prior to a major bottom, or as it is developing, there may be some fundamental clues that a new bull market may emerge soon. They are not precise timing signals, but rather they suggest that a recovery may be on the horizon. Following are some examples:

- Base Metals—Watch the base metals, such as aluminum, and especially copper. If they stop falling in a bear market, pay attention. Copper serves as a leading indicator for potential economic recovery-growth, so it may turn up before the bear market ends. In TC2000, the chart MG132 represents copper. Alternatively, periodically check the chart of a stock that is a fairly pure copper play, which acts as a proxy for the group, such as Southern Copper Corp. (SCCO) or Freeport McMoran (FCX).

- Economic Cycle Research Institute (ECRI) Weekly Leading Index (WLI)—ECRI provides guidance about the economic conditions through their WLI report. If the WLI's annualized growth rate starts making upticks prior to the market bottom, it hints of improvement on the horizon.

- Economic Reports—Important economic data, such as the weekly and monthly employment reports, Retail Sales, the Gross Domestic Product (GDP), and so on, provide clues about the health of the economy. Many economic reports may start to show improvement, even if it is just "less bad." A shift from very negative to less negative shows a trend toward improvement.

When the continuous flow of bear market bad news no longer takes the market down, it's time to be alert for the emergence of a bull market. Remember, the market is a discounting mechanism. It anticipates economic improvement sometimes months in advance. Thus, when the market holds steady, or starts to go up, even though it seems as if it shouldn't, the market is looking ahead to recovery.

An Intermediate-Term View of a Reversal

There's an old Wall Street adage that says, "They don't ring a bell at the top or bottom."The precise turning points of major trends are easy to spot when analyzing past data. However, it is difficult to nail them in real time. It would be so nice to go long right at the bottom, close our eyes, and just enjoy riding the major wave all the way up to its final peak. However, the fact that the market tends to develop through a series of intermediate-length movements makes that difficult. And those zigzag moves often start right from the bottoming process. Remember, the *V* reversal of March 2009 was a fairly rare phenomenon.

Look back at the example on the left in Figure 8.2. Let's say an investor did happen to get in right as the 2002 bottom formed on the Dow (at the head of the head-and-shoulders bottom pattern). The market rallied over 22 percent from the October 2002 low to the November 2002 high. However, it declined almost 16 percent from the November 2002 high to the March 2003 low (the right shoulder) as it worked its way back down for a test of the bear market low. After having his funds committed for about five months, that investor, who had nailed the very bottom and just held on, was nearly back where he had started.

Yet for those participating in the intermediate-term market movements rather than employing a buy-and-hold method, the run up off that bottom, and the subsequent reversal of most of that run, were two completed trends that could have been traded. Those who wish to take a more active role with their investment moneys may choose to get in and out of the market based on buy and sell signals. They may also benefit from both the up and the down trends by going long and short, rather than getting aboard only on the long side and holding on through what are often significant gyrations. But that entails developing the knowledge and skill set to do so successfully.

Mind you, I'm not suggesting that investors must be constantly getting in and out of the market. There may be some fairly long stretches of time within a major trend where the market moves along pretty smoothly with just minor interruptions. There have been some stretches of three to six months in the current bull market. During such phases, a core position may be held for quite some time without the need to exit the position, and without getting stopped out. But for me, there are limits on how much drawdown I'll accept, which keeps me from holding a position through a significant retracement. I'd rather exit proactively or get stopped out, and look for a re-entry opportunity, than watch much, and sometimes all, of the gains that had accrued in a trade evaporate.

Let's take a look at a bear market reversal from an intermediate-term frame of reference rather than trying to figure out at what point a new bull market was under way. That frame of reference means monitoring and participating in intermediate-term trends in both directions. By doing so, I don't typically miss out on the early upward moves in a new bull market, even if I don't yet realize it is a bull market. Figure 8.4 highlights some intermediate-term movements on the Dow leading up to the March 2009 bear market reversal, and as it occurred.

From November 21, 2008, through January 2, 2009, there was a bear market correction against the major downtrend. As price began to rise, an

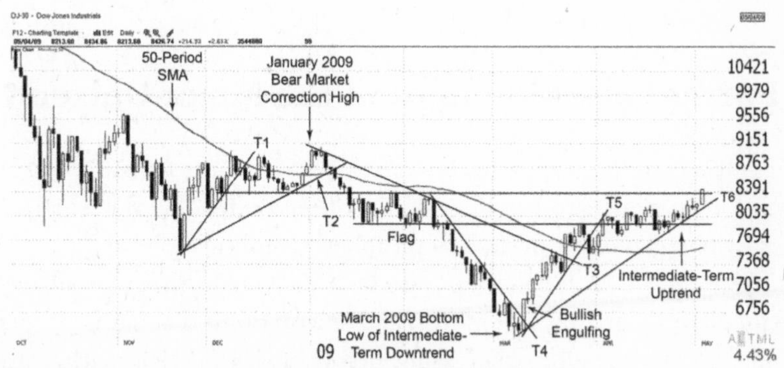

FIGURE 8.4 Intermediate-Term Market Trends
Source: TC2000® chart courtesy of Worden Brothers, Inc.

up trendline (T1) was drawn connecting the bottoms. That line was broken, alerting that a potential reversal back to the downside may be occurring; however, price moved primarily sideways. A new up trendline (T2) was drawn. When that line was broken, once again it alerted that the correction may be ending and another leg down beginning.

After the first push back down out of that bear market correction, price consolidated for several days, setting up a bearish flag before declining again. That allowed for a downward sloping trendline to be drawn (T3). It also created a price setup for shorting. As price accelerated downward into the March 2009 low, a tighter trendline was drawn (T4) representing the steeper slope of the trend.

As price turned up from the March 2009 low, starting from a Bullish Engulfing pattern, the tight down trendline (T4) was quickly broken. As price surged off the bottom, it didn't take long before the looser down trendline and the 50-period SMA were also broken. As price moved up into a new intermediate-term uptrend, rising bottoms formed, allowing the first up trendline to be drawn (T5). It was adjusted a couple of times as minor pullbacks and consolidation occurred while the ascent continued. Price also broke up through resistance identified by the horizontal lines.

The point of this example is to illustrate how a trader may have been working the long side during the intermediate-term upward move off the March low without realizing he was actually participating in the first leg up of a new bull market. Remember, at some point one of the down legs in a bear market will be the last one—the one that puts in the bear market low. And one of the intermediate-term upward moves will eventually be the first leg up of a new bull market. That's the beauty of closely monitoring the intermediate-term trends that develop within the major trends.

■ Further Development of the Major Uptrend

After getting off the ground, the bull market may get into a rhythm of trending up for intermediate-length periods of time (extending the trend), followed by corrections or periods of prolonged consolidation.

In Chapter 11, a detailed case study is provided dissecting all of the intermediate-term upward moves and corrections that have occurred within the current bull market. Thus, before reviewing that market study, following is some background on declines that tend to occur within major uptrends.

The Declines within the Major Trend

As a bull market develops, there will typically be a significant number of minor interruptions of the trend along the way—pullbacks and periods of minor consolidation. There will be a lesser number of more significant interruptions of the trend as well—corrections and more substantial periods of consolidation. Those events were all defined and illustrated in Chapter 4.

Minor pullbacks of about 1 to 3 percent occur quite frequently. After a push up, the market can quickly get overbought on a short-term basis. Many swing traders will sell in order to lock in profits from the prior upswing, causing the market to dip for a bit (or in some instances move sideways). Deeper declines tend to occur when the market gets overbought on an intermediate-term basis. The selling gathers momentum and takes price lower.

The declines within a bull market are often met with buyers. That happens relatively quickly in the case of market pullbacks and minor corrections; and by those happy to get into long positions at what are sometimes significantly lower prices during a deeper correction. It's a bull market and a buy-the-dips mentality has taken over.

Size of the Decline I find that it helps to assign a degree of magnitude to a bull market decline in order to have a shared understanding of the semantics. Thus, Table 8.2 provides the general guidelines I've devised *in regard to the broad market averages* to define the declines that occur.

There is some subjectivity in charting, and there is not a standard set of labels that all chartists adhere to. Some chartists would argue that a 3 percent decline is a correction; others will refer to it as a pullback. Some chartists make no distinction between market pullbacks and market corrections. They may refer to them all as pullbacks, or all as corrections.

I make a distinction between the minor dips (pullbacks) and the more significant declines (corrections). It's a matter of semantics. But I think by doing so, it assists in the learning process. And for those who pursue additional study with me through the options available on my website (www.tinalogan.com), it helps maintain consistency and they are able to easily follow along with me because they understand how I categorize various technical events. In other words, they learn and understand what I think is my commonsense market language.

TABLE 8.2 Bull Market Declines

Size of Decline	Category	Commentary
1% to 3%	Market Pullback	A dip of only 1 to 3% on a major average isn't very significant. I'd categorize it as a pullback, or maybe a deep pullback if it were about 3%.
3% to 5%	Minor Correction	This is a relatively minor correction; it often equates to a decline to about the 50-period SMA. These declines don't shake up traders too much and may offer good opportunities to buy the dip.
5% to 8%	Standard Correction	This is what I'd consider a fairly typical correction. It often equates with a decline to about the 100- or 200-period SMA. Such declines shake up the market a bit and offer an opportunity to enter long positions at nicely discounted prices.
8% to 12%	Deep Correction	This is often touted as a broad market correction; most stocks will get pulled down with the market if it declines this far. This is a pretty deep correction; you'll start to see more bearish interviews and pessimism from guests and commentators on the financial shows.
12% to 16%	Very Deep Correction	The talking heads on CNBC and other venues will start arguing/expressing concerns like "Is the bull market over?" or "Is this a new bear market starting?"
16% to 20%	Minor Bear Market	A decline of about 16 to 20% may be touted as a minor bear market or baby bear. A decline of nearly 17% occurred during 2011 and it was debated whether to call it a correction or a bear market.
More than 20%	Bear Market	The general consensus is a decline of 20% off the bull market closing high has reached bear market territory. A reversal of the major trend may be well under way.

Note: To measure the decline as a percentage, the closing highs and lows are used. Utilize the price percent change (PPC) method illustrated in Chapter 3.

Bull Market Corrections

Once the bull market has advanced for several weeks to a few months, it gets overbought on an intermediate-term basis. The market becomes vulnerable to a selloff. Think of it as pressure building and building. At some point, that pressure must be released—the market needs to consolidate or correct to alleviate the overextended condition.

There may be a few to several corrections within the course of a bull market, depending on how long it lasts, of course. The corrections may vary greatly in duration. They usually last from as little as a couple of weeks up to a few months. They may also vary in magnitude. Minor corrections may be short-term in length, but they are deeper than the very minor pullbacks that are so common.

Deeper corrections can be very unsettling while experiencing them—unless you are in cash, or profiting from them on the short side. When a deep correction occurs, you'll start hearing plenty of bearish, pessimistic talk on the financial shows. Try not to get infected by the dismal talk and just focus on monitoring the market trends. If a bear market ensues, it will reveal itself on the charts and you'll adjust your trading methods accordingly.

As long as the bull market is in force, the corrections prove to be good buying opportunities upon their conclusion. Most stocks tend to move with the market. Thus, during a market correction, many individual stocks get knocked down even if their fundamentals are sound. During the next leg up out of the correction, many of those stocks will move up again with the market.

It is important to realize that a single-digit percentage correction on the chart of the major average may equate to double-digit percentage declines in some individual stocks. Thus, during a correction, I'll closely monitor the charts of certain stocks, or certain sectors or industry groups, for buying opportunities at lower prices, sometimes much lower, than they were in the weeks prior to the correction when the market was overextended to the upside.

Correction Triggers Often there is a trigger, or catalyst, that starts a correction. Traders who understand the ebb and flow of the market get anxious as the market gets overextended and start anticipating a correction may be forthcoming. They are ready to take action if it starts to roll over. One or more events can spook the market and start a correction. Following are some examples of such triggers:

- Target Achieved—The Dow and/or S&P 500 has reached a target that traders are monitoring on its chart. Many experienced chartists monitor these market averages. When an important resistance level is reached, for instance, they may take profits there, initiating a selloff.
- News—A newsworthy event can get a correction started. Following are some examples: a Federal Reserve announcement; an earnings miss or negative guidance on one or more key stocks during earnings season; one or more disappointing economic reports.

A certain trigger may contribute to the start of the decline; however, it is not a requirement. Sometimes there is nothing significant that occurs, but the market is just overextended so a correction ensues.

The inverse may occur to stop a correction's fall. For instance, if the Dow and/or S&P 500 reaches a downside target during the decline, many traders will initiate long positions. Or a positive event or bit of news may be the catalyst that stops a correction and turns the major trend back up.

Bull Market Consolidation

There may be times when, rather than declining and retracing a portion of the prior upward move, price moves primarily sideways. That is, the secondary trend is a sideways move rather than a corrective move. However, it still serves the purpose of alleviating the overbought condition.

During a consolidation phase, you may hear traders and/or commentators refer to it as a "range-bound market." In those cases, in order for the next intermediate-term uptrend to begin, price must break out above the top of the trading range.

When you do hear such comments, though, make sure you understand the context in which they are stated. For instance, I recently heard a commentator on CNBC refer to the recent move to a new all-time high on the Dow as a breakout from a 10-year consolidation. If you were to look at a compressed weekly chart of the Dow for the past decade, you'd see what he means. But the moves across the range he referred to are *thousands* of points (they are entire bull and bear markets), not just minor swings across a trading range that forms within a bull market.

■ The Trends Create Support and Resistance

The intermediate-term movements within the major trend, as well as the short-term movements within the intermediate-term trends, create minor and major support and resistance levels within the new uptrend. The discussion below outlines how that occurs within a bull market, and you may observe the inverse during a bear market.

Figure 8.5 shows the first few months of the current bull market. As price moved up from the March 2009 low, it was not one smooth, uninterrupted run up. Rather, if you look closer you'll see that there were minor pullbacks and sideways movement within the uptrend. Each time price formed a peak and pulled back from it, or moved sideways, that peak created a minor resistance level above price (labeled R1 through R6). In order for the intermediate-term uptrend to continue, price had to surpass each new, higher peak on a subsequent move up.

Each time price pulled back, or based, and then turned back up again, the bottom that formed was a minor support level (S1 through S6). Price often holds at a minor support level during a subsequent pullback; or even later during a deeper decline, as illustrated by the correction in Figure 8.5 to the line at R4.

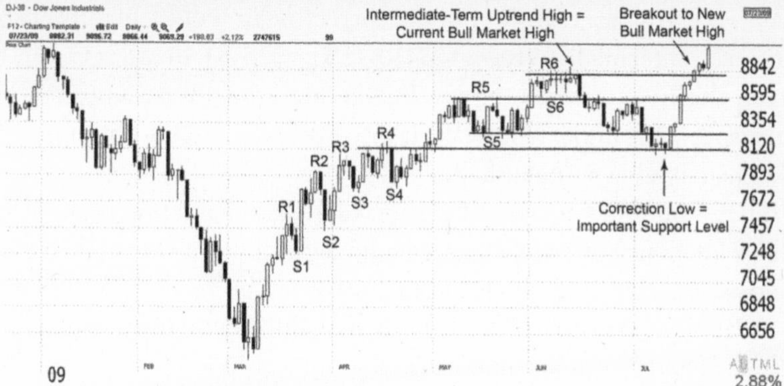

FIGURE 8.5 Support and Resistance Levels Are Formed within Trends
Source: TC2000® chart courtesy of Worden Brothers, Inc.

It is those relatively minor price pivots that create the rising peaks and rising bottoms that identify the *intermediate-term uptrend*. Some end up being more important than others. The horizontal lines drawn on the chart show some significant support and resistance levels. By significant, I mean they meet one or more of the following criteria: The price pivot is prominent (stands out on the chart); it has been touched more than once; or it ends up marking a significant high or low point on the chart.

At some point, often after several weeks to a few months, the intermediate-term uptrend gets overextended and price retraces a portion of the prior uptrend. The intermediate-term top that is left behind as price corrects creates a more significant resistance level above price than a minor pivot that forms on the way up. That top represents the current bull market high—the highest closing price reached so far in the bull market (R6 in Figure 8.5). Realize that we don't actually know yet, as that peak forms, if this is a new bull market. It could turn out to be the end of a bear market rally. And if it does, it is still an important resistance level because it marks the top of that intermediate-length up move.

Once the correction ends and price turns back up, it leaves behind a bottom—the first correction low of the new bull market. It is a prominent and important support level; more so than the minor bottoms formed during the pullbacks or periods of consolidation within the intermediate-term up leg. If the bull market is to keep expanding, that low should provide support if tested during a subsequent decline.

As price continues rising out of the correction, it will eventually encounter the prior intermediate-term top (R6 in Figure 8.5). In order to continue onward, and have a chance of developing into a long-term uptrend, price must surpass that important peak. If price breaks out above it, a new bull market high has been established.

If price continues to rise after breaking that significant peak (R6), it develops into a new intermediate-term up leg as illustrated in Figure 8.6. As price makes short-term swings up, and minor pullbacks or periods of minor consolidation within that next leg up, it continues to form minor peaks (resistance) and bottoms (support) along the way. When the intermediate-term uptrend gets overbought again, watch for another correction to occur; or sometimes a period of consolidation.

Once another correction gets under way, the top of the most recent intermediate-term uptrend marks the current bull market high, and another important resistance level on the chart as illustrated in Figure 8.6. When the correction ends and price turns up again, it creates a new correction low, which is another important support level.

Traders watch those important resistance and support levels very closely. Breaking above prominent resistance, and holding above prominent support, is crucial to the continuation of the long-term uptrend. When you look at a weekly chart, it is those prominent turning points that are the rising peaks and rising bottoms on that time frame.

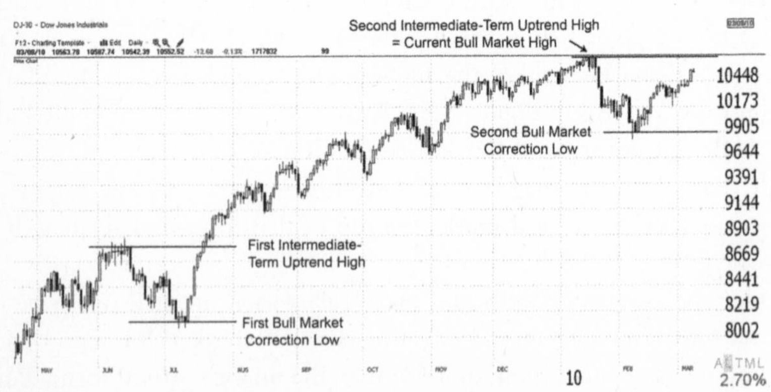

FIGURE 8.6 The Second Intermediate-Term Uptrend and Correction of the Bull Market

Source: TC2000® chart courtesy of Worden Brothers, Inc.

This process goes on and on throughout the bull market. When price breaks out above the last intermediate-term uptrend's peak, every day with a higher close is a new high for the bull market. Once the market stops rising and corrects, it leaves important resistance above. A new bull market high cannot be achieved until price turns back up and breaks out above that resistance. If price consolidates rather than correcting, a breakout above the ceiling of the consolidation constitutes a new high.

The Prior Bull Market's High

At the end of each bull market, you'll see on the chart the highest point reached during that major uptrend—the closing high for that bull market. It not only creates an important resistance level, but it is an important number psychologically. As price declines into a new bear market, it falls farther and farther away from that level. In fact, after several months of a bear market, you'll either have to tightly compress the daily chart or shift to a weekly chart to see it. It is left behind, but certainly not forgotten.

At some point, if the current major uptrend lasts long enough, and rises high enough, price will encounter *the high of the prior bull market*. For instance, the high of the 2002 to 2007 bull market was set on October 9, 2007, at 14,164.53 (refer to Table 8.1). That also happened to be the all-time high for the Dow. Therefore, imagine all the excitement on Wall Street when the Dow approached that level again in 2013. In fact, prior to breaking through that level in early March, the Dow consolidated for all of February below the 14,000 level. Oh, the anticipation!

Once the Dow surpassed the 2002 to 2007 bull market high, it entered new all-time high territory. From that point on, every new higher close meant a new bull market high and a new all-time high. That is heady stuff for traders. It's also great for investors' retirement accounts.

It will typically be well into the current bull market before the prior bull market's high is approached. The Dow fell over 50 percent during the last bear market. A decline of 50 percent takes an advance of 100 percent to recover back to break even. Thus, it can take many months, and often a few years, to recover the gains lost during a typical bear market. There will be exceptions of course. For instance, the 1987 crash was deep enough to put the market into bear market territory. However, in that case the decline was recovered relatively quickly (in a matter of months).

Other Resistance Levels Above

In addition to the resistance levels created by the price action of the new bull market, there may be many other resistance levels above that must be overcome in order for the new bull to continue its upward movement. During the prior bear market (e.g., the 2007–2009 decline), as intermediate-term declines, bear market corrections, and periods of sideways movement occurred, they left their mark on the chart. Thus, once that bear market bottomed out, and a new bull began, price started encountering those important resistance levels above. It has to push up through each of them in order to keep moving higher.

In summary: The new bull market not only creates its own support and resistance levels, but it also encounters those created by the prior bear market.

Additionally, as the new bull emerges, it must move above the 50-, 100-, and 200-period moving averages. And don't forget to take a look at the weekly chart. There may be important price ceilings on that time frame that you can't see in the limited scope of the daily chart, and there are moving averages on the weekly time frame that traders will be monitoring as well (e.g., the 200-week SMA).

The resistance levels above the market provide targets that traders monitor for profit taking points, which is why the market often pulls back, consolidates, or corrects, when significant targets are reached on the Dow and/or S&P 500. However, that doesn't mean price won't push up through those levels at some point—in fact, it must do so eventually or the bull market cannot continue.

■ End of a Bull Market

The bull market ends when price is unable to move up again and surpass the current bull market high. The final top of a bull market is often tested before a bear market begins in earnest. A topping process may develop, which resolves with a break to the downside.

Once it becomes clear that a new bear market is under way, traders shift gears and adjust their trading strategies to work in the downward cycle. Refer to Chapter 9 for more discussion on the start of a bear market.

CHAPTER 9

Bear Markets

There have been many bear markets since trading first began on Wall Street. Bear markets can be quite painful experiences—financially and psychologically—for many investors. A great amount of cumulative wealth may be lost during a bear market. Consider the devastating bear of 2007 to 2009, for example, during which trillions of dollars' worth of Americans' wealth evaporated. On an individual basis, though, some investors will fare very well in that environment while others will experience significant drawdown of their portfolios. It depends on how an investor *protects and directs* his funds during a down market.

Unfortunately, many typical investors do not know how to generate profits during a bear market environment. In fact, many don't take adequate steps to avoid or minimize losses, let alone profit from the decline. They don't sell short for one or more of the following reasons:

- They have never heard of the concept.
- They are fearful of doing so.
- They don't know how to do so.
- They can't do so in their tax-deferred retirement accounts.

Thus, in the past, before the advent of inverse exchange-traded funds (ETFs), some investors chose the safety of remaining in cash during a bear market. Many others held their long positions during the decline, suffering significant drawdown of their account equity with the hope of recovering those losses during the next bull market (the buy-and-hold method of investing).

Inverse ETFs are also known as *bear ETFs*. They are designed to allow investors to profit from a market decline without actually selling short. The

FIGURE 9.1 A Bear ETF Trades Inverse to the Market Average it Represents
Source: TC2000® chart courtesy of Worden Brothers, Inc.

instrument itself is in essence short the market, but the investor trades it long. Hence, the term "inverse." Some investors may choose to utilize an inverse ETF to hedge a long portfolio—basically buying insurance against falling prices. Other investors may choose to trade (or invest in) the inverse ETF as a substitute for shorting the market. *Note*: There are also inverse mutual funds (e.g., Rydex) that may be available to those who don't have access to ETFs in their tax-deferred accounts.

Figure 9.1 shows a two-chart layout with a daily chart of the Dow Jones Industrial Average on the left and the ProShares UltraShort Dow 30 ETF (DXD) on the right. The Dow was declining toward the March 2009 low, whereas DXD was rising during that same period. DXD is a popular choice among traders because it is also a leveraged or "ultra" ETF, meaning it approximately doubles the return of the market average it represents. Investors who prefer less volatility can trade the ProShares Short Dow 30 (DOG), which is a nonleveraged inverse ETF.

The typical investor fears a bear market and embraces a bull market. But ironically, having been burned during a bear market, they are usually late (sometimes very late) getting aboard the next bull market. Most of you who are reading this book are not typical investors; or if you are, you are seeking knowledge so you can take control of and direct your investments rather than be at the mercy of the market. Hence, you are spending the time and effort learning to do things differently, and I applaud you for doing so.

By actively managing your account(s) to protect the gains accrued during a bull market, and selling short and/or utilizing inverse ETFs during a subsequent bear market, it is not necessary to suffer through severe drawdowns of your portfolio during major downtrends.

Bear Markets of the Past 50 Years

Listed in Table 9.1 are the ten bear markets that occurred during the past 50 years. The figures shown are for the Dow Jones Industrial Average using daily market data from TC2000 (version 7). The percentage decline indicated for each of the bear markets is measured from the closing high of the prior bull market to the bear market's closing low.

Although there is general consensus on the start and end dates of most of the past bear markets, there are some instances where different sources list different dates based on their reading of the market. Table 9.1 illustrates my interpretation of the bear markets of the past five decades.

The criterion I chose for bear market classification was a minimum decline of 20 percent from the prior bull market closing high to the bear market closing low. There were ten declines of over 20 percent during the past 50 years. Additionally, the Dow fell over 19 percent during the summer of 1998. However, that decline fell short of meeting the 20 percent criterion, so it was not included in Table 9.1. That severe correction stemmed

TABLE 9.1 U.S. Bear Markets

Dates in Force	Length	Percent Decline	Closing High	Closing Low
Dec. 13, 1961 to June 26, 1962	6.4 Months	−27.10%	734.90 12/13/1961	535.70 6/26/1962
Feb. 9,1966 to Oct. 7, 1966	7.9 Months	−25.21%	995.20 2/9/1966	744.30 10/7/1966
Dec. 3, 1968 to May 26, 1970	17.7 Months	−35.93%	985.20 12/3/1968	631.20 5/26/1970
Jan. 11, 1973 to Dec. 6, 1974	22.8 Months	−45.08%	1,051.70 1/11/1973	577.60 12/6/1974
Sept. 21, 1976 to Feb. 28, 1978	17.3 Months	−26.87%	1,014.80 9/21/1976	742.10 2/28/1978
April 27, 1981 to Aug. 12, 1982	15.5 Months	−24.13%	1,024.00 4/27/1981	776.90 8/12/1982
Aug. 25, 1987 to Oct. 19, 1987	7.9 Weeks	−36.13%	2,722.42 8/25/1987	1,738.74 10/19/1987
July 17, 1990 to Oct. 11, 1990	2.9 Months	−21.16%	2,999.75 7/17/1990	2,365.10 10/11/1990
Jan. 14, 2000 to Oct. 9, 2002	22 Months	−37.85%	11,722.98 1/14/2000	7,286.27 10/9/2002
Oct. 9, 2007 to March 9, 2009	17 Months	−53.78%	14,164.53 10/9/2007	6,547.05 3/9/2009

from the 1997-1998 Asian financial crisis. The decline occurred over a period of about six weeks, and the market had fully recovered less than three months later.

Duration of a Bear Market

According to my calculations based on Table 9.1, the average length of a bear market during the past five decades has been approximately 1.2 years, significantly shorter than the average length of a bull market during the same time span. While that may be the average length and it provides a guideline, they will not all be of average length.

As Table 9.1 illustrates, during the past several decades there have been bear markets ranging from about eight weeks (the 1987 market crash) to as long as about two and a half years. Thus, we can't just rely on the concept of average bear market length to guide our trading. Instead, we can analyze each bear market as it evolves so we can profit from as much of the major downtrend as possible.

Magnitude of a Bear Market

According to my calculations, the average decline of the bear markets during the past 50 years is approximately 33 percent. The most significant decline during that period was almost 54 percent, and the smallest decline was just over 21 percent.

The Significance of October

Looking at Table 9.1, did you notice how often bear markets ended in the month of October? October is sometimes referred to as the "bear killer" because it is notorious for ending bear markets. If you watch CNBC and other financial shows during October, especially if it happens to be a year in which the market is in decline, you'll hear talk of the significance that month holds for the markets.

The bear markets of 1966, 1990, and 2002 ended in October, as did the famous Crash of 1987. During most of 2004, the market drifted downward in a wide descending channel; it was not a bear market, but a slow and somewhat frustrating downward, choppy environment. October marked the low of that channel and the resumption of the bull market. The very deep decline that occurred in 2011 also ended in October.

Economic Recessions

A bear market may be accompanied by an economic recession. The 2007 to 2009 bear market was flanked by a significant period of economic contraction. The recession was so severe it was dubbed the Great Recession. It was the worst recession since the Great Depression that followed the 1929 stock market crash.

Early Development of a Bear Market

The discussion in this segment reveals how bear markets emerge from a bull market top.

Shift from Bull to Bear Market

When a bull market reverses direction, it won't be obvious at first. At the right edge of the chart, you won't know whether the first leg down is just another bull market correction, or whether it is the beginning of a new bear market. Oftentimes after the first leg down, price rallies again for a test of the bull market high. When that occurs, at the right edge of the chart as price is rising back up toward that high, you can't be certain if it will find resistance at/near that level; or whether the index will break up through it, resulting in a resumption of the bull market.

Just like with transitions to new bull markets, there are debates on what determines whether a new bear market is in force. Following are three factors you may see referenced:

1. The index declines by 20 percent off the bull market high.
2. The index closes decisively below the bottom of the last bull market correction.
3. The index closes decisively below the 200-day (40-week) moving average.

The above events will typically occur at different points as a new bear market emerges, and each poses challenges. For example, by the time the index declines by 20 percent, the bear market will be well under way. Remember, the average bear market decline of the past five decades was approximately 33 percent.

As for closing below the 200-day moving average, it has happened a few times already during the current bull market, but price moved back above

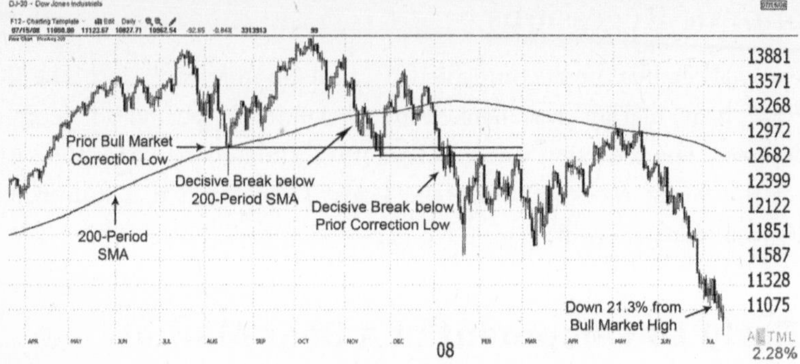

FIGURE 9.2 Factors Used to Identify a New Bear Market
Source: TC2000® chart courtesy of Worden Brothers, Inc.

it. And twice during very steep declines—in 2010 and again in 2011—the Dow closed below the 200-day moving average and the prior correction low, but went on to make new bull market highs.

Figure 9.2 shows a daily chart of the Dow during the transition from the 2002 to 2007 bull market into the 2007 to 2009 bear market. All three of the factors mentioned above are identified on the chart. Clearly by the time the Dow was down 20 percent, it was deeply into the bear market. It occurred much later than the breaking of the important support levels at the prior correction low and the 200-period SMA.

These are guidelines for making a determination of whether a major trend change has occurred from a bull to a bear market. However, traders should not wait until any or all of those factors are present to take the actions of protecting capital, and/or determining if the time is right to sell short in the decline (or go long inverse ETFs).

The Topping Process Trying to time the precise turning point of a new bear market can be difficult. The major shift has a fundamental basis in the business cycle and often takes time to unfold. It also tends to take time because, on a technical basis, most bear markets do not start from a single top reversal. The reversal is more of a transitional process than a specific turning point; therefore, it can take a few to several months before it is officially deemed a new bear market.

The topping process usually involves the market putting in the final bull market high and then testing that high one or more times before a

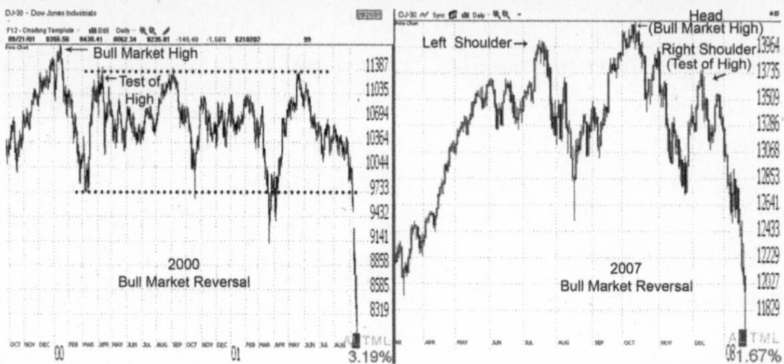

FIGURE 9.3 Comparison of the Last Two Bull Market Reversals on the Dow Jones Industrial Average
Source: TC2000® chart courtesy of Worden Brothers, Inc.

new bear market can gain a foothold. Thus, a typical reversal from a bull to a bear market will be from a double, triple, or head-and-shoulders top; or the market will top out and form a rectangular-type topping process (often referred to as *distribution*) or a rounding-type top. Any of those topping formations sets up a more significant zone of resistance above the market than would occur if the trend reversed from a single top. There are those infrequent occasions, though, when a bull market may reverse direction in an abrupt fashion (most recently, the reversal in July 1990). You may hear it referred to as an *inverted V* or a *spike top*.

Figure 9.3 illustrates a two-chart layout of the Dow. The charts have been tightly compressed to compare the two most recent bull market reversals. The reversal shown on the left started from the 2000 bull market high. After the initial move down, price rallied back up to near the bull market high. Over the next year and a half, the Dow was trapped in a wide trading range (dotted lines). It broke to the downside in September 2001, but later rallied back up inside the wide trading range (not shown) before eventually continuing down and ultimately putting in the 2002 low.

The reversal from the 2007 bull market high is shown on the right in Figure 9.3. After the initial decline off the top, price rallied back up toward the bull market high, falling short of reaching it and creating a large head-and-shoulders top. It's not an ideal pattern—the left and right shoulders are not close enough to the same price level. Nonetheless, the message is clear—a topping process occurred rather than an abrupt bull market reversal.

It is difficult to nail the very top of a new bear market in real time. But that doesn't mean market participants have to hold their long positions deeply into a bear market and lose a significant amount of the profits they had built up in their portfolios during the prior bull market. There are almost always technical indications of a breakdown that can be seen on the intermediate-term trend (daily chart) or the long-term trend (weekly chart). Additionally, using protective stop loss orders will limit the amount of gains the investor forfeits; or the amount of loss of capital for those who got invested at/near the top but have little to no gains accrued.

Nor does it mean missing out on shorting the initial decline off the bull market high if a sell signal is present, or going long using inverse ETF(s). By the time certain barriers have been crossed, and/or enough percentage decline occurs on the market average, to officially deem a new bear market to be in force, you may have already been participating via the intermediate-length trends. Many individual stocks will have already made significant declines by that time.

Moving Averages Turn down and then Cross

As a new bear market emerges, short-term moving averages will turn down quickly, and it won't take long for a fast moving average (e.g., 10-period) to cross below a slower one (e.g., 20-period). However, those short-term moving averages track relatively close to price, so just because they turn down, or even cross, does not mean a trend reversal is imminent. They'll turn up and cross again if what appears to be a new bear market emerging turns out to be just another bull market correction.

Eventually, as the bear market gets going, the intermediate- and long-term moving averages will also turn down and experience crossovers. For example, the 50-period will cross below the 200-period (referred to as a death cross). In fact, price will encounter all those strong moving averages during the decline and will have to break down through those potential support levels.

Observations Prior to the Reversal

In Chapter 8, information was provided about watching for technical warnings prior to or during a market bottom, as well as signs from fundamentals. I won't repeat that discussion here because, as a general rule, the concepts apply inversely to reversals from a bull market into a bear market.

■ Further Development of the Major Downtrend

Once the bear market gets going, it will typically fall into a rhythm of trending down for an intermediate-length period of time, extending the trend, followed by a correction against the major trend; or in some cases, a period of prolonged consolidation.

During the down legs, bounces (relief rallies) and bases/flags are common occurrences. They create support and resistance levels within the intermediate-term trend. Those minor interruptions of the trend may offer opportunities to short the market for another move down; or to add shares to an existing core short position. After several weeks to a few months, the downtrend will be oversold on an intermediate-term basis, sometimes severely so, and a bear market correction ensues serving to alleviate that overextended condition. The turn up into a bear market correction and the subsequent turn back down to resume the major downtrend create important support and resistance levels.

A bear market correction, which may also be called a *bear market rally*, is more pronounced than a minor bounce—it retraces a significant portion of the prior decline. There may be an instance where it retraces all of it, though that should occur infrequently; otherwise, the market would become range bound.

As you monitor the up and down legs within a bear market, watch for warnings of a potential trend reversal. Utilize the tables in Chapters 5 and 6 as quick reference guides for early and later warnings, respectively. You may also pay attention to the market internals discussed in Chapter 7. The detailed discussions of monitoring bull markets included in Chapters 8, 10, and 11 are also applicable to monitoring bear markets, but inversely since the extensions of the major trend are now to the downside and the corrective moves are to the upside. I've included some illustrations and commentary below regarding the first few intermediate-term movements of the most recent bear market of 2007 to 2009.

Figure 9.4 shows a daily chart of the Dow during the first two down legs of the 2007–2009 bear market, with a correction separating them. The first intermediate-length decline off the October 2007 top was just over 10 percent. It was fairly orderly, starting with an initial push down, followed by a bounce of just over 3 percent (labeled B1). The next push down started from a long Bearish Engulfing candle followed by a brief pause and more down movement. The next bounce was a single long candle of almost

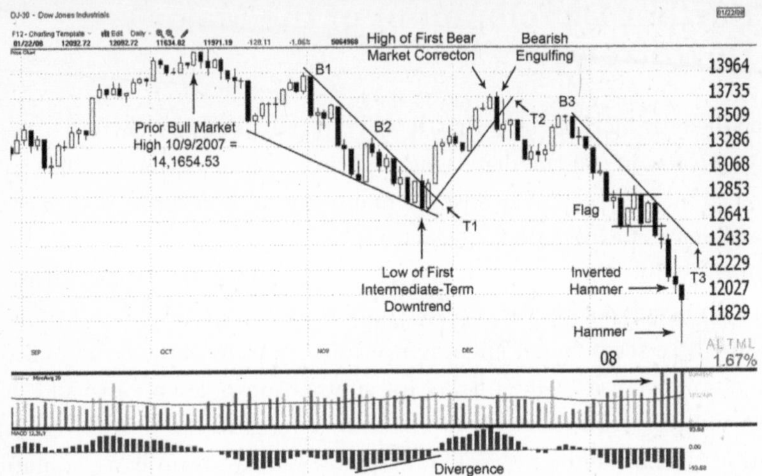

FIGURE 9.4 The First Down Legs and Correction of the 2007–2009 Bear Market
Source: TC2000® chart courtesy of Worden Brothers, Inc.

2.5 percent (B2). A down trendline (T1) was drawn connecting the declining peaks. As the final low of that decline formed, the trendlines identify a bullish descending wedge with a bullish divergence against the MACD histogram shown in the bottom panel. That bottom became the current bear market low and a very important support level. It would have to be broken in order for the bear market to move lower.

Price broke out from the descending wedge moving above the down trendline (T1) and rallying nearly 8 percent during what would become the first bear market correction. At the time, though, at the right edge of the chart, the first leg down off the top had looked like just another bull market correction. And as price rallied during what we now know as a bear market correction, at the right edge of the chart it looked like it was a new up leg of the bull market. That is, until price rolled over again rather than moving above the October high.

The next intermediate-term downtrend began with a Bearish Engulfing pattern and a break of the short-term up trendline (T2). It was followed by a bounce of almost 3 percent (B3). The next push down broke the low of the prior intermediate-term decline, setting a new bear market low. That sharp decline had only brief pauses along the way; it would ultimately be seen as the pole of a bearish flag. The flag is identified by the short horizontal

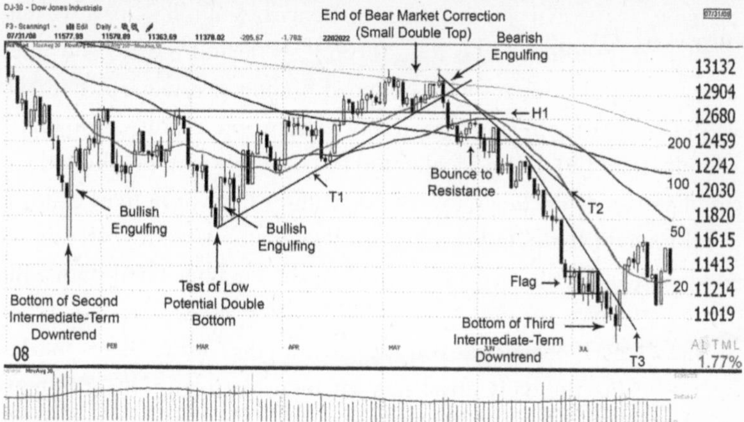

FIGURE 9.5 The Next Correction and Down Leg of the 2007–2009 Bear Market
Source: TC2000® chart courtesy of Worden Brothers, Inc.

lines. Price broke through the bottom of the flag, making another strong move down accompanied by heavy volume. An intermediate-term down trendline (T3) was drawn defining the length and slope of the decline. Back-to-back bullish candlestick patterns formed at the low—an Inverted Hammer followed by a Hammer.

Figure 9.5 shows a daily chart of the Dow with the next two intermediate-term trends shown—a bear market correction followed by another down leg extending the length and magnitude of the bear market. The 20-, 50-, 100-, and 200-period simple moving averages (SMAs) have been added for more detail on this chart.

At the left side of the chart, in late January 2008, price started the move up from the bottom of the second intermediate-term downtrend with a Bullish Engulfing candle. The move stalled and price turned back down for a test of that prior low, creating a potential bullish double bottom pattern. The move up from that low also started from a Bullish Engulfing candle, ultimately resulting in a run up (bear market correction) of over 11 percent.

During that rise, price broke through resistance at the horizontal line (H1) confirming the double bottom. However, it didn't move much higher before finding resistance at the 200-period SMA. Price dipped back to the prior ceiling (H1), which reversed roles from resistance to support. Price rallied back up to the May high but was not able to surpass that peak, stalling again at the 200-period SMA and setting up a potential small double top.

The next leg down started from a Bearish Engulfing pattern closing below the up trendline (T1), the 20- and 50-period SMAs, and line H1. After that first push down, price bounced finding resistance at line H1 and the 50-period SMA, offering a good short entry opportunity. A down trendline was started (T2). Price accelerated into the July low, breaking the prior intermediate-term decline's low and setting a new bear market low. The sharp fall formed the pole for a bearish flag. A steeper down trendline was drawn (T3), which was easily broken when the decline ended with a Bullish Engulfing pattern.

For practice, I challenge you to review the entire bear market of 2007–2009 using the daily chart in your own platform. Observe how the up and down legs formed and when the prior bear market low from the 2000–2002 decline was surpassed. Yes, this examination takes some time, but you'll learn a lot by going through the process.

End of a Bear Market

During a bear market, flashy rallies can occur, which lead many to believe the bottom is in. When the rally fizzles out and the major trend resumes, they realize it was just another correction of the long-term downtrend. Price makes another scary decline back down toward the prior low, and market participants watch with trepidation to see if it provides support.

This is how bear markets evolve; on and on it goes, making downward moves and bear market rallies (or consolidation) until it runs its course and an actual long-term trend reversal occurs (a shift from bear to bull market). Finally, the bulls come forth with sufficient strength to propel the market into a sustainable uptrend—a new bull market.

CHAPTER 10

Monitoring the Market Trends

As you have probably come to realize by now, monitoring the progress of intermediate-term trends is one of my primary activities. I monitor those trends on the stocks in which I hold open positions, and often on those for which I am looking for an opportunity to initiate a new position. Additionally, the intermediate-term trends of the broad market *guide my overall trading activities*. They dictate the primary direction to focus trades and the tactics used at any given time for core positions, as well as swing trading activities since swing moves occur within intermediate-term trends.

This chapter focuses on monitoring the intermediate-term movements, both up and down, of the broad market. Although this activity is very important, the job of doing so doesn't actually take excessive amounts of my time and attention each day. Rather, it is just part of an ongoing routine that requires periodic tasks, such as adjusting sloped trendlines and horizontal support and resistance lines, and watching for indications of potential weakness of the trend so I'm prepared when a trend reversal occurs. By prepared, I mean to protect capital invested and gains accrued in open positions, and to be ready to trade in the opposite direction when a trend reversal occurs.

Although monitoring the market trend does require regularly checking its progress, it is the everyday tasks that take more of my time and attention, such as the following:

- Looking for trading candidates that have strong potential for success without exposing capital to excessive risk.
- Monitoring open positions and executing orders.

- Tracking short-term price movements on charts of stocks for entry and exiting signals; and on the Dow Jones Industrial Average to help guide overall trading decisions.
- Monitoring the market internals.
- Staying in tune with news and events that impact the market.
- Running scans and browsing through my watchlists that require regular review.

When managing a specific swing trade, or swing trading around a core position (the Lock and Reload technique mentioned previously), I'm actually very focused on the short-term trend on the chart of that stock. Additionally, the swing moves on the chart of a major market average (e.g., the Dow) may influence the swing moves that occur on many individual stocks. For instance, if after an upward price swing the Dow pulls back (a minor trend interruption), many stocks will pull back as well. Thus, I continually monitor the strength of the short-term market trends and watch for signs that the minor trend may change direction. Basically, the intermediate-term trend provides the overall guidance, but the short-term movements provide the entry and exiting opportunities.

Day trading requires monitoring intraday charts. I'm not a day trader per se, since I do not close out my account to cash at the end of each day. However, I do take positions that would be considered day trades. On some days that could take up a significant amount of time during a trading session, depending on how many trades are opened and closed. Or if day trading around a swing position, it means watching for chances to take some profits on intraday price runs and then adding back shares to the position if an opportunity arises (the Lock and Reload technique taken down to a lower time frame).

As for the long-term trend, I'm always aware of the major trend of a stock I trade, as well as that of the broad market. But I don't have to spend much time specifically focused on the long-term trend itself, because it is incorporated into my activities of monitoring the intermediate-term trends within it.

As illustrated in Chapter 3, most long-term trends are strung together by a few to several intermediate-length moves. Those moves are either in the direction of the major trend (extending it), or against the trend (correcting it). There may also be periods of sideways movement interrupting the major trend. Those intermediate-term movements are easier to follow and monitor than the major trend, which is significantly longer; and by continually monitoring them, I am indirectly monitoring the long-term trend.

The *last leg up* in a bull market, and the *last leg down* in a bear market, is usually an intermediate-length move leading to the final top or bottom, respectively (Figure 10.1). Therefore, when I'm monitoring an intermediate-term trend for signs of weakness, at some point I'll be seeing what will ultimately turn out to be the end of the long-term trend.

The *first leg up* in a new bull market, and the *first leg down* in a new bear market, is usually an intermediate-length trend coming off the bottom or top, respectively (Figure 10.1). So here again, by monitoring the intermediate-term trends as readily as I do, I don't miss a chance to participate when a long-term trend changes course.

Figure 10.1 shows a two-chart layout of the Dow, which illustrates the points above. The dotted lines on the charts show where intermediate-term trends start and end. The daily chart on the left shows the top of the 2002 to 2007 bull market, an intermediate-term uptrend; and the first leg down into the 2008 to 2009 bear market, an intermediate-term downtrend. The daily chart on the right shows the last leg down of the 2008 to 2009 bear market, an intermediate-term downtrend; and the first leg up of the current bull market, an intermediate-term uptrend.

In addition, I do chart analysis using multiple time frames. When I'm monitoring the intermediate-length trends within a major trend, I periodically shift up to the weekly chart to get a bigger picture view of the entirety of that trend; and to identify the major support and resistance levels. Thus,

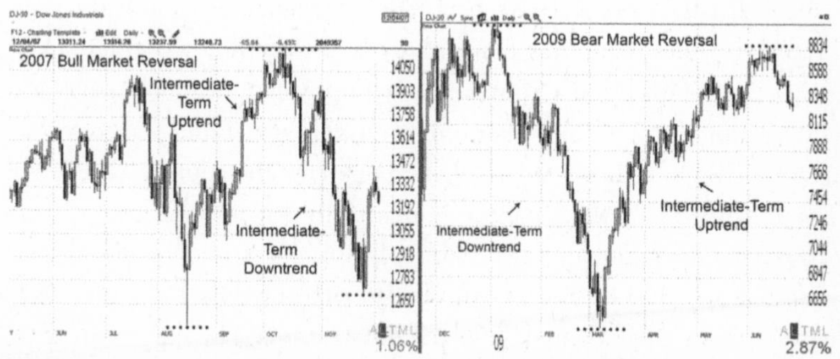

FIGURE 10.1 Intermediate-Term Trends at the Beginning and End of Bull and Bear Markets
Source: TC2000® chart courtesy of Worden Brothers, Inc.

I'm always aware of the major trend, but I can't trade the "whole trend." A major trend may last for several years. Therefore, the shorter trends within it are where my activities are primarily focused.

Even for a long-term (core) position, it is unlikely to remain intact for an *entire* bull or bear market. For me, a trend-following strategy does not mean holding on no matter what occurs—that would be more in keeping with the buy-and-hold mantra, to which I don't subscribe. Rather, with core positions I can tolerate a certain amount of drawdown during corrections, but my risk tolerance has limits. Eventually, a retracement of the trend will be deep enough to encourage exiting, or trigger a stop loss order. Remember, there was a nearly 17 percent decline during 2011. Even a prolonged period of sideways movement may be enough in some cases, either because the swings across the consolidation area are deep enough, or a volatility-based stop is pulled in tightly enough to trigger. If stopped out of a core long position, I'll watch for an opportunity to get back aboard the major trend (e.g., after a correction has run its course).

What I want to emphasize from the above discussion is that even though the time and effort spent on the actual tasks of monitoring the intermediate-term trend are not excessive, they are extremely important for guiding my overall trading focus. The importance of an activity should not be measured by how much time it takes, but rather by how critical it is. Basically, I tend to busy myself with daily trading-related tasks, while regularly checking in on the intermediate-term trend to gauge its progression.

You may, at first, get the impression while reviewing this chapter that it is a very time-intensive activity. But perhaps it just seems that way because it takes me so many pages to explain how I do it! That's why I provide bulleted or numbered lists, and tables, in many of the chapters—to summarize the content of the discussions. Once a trader understands the concepts involved, and then becomes efficient with performing the related tasks, it becomes part of his regular routine along with various other repetitive tasks. Trading is not all thrills and excitement; much of a trader's success (or failure) comes down to how effectively he performs the routine tasks involved.

The discussion in this chapter is primarily focused on monitoring the intermediate-term movements within the major trend on the chart of a market average that represents the broad market. The Dow and S&P 500 index charts are used primarily in the illustrations. They are both large-cap indices widely utilized by chartists. The bull market that is currently in force is used for this instruction; however, the concepts can also be utilized during a bear market but with the focus on the major downtrend in those instances.

Monitoring the Intermediate-Term Uptrends

Let's start with the intermediate-term upward movements, which serve the purpose of extending the duration and length of the bull market. While the market is moving upward for a period of time in the direction of the major trend, I trade primarily long positions and continually monitor the market's trend to gauge its strength.

For me, this is the time to really work the long side—it is an *up leg in a bull market*. For instance, I frequently utilize bases/flags and pullbacks against the uptrend as setups, either for initiating or adding to a position. Since the market is trending during this phase, and often quite strongly, I favor core and swing positions. I may even do some day trading around swing positions; and/or if time allows, some specialized bullish strategies (e.g., a morning-gap-reversal type of strategy) that tend to work well in that environment.

I maintain that bullish stance until such time as the trend begins to age to the point where it is considered to be overbought on an intermediate-term basis, and/or warnings of a potential trend reversal emerge. Those warnings may be technical signs such as those outlined in Chapters 5 and 6, and/or signals from my scanning activities and the market internals.

What do I mean by aging to the point of being overbought? Recall that an intermediate-term trend typically lasts from about one to three months; and the movements that are in the direction of the major trend tend to last longer than the corrective moves. Thus, once an upward move approaches the far end of that range, I am very aware that its remaining days are numbered. I continue to work that trend until it has run its course, because we don't know precisely how long the move will last; but I strive to avoid becoming complacent with my trading activities, which can lead to being caught off guard when a reversal occurs.

Note: In Chapter 11, I've included a table that lists all the intermediate-term uptrends of the current bull market along with the percentage rise and duration of each upward move.

The longer the intermediate-term uptrend goes on, the more overbought it gets, and the more anxious bullish traders will become because they know a corrective move is around the corner. Some of the intermediate-term up legs in the current bull market lasted from about four to six months. So imagine how overextended the move feels to the market participants by that point! The pundits on the stock shows will be clamoring for a correction by then. But because some of those trends have lasted that long, it is an argument for not prematurely exiting a trend just because it is aging. An overbought market can get more overbought and stay that way for some time. Instead, take advantage of the trend and monitor it until its eventual end.

I continually monitor the uptrend during its entire lifespan, but as it extends to a few months or beyond, I become even more vigilant. The aging of the trend alone is not enough to cause me to close all long positions, nor to start shorting the market. I must see actual sell signals before taking those steps. However, as the trend gets overbought, I do tend to get more cautious; especially if the aging of the trend is accompanied by one or more early warnings of a potential trend reversal. I continue to work the long side, but get even more selective than normal with the setups I trade, and more conservative with my trade management (details are provided later in this chapter in the discussion of responding to market trend reversal warnings). The goal is to capture as much of the uptrend as possible, but minimize exposure to a potentially sharp and fast market decline as the trend enters the more vulnerable stage of its run up.

Maintain Trendlines

One of my primary tasks for monitoring the intermediate-term uptrend is to maintain support trendlines in order to observe when a trend may be reversing direction, and resistance trendlines as visual cues for potential barriers above. I utilize both sloped trendlines and horizontal support and resistance lines as described below.

Intermediate-Term Up Trendline(s) An intermediate-length upward-sloping trendline is drawn below the prominent rising bottoms. In some cases there is more than one up trendline (e.g., recall prior discussions of loose and tight lines and internal and external lines). I continually adjust the line(s) upward as long as the intermediate-term trend is in force. A steepening of the trendline slope, or a break of a strong trendline, is among the warnings of a potential trend reversal. For those reasons, this is an important part of the monitoring process in my opinion.

An intermediate-term trendline is typically broken during a market correction. However, price need not always decline that much to break the trendline (especially if it has become tightly fit to price). In some cases, it will be broken during a market pullback, or if price bases sideways for a period of time. If the trendline is broken by a minor trend interruption, and then price recovers rather than breaking down further, the trendline can be redrawn to reflect the current length and slope of the uptrend as illustrated in Figure 10.2.

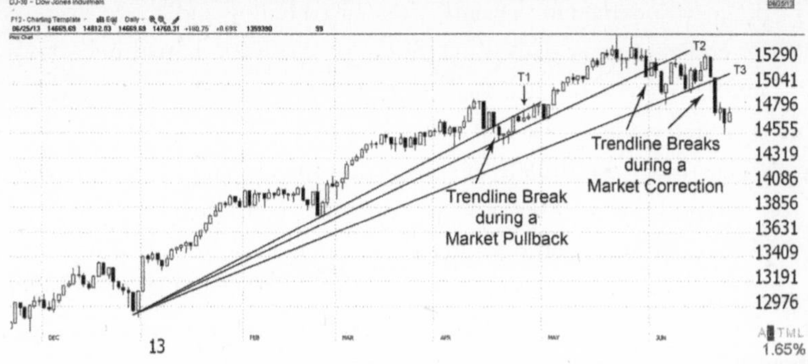

FIGURE 10.2 Intermediate-Term Up Trendlines
Source: TC2000® chart courtesy of Worden Brothers, Inc.

Figure 10.2 shows a daily chart of the Dow during the latter part of the intermediate-term up leg that lasted from November 2012 to late May 2013. The chart shows where, at particular times in the trend's evolution, three specific trendlines were drawn, and when they were broken.

The first trendline (labeled T1) was broken during a market pullback from April 15 to 18—a decline of only 2.2 percent. Once price turned back up out of that pullback, it formed a new price pivot (a bottom). A new up trendline was drawn (T2). That line was continually extended upward, and slight adjustments to the slope were made as warranted, until late May 2013.

From May 29 through June 5, price pulled back almost 3 percent, breaking the up trendline (T2). At that time, at the right edge of the chart, it would have appeared to be just another market pullback. Price turned back up forming a new bottom. At that time, a new trendline (T3) was drawn. It was extended upward, and slight adjustments made to the slope, until it was broken on June 20. At that time, at the right edge of the chart, it became apparent that the market was experiencing a correction. Many stocks are influenced by the broad market movement. Thus, by this time, a stop order on an individual stock may have already been triggered; or the chart of that stock may have previously flashed a warning(s) encouraging the trader to close the position, or at least take partial profits to reduce exposure to more downside.

Horizontal Support and Resistance Lines I also maintain horizontal lines to identify support and resistance levels. Recall from Chapter 8 that minor support and resistance levels are created from the up and down price swings (and periods of minor consolidation) as the uptrend develops. They show where potential near-term barriers are located below and above price as the trend zigs and zags its way upward. Some of those levels will become more significant than others. For instance, a line may reverse roles from resistance to support, or vice versa. A line that is touched multiple times will be monitored by many chartists. Additionally, at some point the intermediate-term uptrend will top out, and that will become an important resistance level.

I may also maintain some longer-term horizontal lines from the distant past that are still relevant, and that I continue to extend to the right edge of the chart. You'll see some of the meaningful past support and resistance levels in the case study of the current bull market in Chapter 11.

As illustrated on the daily chart of the Dow in Figure 10.3, I'll often start a very near-term line—a relatively short horizontal line. For instance, at the time the bases illustrated in Figure 10.3 were forming, I maintained short horizontal lines (e.g., H1 and H2) on the daily chart. I knew price would have to break the upper line in order to continue the uptrend; and a break of the lower line could warn of a potential trend reversal.

I'll extend the line to the right if price is still using that line for support and/or resistance as illustrated by line H3. I'll extend a line all the way over to the right edge of the chart if it comes into play again in the future. That is, if price approaches that line again during a market pullback or a deeper correction as illustrated by lines H4 and H5. Line H6 was extended to the right edge because it represented the top of the prior intermediate-term uptrend, which was also the bull market high at the time, making it an important resistance level. The market had to move above it in order for the major trend to continue its rise, which it did in July 2013 (not shown).

FIGURE 10.3 Horizontal Support and Resistance Lines
Source: TC2000® chart courtesy of Worden Brothers, Inc.

Once broken, a resistance line often becomes support below price. Sometimes it occurs right away, and sometimes later on. Line H4 in Figure 10.3 shows both examples. After breaking out just above the base shown between lines H3 and H4, price immediately dipped back to the base top. Several days later that line was tested again, and yet again in June during the market correction shown at right edge of the chart.

Continuous Monitoring and Trendline Cleanup The lines I currently have drawn on my charts are not all present in many of the examples in this book because I don't want to distract from the price movement I point out during a specific discussion. However, you can bet that as soon as I was done capturing all the illustrations for publication, I redrew all the pertinent trendlines because they are important to my ongoing analysis. I continually adjust the sloped and horizontal lines and share my chart each week, along with market commentary and educational topics, in my affordable weekly report (yes, I know that was a shameless plug!).

Figure 10.4 shows the primary sloped and horizontal lines I have drawn on the daily chart of the Dow at the time of this writing. Some of the past lines shown in Figures 10.2 and 10.3 have been erased. I'll periodically go back and delete the unnecessary sloped and horizontal lines so the chart doesn't get overly cluttered. However, the strongest of the lines, and the ones closer to the right edge of the chart that are in play, or may become so again soon, remain on the chart. I continue to extend them to the right edge until they are no longer meaningful. But even that may only be temporary. A line may come into play again in the future (e.g., during a market correction), and if so, it can

FIGURE 10.4 Sloped Trendlines and Horizontal Support and Resistance Lines
Source: TC2000® chart courtesy of Worden Brothers, Inc.

be redrawn at that time. Some lines become very strong, long-term lines and they may remain on my charts for a prolonged period.

The analysis of the intermediate-term movements is done on the daily chart. Thus, the primary trendlines for those movements are maintained on that time frame. I also periodically check the weekly chart and am aware of the longer-term sloped trendline(s) as well as the major support and resistance areas, including important moving averages, on that time frame. *Note:* There will be times when a long-term line intersects with an intermediate-term line.

Market Trend Reversal Warnings

Another of my primary tasks for monitoring the uptrend of the market is to watch for warnings of a potential trend reversal. Chapters 5 and 6 were devoted to recognizing signs that a trend may be losing momentum, or in the process of reversing direction. The early and later trend reversal warnings covered in those chapters apply to trends on the charts of stocks. They also apply to index charts. One or more of those warnings may occur prior to, during, or soon after a change in the direction of the market trend. They are all listed again in Table 10.1, and you may return to Chapters 5 and 6 to review the detailed discussion.

I mentioned in Chapter 5 that there were some additional trend reversal warnings that do not apply to the charts of individual stocks, but rather can be used to *gauge the health of the trend of the broad market*. Those warnings are from market internals, and noticeable shifts in sentiment measures and certain scans. They are addressed in this chapter and have been added to the list of trend reversal warnings in the middle of Table 10.1. These concepts will also be referenced in Chapter 11.

When the broad market average shows a healthy uptrend, it is because many stocks are rising pushing it up. When the trend of the broad market average reverses direction, it is because many stocks have reversed direction pulling it down. Then more stocks will follow the market down during the selloff, regardless of their underlying fundamentals. The movement of most stocks is influenced by the broad market (and/or by the sector to which that stock belongs). A warning(s) of a potential reversal of the trend of the market average suggests many stocks have lost momentum, and some may already be shifting direction. Hence, that may influence the decisions a trader makes in regard to some or all of his open long positions, and pending orders for initiating new positions. That is, he may take some defensive action to preserve the gains in open positions, and avoid exposing more capital on the long side when there are signs pointing to a potential market decline.

Monitoring the market internals, along with the chart of the market average, can help draw attention to weakness in the market trend. Following is some discussion of the "Market Internals, Sentiment, and Scans" listed in the middle of Table 10.1.

Market Internals Many experienced traders pay attention to market internals, which measure the momentum of the market trend. One gauge they look at is the number of stocks making a new 52-week high or a new 52-week low (referred to as new highs and new lows, respectively).

This is one of the best measures to use for confirming the strength of the market trend; and for signaling weakness of the trend that may precede a trend reversal. During a bull market, clearly a large number of stocks will be rising and, therefore, setting new highs. During an up leg within the major market uptrend, expect the number of new highs to expand as many stocks move up. During a market correction, the number will drop back

TABLE 10.1 Warnings of a Market Trend Reversal

Early Trend Reversal Warnings	
Uptrend	***Downtrend***
Bearish Climax Move	Bullish Climax Move
Bearish Divergence—Price vs. Indicator	Bullish Divergence—Price vs. Indicator
Failure to Break Prior Peak	Failure to Break Prior Bottom
Change of Slope—Steeper Rising Trendline	Change of Slope—Steeper Declining Trendline
Break of Tight Rising Trendline	Break of Tight Declining Trendline
Approaching a Strong Ceiling	Approaching a Strong Floor
Bearish Candlestick Reversal Pattern	Bullish Candlestick Reversal Pattern
Early Broad Market Trend Reversal Warnings (Market Internals, Sentiment, and Scans)	
Uptrend	***Downtrend***
Bearish Divergence—Index vs. Market Internals	Bullish Divergence—Index vs. Market Internals
High Positive Market Sentiment Readings	High Negative Market Sentiment Readings
Notable Change in the Count of Certain Scans	Notable Change in the Count of Certain Scans
Later Trend Reversal Warnings	
Uptrend	***Downtrend***
Breakdown through Support	Breakout above Resistance
Break of Up (Support) Trendline	Break of Down (Resistance) Trendline
Breakdown below a Strong Moving Average	Breakout above a Strong Moving Average
Change in Direction of Peaks	Change in Direction of Bottoms

since many stocks will move down so they won't be making new highs. Conversely, during a bear market, a significant number of stocks are declining, thereby making new lows. During a down leg, the number of new lows will expand. That number will decrease during a bear market correction.

By regularly tracking the number of stocks making new highs and new lows, you may recognize important changes, either in the numbers themselves and/or in the trend of those numbers. In either instance, it may serve as an early warning because it occurs before the market actually reverses direction as follows:

1. Sentiment—If the number gets particularly high, a trader may view it as a contrary signal. There is often excessive bullishness (new highs) prior to the market putting in a top. Excessive bearishness (new lows) may occur prior to a market bottom. Thus, be on the alert for a potential market trend reversal when a reading gets very high.
2. Divergence—If the number of new highs starts declining noticeably (trending down), but the market is still rising (trending up), it is a negative divergence between the market and the internals. Conversely, if the number of new lows diminishes noticeably but the market is still falling, it is a positive divergence.

As part of their trading routine, active traders may choose to keep track of the total number of stocks making new highs and new lows each day for the New York Stock Exchange (NYSE). Your broker may supply this information. Alternatively, you can get the hourly numbers on Briefing.com (under Market Internals), or get the data delayed by 15 to 20 minutes on Yahoo! Finance (www.finance.yahoo.com/market-overview). On Yahoo! Finance, look under Market Stats/Advancers & Decliners. New Highs and New Lows should be listed in the same table. Track the numbers in a spreadsheet or by writing them down in your trading journal. After some time tracking the numbers, you should start to notice when there are high readings (sentiment). To note changes in the trend of the new highs or new lows, watch for a divergence against the market average, or watch for the ratio of stocks making new highs versus new lows to start improving or deteriorating.

Sentiment Measures Sentiment is an important concept in market analysis. It reveals the emotional mindset of the market participants. There are different ways to measure sentiment. For instance, tracking the new highs and new lows as mentioned above is a means of gauging sentiment and can be used for monitoring the health of the market trend. And for short-term price swings, sentiment is revealed in the candlesticks. They show the bullishness (white or hollow candles), bearishness (black or shaded candles), and indecisiveness (small-bodied candles or Doji) of market participants. Many traders use candlesticks as a visual gauge of market sentiment to assist with swing trading.

There are also some specific indicators for measuring sentiment, including the following popular choices:

- CBOE Volatility Index (VIX)
- Put/Call Ratio
- Sentiment Surveys (such as those conducted by Investor's Intelligence)

Oftentimes, market participants tend to be overly bullish at a top and overly bearish at a bottom. Thus, sentiment may serve as a contrary and leading indicator—high positive readings may precede a market top, and high negative readings may signal a potential market bottom. An example of a high positive market sentiment reading would be noticeable upticks, or steady high readings, in a sentiment survey.

I don't suggest betting the farm on sentiment readings alone. There may be periods where their readings are more, or less, reliable than during other times. I recommend using a combination of tools for analysis rather than relying on one single indicator.

Notable Changes in Scan Counts Traders may use scans to specifically identify strength or weakness in the market trend. For instance, they may regularly run a scan to identify the number of stocks trading above or below their 200-period simple moving averages, which is another means of monitoring the strength of the market trend.

Traders may also utilize scans for finding potential trading candidates. For instance, during an up leg in a bull market, I regularly run scans to find setups for long positions, and to catch stocks that are breaking out. However, in that environment, I also run scans looking for negative signs (e.g., stocks forming bearish reversal bar patterns or breaking down through support). Normally, there would not be a significant number of hits in those negative scans, because most stocks would be trending up with the market. Therefore, if I observe a notable increase in the number of negative scan hits, but the market is still rising, it serves as a warning that the uptrend may be in danger of reversing. Here again, it is a negative divergence of sorts, but this time between the market and the scan results. It is another internal strength measure.

During downward legs in a bear market, I run scans for shorting candidates. However, I also run scans looking for positive signs (e.g., stocks forming bullish reversal bar patterns or breaking up through resistance). A notable increase in the number of positive scan hits while the market is still falling sends a signal that the downtrend may reverse direction (positive divergence).

Responding to Market Warnings

When a warning(s) of a potential trend reversal emerges on the chart of an individual stock, it has implications for that particular stock. And, in some cases, it may have implications for one or more other stocks because sometimes like-kind stocks will move in sympathy with each other, at least temporarily. For instance, if Caterpillar, Inc. (CAT) breaks down, Deere & Co. (DE) may follow, or vice versa.

If a trader sees one or more warnings that a stock he owns may be weakening, he may choose to take some defensive measures to protect the profits that have built up in that trade. Recall that there were some suggestions provided at the end of Chapter 5 for responding to such warnings.

When a warning(s) occurs on the chart of a major market average, and/or between the market average and the internals, it has *broader implications*. For instance, if the broad market average is overbought and a correction ensues, many stocks will decline. Although most stocks do tend to move in the general direction of the broad market, many of them will rise or decline much more than the market indices on a percentage basis. Say, for example, the market declines 7 percent during a correction, many stocks may experience double-digit declines during that descent.

If a trader sees one or more warnings appear on an index chart that represents the broad market (e.g., the Dow), he may take defensive action on his trading activities as a whole. Traders may adjust their strategies because those warnings suggest the market environment may be changing. Listed in Table 10.2 are some actions to consider for responding to warnings that the market trend may be weakening, but has not yet changed direction.

The trend is your friend until it ends. The suggestions in Table 10.2 allow traders to continue to benefit from the market trend, but reduce their exposure in the event of a reversal. Even with protective stops in place on all open positions, when a market trend reverses direction the initial move may be swift and sharp. Many stocks will make fast moves if the broad market punches through a strong support level; or up through resistance in a down-trending market. You may hear this referred to as *melting down* or *melting up*, respectively.

TABLE 10.2 Responding to Market Warnings

Limit Size of New Positions	Decrease the size of any new positions initiated in order to minimize exposure to a market correction while still benefiting from the trend, which has not yet changed direction.
Reduce Size of Open Positions	Sell some shares of existing open positions in order to lock in some profits and reduce the amount of exposure to a potential market reversal.
Decrease Number of Open Positions	Decrease the number of trades being managed to avoid having to attend to a significant number of positions if a trend reversal begins. For instance, close out positions that are near targets and/or those that are performing poorly.
Curtail Use of Margin	Reduce or eliminate the use of margin for extending buying power for long positions. The goal is to reduce exposure now, and the use of margin increases exposure.
Protect Capital that Is Invested	Always maintain and closely monitor protective stops on every position; or mental stops or alerts for very disciplined traders.
Prepare to Short	Begin looking for trading candidates to sell short if a reversal gets under way, or prepare to utilize inverse ETFs.
Reduce Hold Time of Trades	As the market gets more overbought, and/or more warnings arise, shift trading activities to holding for shorter periods of time (e.g., shift to day trading).
Go to Cash	If quite concerned, it is okay to put the account in the safety of cash. Too much time spent in cash unnecessarily brings with it opportunity cost, though, so I don't suggest this choice as a replacement for regular market analysis.

Stop loss orders become market orders when triggered, so they may suffer a lot of slippage in a fast-moving market. For that reason, when you see one or more warnings that the market trend may be weakening, you don't have to just leave it in the hands of your stops to get you out. You may choose to take a proactive stance on your open positions and reduce exposure to that type of sharp selloff (long positions) or rally (short positions).

The above practices fall under the role of money management. Unfortunately, many aspiring traders overlook prudent risk management practices, which is one of the primary reasons why so many newcomers fail in this business. Managing risk is the most important element for long-term success.

Monitoring a Bull Market Correction

Now let's shift to the process of monitoring the corrective moves against the major uptrend. When an up leg within a bull market has run for a while (typically several weeks to a few months), it becomes overbought on an intermediate-term basis. It is often followed by a retracement of a portion of that uptrend, which serves to alleviate the overbought condition. In fact, during a correction, the market often gets oversold, creating the conditions for another leg up to follow. The market tends to alternate between overbought and oversold conditions.

Recall that a correction may be triggered by an event, such as the Dow reaching an upside target being monitored by many traders who take profits at that level; or some news or economic report the market doesn't like. But sometimes the intermediate-term upward move just ages to the point where seemingly everyone is proclaiming it to be overextended and finally the pressure is relieved by a correction.

A correction is often much shorter in duration, and of less magnitude than the prior up leg. It retraces a significant portion, but not all, of the prior intermediate-term uptrend. There will be exceptions, of course. For example, there may be instances when a correction lasts longer—some will go on for several weeks and some for several months. And there will be instances where the correction is deeper, erasing the entire prior uptrend, and in some cases even continuing beyond that prior correction low. You'll see two such examples in the case study in Chapter 11.

There will also be instances where the correction is mild. It may even be comprised of a short-term downtrend rather than an intermediate-length correction. That is, it is deeper than a standard market pullback, but not as deep as a standard correction. I refer to those interruptions as *minor corrections*. In a strong bull market, in some cases just a relatively minor correction (e.g., a decline to about the 50-period SMA) is enough to reset the clock for another intermediate-term uptrend; or at least it eases the overbought condition and allows the current intermediate-term uptrend to extend farther.

Note: In Chapter 11, I've included a table that lists all the corrections of the current bull market along with the percentage decline and number of days of the correction.

As a bull market correction begins, the question is how far will it fall? If you want to participate on the long side during the next leg up, closely monitor the correction in order to recognize when an upside reversal occurs. Once a new up leg gets under way, there is often plenty of potential for profits. That's why it pays to focus on recognizing when a new up leg may be starting after a correction—in order to work that upward movement again on the long side.

If you wish to open one or more short positions, monitor the decline for a good reward-to-risk entry opportunity (e.g., a bounce to an area of resistance). When participating in a correction by shorting, monitor the decline in order to protect the profits built up in your short position(s).

TABLE 10.3 Monitoring a Correction	
Bull Market Correction	**Bear Market Correction**
Support Below	Resistance Above
Fibonacci Retracement Levels of Prior Uptrend	Fibonacci Retracement Levels of Prior Downtrend
Bottoming Price Action	Topping Price Action
Positive Divergence—Index versus Technical Indicator	Negative Divergence—Index versus Technical Indicator
Positive Divergence—Index versus Market Internals	Negative Divergence—Index versus Market Internals
Bullish Candlestick Pattern or Western Reversal Bar	Bearish Candlestick Pattern or Western Reversal Bar
Notable Change in Scan Hits	Notable Change in Scan Hits
Break of Resistance Trendline	Break of Support Trendline

We can't know for sure how far the market will fall during a correction, or when it will stop falling, but there are well-known chart points and indicators, and chart formations, we may observe. Traders tend to take action at those levels, which may stop the market's fall. I watch for the technical events listed in the column titled Bull Market Correction in Table 10.3, which may bring about an end to the correction.

The Bear Market Correction column in Table 10.3 should be used during a bear market to monitor a correction against the major downtrend (a bear market rally). For a bear market correction, the question is how far will it rise? In that scenario, traders look for an opportunity to participate on the short side again once the upside correction ends. And during the rise, traders may execute long positions and they must protect the gains accrued. Since we don't know how far the market will rise during a correction, monitor the chart as the price advance evolves, watching for warnings that may lead to an end of that bear market correction and a resumption of the major downtrend.

The events in Table 10.3 should be quite familiar by now. They include some of the warnings of a trend reversal included in Chapters 5 and 6, as well as some of the warnings related to scans and market internals, which were mentioned in Chapter 7 and again in this chapter. Watch for signs of a trend reversal during both up and down trends.

A bull market correction can be a great opportunity to buy stocks at lower prices. I don't want to miss out on much of the next upward move. Hence, I watch the correction like a hawk using the daily chart to monitor it for developments that signal the correction may be ending. And if I've sold short into the correction, I'm monitoring the trend to avoid getting caught short unaware if the major uptrend reasserts itself. The goal is to participate in as much of a trend as possible, in whichever direction we are trading, while not deluding ourselves into thinking we can always nail the very tops and bottoms of the trends!

This segment provides detailed instruction on how I monitor a bull market correction. The concepts work inversely for monitoring a bear market correction. This information applies to monitoring a correction that occurs on a market average; however, most of the guidelines can also be applied to monitoring a correction on the chart of an individual stock, sector, industry group, and so on.

Support Below

Monitor areas below on the chart where price may find support. Following are some logical levels where traders may initiate long positions, and for shorts to cover, which may stop the decline:

- Strong Moving Averages—If it turns out to be just a minor correction, price may find support at/near the 50-period simple moving average (SMA). During deeper corrections, price may test the 100- or 200-period SMA.
- Price Pivots—A single prominent price pivot, multiple pivots (e.g., the top of a prior trading range), or a tight area of congestion (a base) may be present on the chart.
- Gap Opening—Price may fill back into a prior gap. The gap's opening may provide support. *Note:* This only applies to stocks, and indices where gaps may form on the chart (not all index charts will reflect gaps, or they may occur infrequently).

Figure 10.5 shows the most recent correction the Dow experienced. During May–June 2013, the market corrected down to prior support. As mentioned previously, a horizontal support line drawn across the top of the small base that formed during March (H1) was quite significant.

The 100-period SMA was also there for additional support. Price pierced that moving average intraday, as evidenced by the bar's long lower shadow, but closed just above it. Recall that the 100-period SMA is approximately equivalent to the 20-week SMA. Thus, even though you won't hear about it as much as the 50- and 200-period SMAs, it is a strong moving average.

Speaking of the 50-period SMA, I bet many of you are wondering, "Price bounced at the 50-period SMA (and line H2), so why didn't you think that was

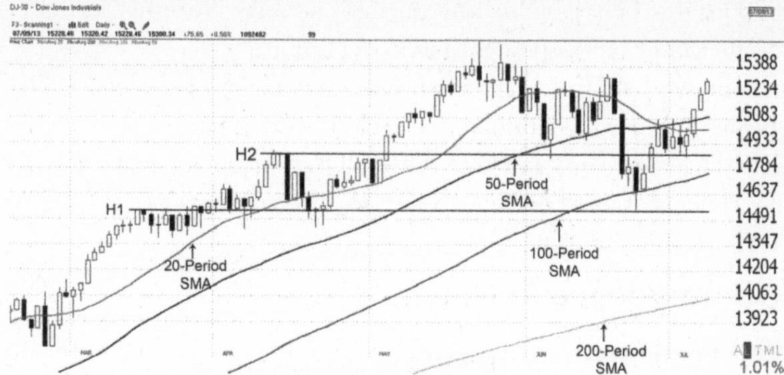

FIGURE 10.5 The Market Correction Ended at an Area of Support
Source: TC2000® chart courtesy of Worden Brothers, Inc.

the end of the correction?"There is discussion about this situation, and how to handle it, later in this chapter in a segment called "Beware of False Starts."

Fibonacci Retracement Levels

During a correction, price will often retrace from one-third to two-thirds of the prior upward move. Pay attention to the well-known Fibonacci retracement levels of 38, 50, and 62 percent. Figure 10.6 shows a daily chart of the

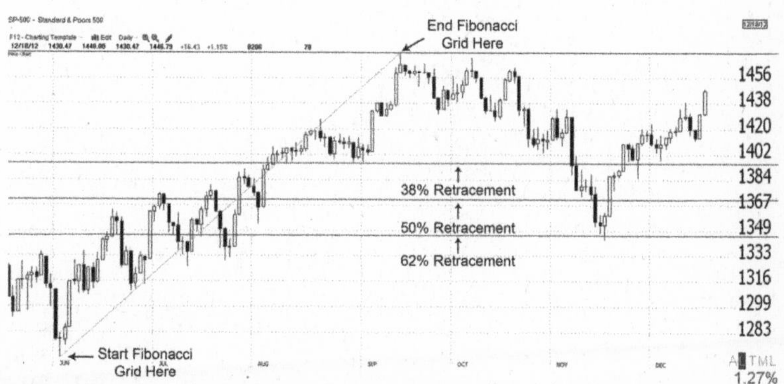

FIGURE 10.6 The Market Correction Ended at the 62 Percent Fibonacci Retracement Level
Source: TC2000® chart courtesy of Worden Brothers, Inc.

S&P 500 Index. After correcting during October–November 2012, price bounced right at the 62 percent Fibonacci line.

I recommend plotting a Fibonacci grid across the prior uptrend as a correction begins in order to identify those levels. You don't have to leave the grid up if you find it bothersome, but note the levels in your trading journal; or if there is other support at/near that level, draw a horizontal support line on the chart.

Bottoming Price Action

During a market correction, watch for bottoming price action as the decline progresses. In some cases, the bottoming action will be a well-known reversal pattern, such as a double or head-and-shoulders bottom. Price puts in the correction low, bounces, and then drops back down to/near that level for a test of the correction low. An example is illustrated at the bottom of a deep correction on the chart of the Dow Jones Utility Average in Figure 10.7. After forming the correction low (the head), price dipped partway back toward the head then turned up again, forming the right shoulder of the pattern.

These are relatively large patterns that take some time to form. I find that often when the correction is deep (Figure 10.7) and/or volatile, such as after the Flash Crash in 2010 and the 2011 decline, this is when a larger bottoming pattern may form (though there are exceptions). Those two events will be illustrated in Chapter 11.

A correction often ends in a much quicker fashion. In some instances, it will be a very small version of a bottom reversal pattern. So small that

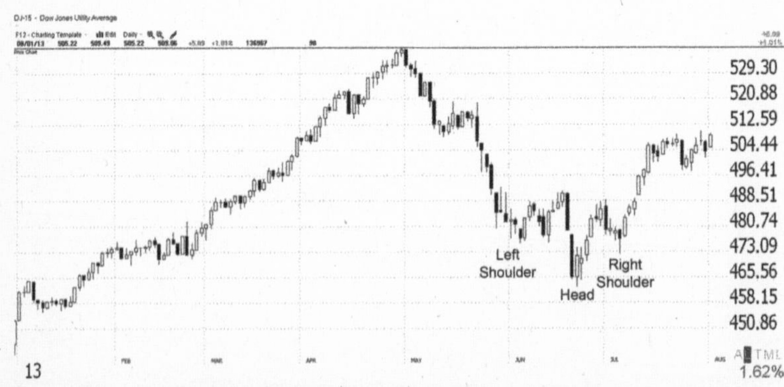

FIGURE 10.7 A Head-and-Shoulders Bottom Formed after a Deep Correction
Source: TC2000® chart courtesy of Worden Brothers, Inc.

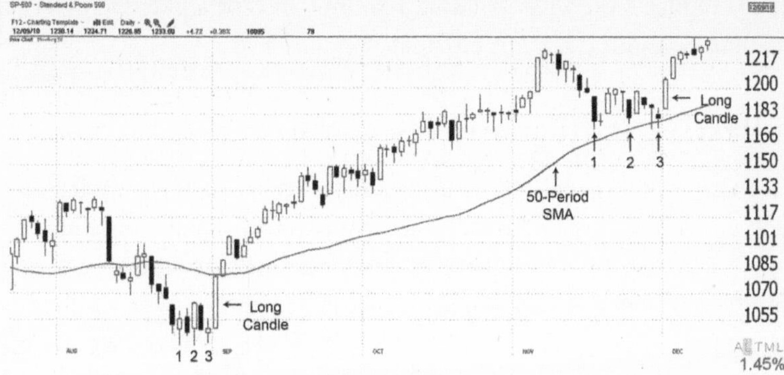

FIGURE 10.8 Bottoming Action Occurred after Market Corrections
Source: TC2000® chart courtesy of Worden Brothers, Inc.

it is really just a double or triple "tapping" action. But it has the effect of price putting in a low and then testing it once or twice immediately after. Experienced traders know the importance of this price behavior.

Figure 10.8 shows a daily chart of the S&P 500 Index during 2010. The August and November corrections both ended with the small triple-tap movement mentioned above. They are not triple bottoms on the daily chart. They are simply too small to meet the criteria—they don't contain enough bars, and are not deep enough. But remember that a price swing on the daily chart is a downtrend on lower time frames. Thus, if you were to look at this little triple-tap action from an intraday perspective, it would be a very obvious triple bottom to those viewing the intraday time frames.

While these small bottoming patterns may not be enough to reverse a major downtrend, they are enough to put in the bottom of a correction within a long-term uptrend. Remember, it is a bull market and many traders have a buy-the-dip mentality. They don't want to miss out on the next leg up any more than I do. They are looking for those re-entry opportunities.

Positive Divergence

Keep an eye on the declining bottoms in price during the correction by comparing them to an indicator that measures the downward momentum of the trend, such as the MACD histogram or the RSI. The indicator may turn up as price is still declining, flashing a positive divergence—an early warning of a potential end of the correction. Several examples are illustrated in

Chapter 11. Also watch for oversold readings and/or a positive divergence between price and the market internals.

Candlestick Pattern or Western Reversal Bar

Watch for the emergence of a candlestick reversal pattern. Quite often a new leg up from a correction starts from a reversal signal consisting of one bar (e.g., a Bullish Engulfing pattern or a Hammer) to a few bars (e.g., a Morning Star). Many examples are provided in the market case study in Chapter 11. There may also be instances where a key reversal or an outside day marks the end of the correction.

In some cases, the candle may not fit the criteria of a specific candlestick reversal pattern; however, the candlestick line itself sends a message. Remember, candlesticks reveal the sentiment of market participants. For example, in Figure 10.8, as the S&P emerged from the August and November 2010 corrections, the new up leg started from a long bullish candle in both instances.

Sometimes volume helps to confirm the move. Heavy volume often accompanies the long candle or the candlestick reversal pattern. In the instances in Figure 10.8, the market volume (not shown) was not remarkably high during either of those long candles; however, volume has been tricky throughout much of the current bull market. The typical price to volume relationships have not been present at times during this major uptrend, which has been frustrating for many chartists because volume is one of our primary tools. However, we must adjust to the market conditions. And that doesn't mean the typical relationships won't resume at times as the current bull market progresses, or be prevalent again in future bull markets.

Notable Change in Scan Hits

If you regularly run scans looking for charting events that suggest bullishness (e.g., a breakout scan), you may notice the number of hits starting to increase as the bottom of the correction forms. Thus, during the correction, continue to monitor the scan hits on bullish scans for clues.

Monitor the Correction with a Trendline

A market pullback is a minor event. It is typically relatively brief and price declines no more than a few percentage points. Thus, often the *first push down* into a correction looks like it is just a pullback within the uptrend when viewed at the right edge of the chart.

That first move down is often followed by a brief bounce, or some minor sideways movement. At that time, at the right edge of the chart, it looks like the market is done pulling back and is preparing to move up again. But instead, price turns down again. At that point, I surmise that the market is experiencing a correction. Oftentimes, the intermediate-length up trendline that was drawn below the rising bottoms during the up leg has been broken by that time.

It is also at this point that it is often possible to start a down trendline to use for monitoring the correction, because there are two pivots for connecting the line: the peak that formed the end of the prior uptrend, and the lower peak formed by that first bounce or period of sideways movement as illustrated in Figure 10.9. Drawing such a line across the correction peaks traps the price action below it—it is a resistance trendline. When price breaks up through that trendline, the correction may be ending.

I usually maintain a down trendline across the correction peaks when monitoring the market, and I often do so on charts representing sectors and industry groups, as well as on stocks I'm monitoring for a re-entry on the long side. I often refer to it as a "correction trendline."

Just like with any sloped trendline, the correction trendline is not static; it may need to be extended downward, and the slope may need to be adjusted slightly, one to several times as the correction develops. During a bear market correction, draw an up trendline below the bottoms and continue extending it upward (and adjusting the slope as needed) to be alerted when the correction ends and price turns down again.

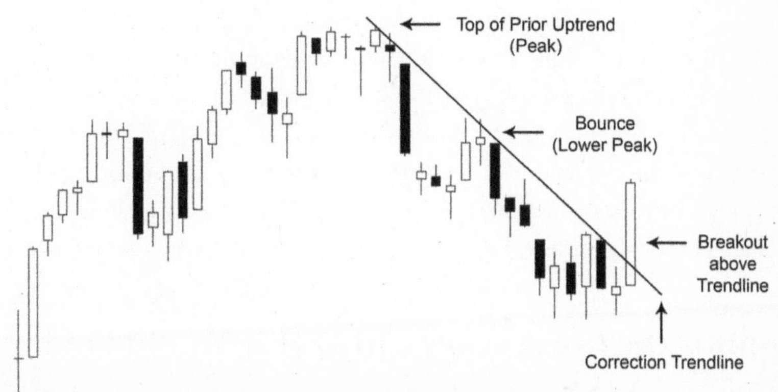

FIGURE 10.9 Draw a Correction Trendline to Monitor the Decline

Some chartists will argue that a trendline is not valid until it has three touches on the line. For the purpose of maintaining a correction trendline, I don't suggest adhering to that rule. The purpose of this line is specifically to monitor the decline during the correction (or the advance during a bear market correction), watching for signs of an end to that retracement. I'm not concerned about the number of touches on this line; as long as there are two, which are needed to draw the line, that's fine for this particular task.

There won't always be some support below, or bottoming action to catch your eye, at the end of the correction. But with a trendline drawn, you'll see when price breaks out above it and can participate in the next leg up. Thus, while you may not nail the very end of the correction, especially if there are no other signs, using the trendline will still allow you to participate in much of the next up leg.

To make sure you won't miss the trendline break, you can set an audible alert to trigger upon the break of the line. You'll need to adjust the alert's price each time you adjust the correction trendline downward (or upward during a bear market correction). It is easy to determine the price along the trendline. If the pointer in your charting platform includes a horizontal line that bisects it, drag the horizontal line to the point on the trendline where price would pierce the line if it were to move through it right now. Your charting platform may even have a feature that allows users to set an alert based on a trendline break that automatically adjusts whenever the trendline is adjusted.

Using a trendline in this manner to "stalk" the decline can be very helpful. Say, for instance, none of the other events listed in Table 10.3 occur alerting of the potential end of a correction. I'll notice when the down trendline is broken. That is, in the absence of any other signs, the trendline will eventually be broken as price turns back up out of the correction; sometimes sooner than later depending on the proximity of the trendline to the price action.

Using a down trendline to monitor the correction is not a perfect or foolproof technique. For example, there will be times when the line, especially if it is relatively tight, experiences a false break. Thus, it is preferable to have more evidence that the correction is ending; and often there are multiple signs. But there might be times when there is no other evidence, so maintaining the down trendline may be the first real sign when the market comes out of the correction.

Monitor the Correction with a Horizontal Line

There may be instances where a horizontal resistance line is also helpful. As the correction evolves, a prominent price pivot or a period of minor

FIGURE 10.10 Draw a Horizontal Line to Identify a Breakout

consolidation may form, which, if broken, would suggest the correction may be ending.

In Figure 10.10, because the last swing down of the correction was quite steep, it left the correction trendline relatively far away from price. However, when the decline stopped, price moved sideways for several days, setting up a shallow base (a short horizontal line identifies the base top). Price broke out above the base top much earlier than the breakout above the correction trendline. *Note:* Don't be concerned about the number of touches on the horizontal line for this task. The line is only being used as a visual cue to identify the move above resistance.

Convergence of Signals

When two or more of the technical events listed in Table 10.3 occur at/near the same point, it is a convergence of signals. The likelihood increases, as does my confidence, that the correction may be ending. For instance, say the Dow were to decline to the 200-period SMA and formed a small double bottom pattern there, it would certainly get my attention; especially if that level also happened to be a 50 percent retracement of the prior up leg. That would be three signs converging at/near the same level.

■ Be Ready to Pounce after the Correction

The point of the above instruction is to look for evidence that a market correction may be ending. Keep a watchlist of preferred stocks and ETFs ready to go long when the correction is over, and/or run positive scans to find good-looking reversal and breakout candidates. Like a cheetah stalking its prey, you must be ready to strike when opportunity glides across your path like a gazelle.

By continually monitoring the broad market trend, and the charts of stocks I want to own, I'm prepared when an opportunity presents itself. It is very disheartening to look back at the market, or a stock, after a trend is well under way, and realize you hadn't done the work to catch that trend. To me, this is a discipline issue. Monitoring the market trend is a daily task for me, as are managing watchlists (e.g., using alerts or pending orders), paying attention to market internals, and so on. If I get lazy with my work and miss an opportunity, it is nobody's fault but my own.

The signs described above may seem like a lot to watch for at first, but trust me when I tell you that as you gain experience, it won't seem overwhelming. Until you become proficient at monitoring the price action during a correction, use Table 10.3 as a quick reference guide.

Beware of False Starts

I stated a few times above that the correction "may be ending" because sometimes it will fool you. There might be signs that it is ending, and price starts upward again, but then turns back down. It is a false start to the new up leg. It is sort of like during a race when one of the runners jumps the gun off the starting line.

When that occurs, price may break down through what you thought was the correction low and continue downward, extending the length of the correction and increasing its magnitude (refer back to Figure 10.5 for an example). You're now on the wrong side of the market. In those cases, you'll realize it wasn't done falling after all. If you've entered one or more long positions, you may be stopped out, depending on how much farther price falls and where you've placed (or trailed) your stop order.

Other times, price will turn back down and test the correction low, and find support there as illustrated in Figure 10.11. That sets up a stronger bottom from which the next up leg is able to gain strength. If you have already entered one or more long position(s), as long as the stop has not been triggered, stay with the trade(s) to give it a chance as price begins to rise. The

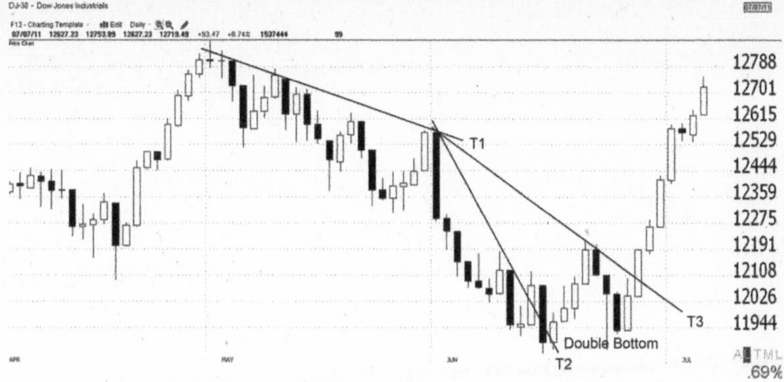

FIGURE 10.11 A Test of the Correction Low Occurred Prior to the Move Up
Source: TC2000® chart courtesy of Worden Brothers, Inc.

potential for a false start to occur, which then holds at the correction low, should discourage adjusting a stop upward too quickly, or too tightly. Sometimes price will wiggle around that correction low a bit and stop the trade out unnecessarily if the stop is set too tight.

Figure 10.11 shows a daily chart of the Dow. A correction occurred during May and June 2011. For several weeks, price declined at the slope indicated by the looser of the correction trendlines (T1). The correction then accelerated downward. A tighter down trendline was drawn (T2) representing the new slope of the correction. That trendline was broken and it appeared as if a new leg up was starting. However, price declined back to the correction low where it bounced, setting up a double bottom pattern. If the correction trendline is broken but price falls back down and holds at the correction low, redraw the down trendline connecting it to the new peak that has formed (T3).

Monitoring Bull Market Consolidation

Sometimes rather than retracing a portion of the uptrend, price will consolidate for several weeks to a few months. This also serves the purpose of alleviating the overbought condition, allowing for another upward move. Figure 10.12 shows a daily chart of the S&P 500 during the 2002–2007 bull market. After consolidating in a trading range for several weeks, the index broke out, setting a new bull market high.

When consolidation occurs, maintain a horizontal resistance line at the upper boundary to provide a visual cue for the ceiling (labeled H2 in

FIGURE 10.12 Consolidation during a Bull Market
Source: TC2000® chart courtesy of Worden Brothers, Inc.

Figure 10.12). Watch for an upside break to resume the major trend. The horizontal line makes it easy to see when a breakout occurs. Since the breakout point is usually clear, you may choose to set an audible alert for the breakout to ensure you don't miss it.

Note how, after breaking out, price pulled right back to the ceiling of the trading range—prior resistance became new support below. When price held that support level and turned back up, it was a good time to enter, or add to, long positions. There may be a few weeks to a few months (sometimes more) of upside movement that follows the consolidation. Remember, this is a relatively significant interruption of the major trend, which allows it to rest up for another move.

There is no guarantee the uptrend will resume. There will be instances where, instead of breaking to the upside, price breaks down below the floor of the consolidation area. Therefore, also maintain a horizontal support line(s) on the chart (H1).

■ Beware of a Break in the Market's Rhythm

I think of the way in which the market has a tendency to trend for periods of time, followed by corrections (or consolidation), as the market's rhythm. It can go for long stretches with fairly orderly movements up and down. However, there may be times when the market's rhythm gets off track for a while, sometimes way off track. In fact, an analogy that may work is that of the market shifting from a waltz to jumping into a mosh pit!

During the current bull market, a significant break in that rhythm has happened twice so far. First, after the Flash Crash in 2010. For several weeks following that event the market became very volatile, whipping up and down. The market environment became very volatile again for a few months during and after a very deep correction in 2011. From the closing high of April 29 to the closing low of October 3, the Dow declined 16.82 percent. It truly felt, at the time, based on the chart action as well as market fundamentals, that the market was shifting to a bear. That sharp decline occurred during the time when our elected officials in Washington D.C. were wrangling over raising the debt ceiling, and the subsequent downgrade of the U.S. credit rating by Standard & Poor's. Incidentally, here we are in the summer of 2013 coming up on another debt ceiling showdown, so watch for the market to potentially get whipsawed again.

I maintain an ongoing market study of the volatility of the Dow, the S&P 500, and the Nasdaq Composite indices using average daily range as a gauge for volatility. During those wild weeks following the Flash Crash, the Dow's average daily range was as much as 2.5 to 3 percent, with it running as high as 3.5 percent for a short stretch; whereas a more normal reading would be closer to 1 to 1.25 percent.

I want you to see what wild and whippy looks like, so when I refer to those periods elsewhere in my training, or mention times of very high market volatility, you have a picture in your mind. Figure 10.13 illustrates a two-chart layout with the daily chart of the Dow shown in both panels. The highly volatile period during and after the May 2010 Flash Crash is shown on the left. The high volatility decline into the November 2011 correction low, and the period that followed, is shown on the right. The volatility remained high as the Dow broke out from that consolidation.

During those periods when the market trend moves rapidly up or down, significant gains can be made by traders who are on the right side of the trend and know how to handle the extreme volatility. During the periods when the market thrashes back and forth, which occurred during the trading range in 2011 shown on the right in Figure 10.13, it is easy to get "whipped around like a rag doll," to use a quote from one of my clients.

When the market gets that choppy, I find it is easier to day trade—scalping for brief periods, or riding the intraday trends while they last. A trend-following strategy on the daily chart could get whipsawed badly during that type of consolidation. For some traders, it is just best to sit aside in the comfort of cash protecting capital so they "survive to trade another day." I've done that at times as well. There is no shame in seeking the safety of cash.

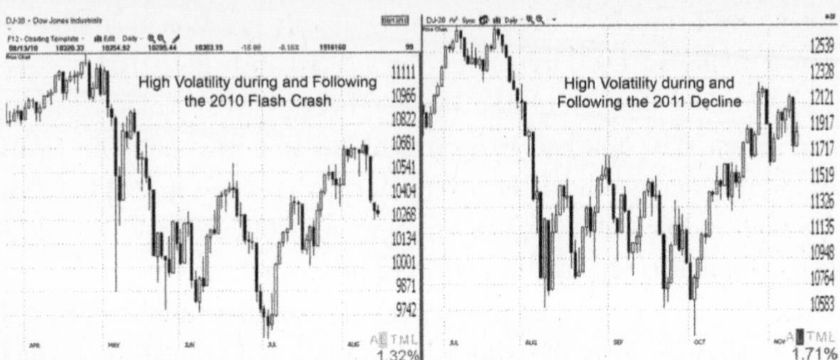

FIGURE 10.13 Periods of Very High Market Volatility
Source: TC2000® chart courtesy of Worden Brothers, Inc.

No matter what they say about cash being cold and hard, it can actually be a warm and comfy place to hang out for a while!

Eventually the market settled down from those highly volatile periods and picked up its rhythm again, and I was able to go back to monitoring the intermediate-term up movements, and the corrections, using the methods I've described in this chapter. And emerging from the volatility allowed me to go back to holding positions for longer periods of time.

■ Profiting through Working the Trends

So far the discussion in this chapter has been primarily devoted to showing you how I monitor the intermediate-term uptrends, and the market corrections, during a bull market environment. Now the focus shifts to how I direct my overall trading activities in that environment in order to generate profits from those trends. *Note:* The methods are inverse in a bear market environment.

I'll start by providing an analogy that will give you a model of how I approach working the trends, both up and down. Let's put you in your car and take a hypothetical drive up into the hills. You are now driving along an upward-sloping highway at pretty good speed. It's not a straight line, but it is a fairly smooth drive with just slight shifts along the road. The highway conditions remain that way for quite some time.

You're enjoying the scenery as you continue driving up the hill when you notice a road sign warning that there is a steep downgrade ahead and indicating you should prepare to slow down. Unfortunately, though, nobody bothered to note on that sign exactly when the down slope would begin, nor how steep it would be. You slow down a bit, and as you continue on, you see another sign warning that you are getting closer to the steep downgrade; and once again you are advised to slow down, but still you're not sure when you'll see that decline begin.

It's been a nice drive up the hill, but you're feeling a bit anxious now not knowing exactly what lies ahead. You slow down some more, and grip the steering wheel a bit tighter, as you continue driving along anticipating the down slope that certainly must start soon. You've changed your driving technique from a fairly relaxed state to driving more defensively in order to make sure you maintain control of the vehicle. You must protect your assets, which are (1) your person and (2) your automobile.

You finally reach the summit, cross over it, and start the journey down the other side. The downgrade is fairly steep, and requires paying close attention to maneuver safely through the slight shifts in the road along the way. Eventually, you see indications on the horizon suggesting you're getting close to the end of the down slope.

You reach the bottom; but before starting up the next hill, you encounter a couple of curves in the road. You proceed with caution, taking it slowly at first. When it's clear those hurdles are behind you, and the road that lies ahead looks pretty smooth again, you step on the accelerator to bring the car up to cruising speed. You relax your grip on the steering wheel a bit and start enjoying the scenery again as you drive up the next hill. And just when it seems you've been driving uphill for quite a while, there it is, another road sign warning you to slow down again to prepare for another downgrade.

Trading the Smooth Runs and Maneuvering the Turning Points

The intermediate-term market trends are similar to the hills you just drove up and down on your imaginary road trip. But now you are trading the market instead. So let's take the above analogy and apply it to trading market trends, incorporating what you learned earlier in this chapter, as well as in prior chapters.

Trading during the Uptrend An intermediate-term uptrend is like the relatively uneventful drive up the hill. During a fairly smooth leg up is when it pays to step on the accelerator with long positions. There have been quite a few such opportunities during the current bull market, as you'll see in the case study in Chapter 11. The upward move is likely to last for a while, so take advantage of it. Ride the wave up with core positions, and/or swing trades if you like. I often do both during this phase.

It is during those upward stretches of several weeks or longer that I tend to trade most assertively on the long side. Minor pullbacks and bases/flags that form within the uptrend are like the slight shifts along the highway. They make good trade setups for entering new long positions, or adding to existing positions.

Trade the uptrend until it ages to the point of becoming overbought on an intermediate-term basis, while also watching for warnings of a potential trend reversal. Those warnings are like road signs that alert the driver to prepare for a decline ahead. They are the early and later warnings described in Chapters 5 and 6, respectively, as well as the market trend warnings (e.g., market internals) described in Chapter 7.

You won't know precisely when the uptrend will end. However, as it continues to age it becomes more vulnerable to a correction. If you see a sign(s) that warns of weakness for the market trend you can take precautionary measures. Just like the driver who, by slowing down and driving more defensively takes action to protect himself and his automobile, you must protect your assets. Your assets are (1) your trading capital and (2) your psyche. The precautionary measures a trader takes may include reducing position size, curtailing the use of margin, and so on (refer to Table 10.2).

Trading during the Correction A correction is obviously like the down slope the driver experiences after crossing over the summit. Once the uptrend gives way to a correction, you can shift from focusing on long positions to working the downside, while also being watchful for signs that the correction may be ending. During a market retracement, a trader may direct his activities as follows:

- Sell Short—Use shorting techniques to benefit from the decline.
- Go Long Bear ETFs—Use inverse ETFs, or leveraged inverse ETFs, to benefit from the decline.
- Go to Cash—If a trader cannot sell short because his is a tax-deferred account, and he has no access to bear funds/ETFs, it is okay to stand aside and focus on preservation of capital during a market decline.

A correction usually only lasts from a few weeks to a couple of months; some will only last a couple of weeks or so. Thus, my trading focus during that time is usually short-term. Based on my calculations of the corrections that have occurred so far during the current bull market, the average market correction has lasted a little over six weeks. And if the near bear market of 2011 were excluded, the average duration would drop to about four and a half weeks.

Some bull market corrections can produce good profits through trading activities, while others won't end up lasting long enough to really work the downside vigorously. During some corrections, you may even end up mostly treading water rather than generating significant profits. You may find, as I often do, that day trading, or guerilla trading (holding trades for one to two days), is often easier than trying to take swing or core trades during a corrective move.

When you review the market case study in Chapter 11, make sure to note that some of the market corrections would have been nearly over by the time some traders would have felt confident just starting to sell short. For instance, some corrections will only consist of two pushes down. The first looks like just another pullback within the uptrend. The second push down reveals that a correction is likely under way, but that swing down may put in the bottom (see Figure 10.5). This is why I mentioned above that my trades during corrections are often short-term in nature. I tend to work the long side more assertively in bull markets, and the down side more so in bear markets.

Do keep in mind, though, that individual stocks may decline significantly more on a percentage basis than the market averages. Additionally, there are now leveraged ETFs that track the market averages, which can enhance profitability. Hence, there will be instances where handsome profits are made in specific trades even though the duration of the market decline may be limited.

If a trader does not wish to attempt trades during a market correction, he may choose to stay in cash and closely monitor the correction for signs of a reversal in order to participate on the long side again. However, during a bear market, the downward movements will typically be longer than the corrections. Thus, in that environment, I'd suggest taking advantage of the opportunities to profit on the downside. The advent of the bear ETFs has made it much easier to participate in a down market.

Trading after the Correction By the end of a correction, the previously overbought condition has been alleviated; and in fact, the market is often considered oversold by that point. Once price turns up again, we can *restart* *the clock* on a new intermediate-term uptrend. That is, it is a new leg up and there is the potential for several weeks to a few months of uptrend as the bull market continues its trek higher. Between the correction low and the top of the next intermediate-term leg up, there is the potential of making some great returns again in swing and/or core positions on the long side.

As price turns up from the correction low, it is again a time of uncertainty. Remember, the market may start back up but then turn down again, extending the correction; or it may rally a bit but then decline for a test of the correction low before a new uptrend gains momentum (see Figure 10.11). Therefore, I don't recommend loading the boat with long positions just as it appears the bottom is in for the correction. Instead, I suggest easing back into long positions starting out with limited size (e.g., a half position) and a limited number of positions. To use the driving analogy again—give it a little gas. If it turns out it wasn't the end of the correction after all, you won't have too much exposure and you'll be stopped out with minimal damage.

As the uptrend proves itself, it is okay to get more assertive with long positions (step down on the accelerator). That means increasing the position size and/or number of positions, putting on swing and core trades, and sensibly using margin to extend buying power (only recommended for experienced, disciplined traders).

The Turning Points The turning points of the trends can be the most challenging times. Those are the times when a reversal is due to occur, but you're not sure when it will get started. And it can look like it is getting started, but fool you by turning back the other direction before finally making its move in earnest. That's why I tend to get more conservative with my trading activities when it appears an intermediate-term uptrend may soon break down. And it's why I don't put the accelerator all the way to the floor right off a correction low.

In summary: Take advantage of the trending periods. Reduce exposure to a potentially sharp reversal when the intermediate-term uptrend is showing signs of weakness. Limit exposure at first when coming off an oversold level after a correction.

CHAPTER 11

Current Bull Market—Case Study

This chapter provides in-depth analysis of the most recent bull market that began in March 2009, and is still in force at the time of this writing. This may be the most extensive market review you'll ever experience in one sitting. But I sure wish someone had taken me through such an exercise very early in my trading career—it would have shaved a lot of time off my learning curve.

Reviewing this detailed case study is a very important exercise. All of the concepts described in the prior chapters will be put to work here. You'll take a walk with me through the up, down, and sideways movements that have occurred on the chart of the Dow Jones Industrial Average over the past few years, looking at those technical events through my eyes.

All of the specific intermediate-length uptrends and corrections that have occurred during this bull market will be dissected using the daily chart. It should actually start to feel fairly repetitive by the time you reach the last page. If so, that tells me you are absorbing the concepts and can move on to analyze market trends on your own with confidence.

After completing this review, I strongly encourage you to continue the analysis on your own as this bull market goes on to complete its life cycle, and eventually gives way to another bear market. After reviewing this chapter, for additional practice I suggest using your charting platform to

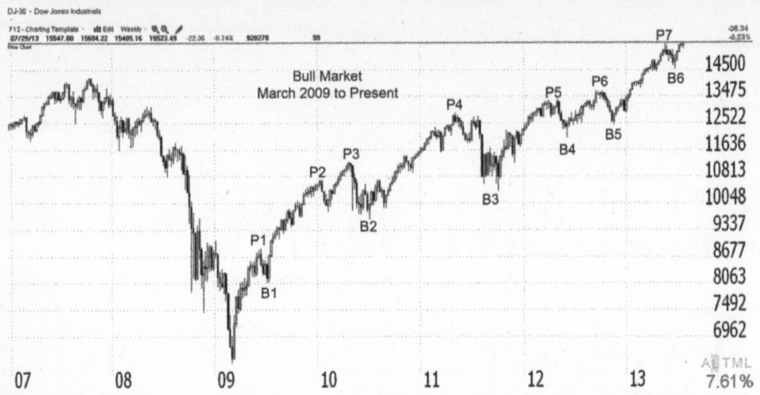

FIGURE 11.1 The Current Bull Market Shown on a Weekly Chart of the Dow

Source: TC2000® chart courtesy of Worden Brothers, Inc.

perform your own analysis of the current bull market on other indices, such as the S&P 500 and the Nasdaq Composite.

Before we get started, take a look at the weekly chart in Figure 11.1. A glance at this time frame allows you to see the entirety of the major uptrend to date. It is a relatively long and strong bull market. The prominent peaks (labeled P1 through P7) have been rising for over four years. Those peaks represent the highs of several of the intermediate-term uptrends that formed within, and extended, the major trend. The prominent rising bottoms (B1 through B6) represent the lows of several of the market corrections that formed within the major uptrend.

Following are two well-known Wall Street adages:

- Don't Fight the Trend.
- Don't Fight the Fed.

I don't recall a time in which those two mantras held stronger implications than in the current bull market. This market has marched upward for the past few years, in spite of sluggish economic growth, stubbornly high unemployment, pressures from the debt issues domestically and in Europe, and the continuous wrangling in Washington, D.C. over concerns like tax rates, health care reform, budget deficits, and sequestration.

This uptrend has been largely fueled by the monetary policy of the Federal Reserve (the Fed) prior to and during the bull market's lifespan. Whether or not you agree with the Fed's very accommodative stance, and the actions

FIGURE 11.2 The "V" Bottom Reversal from the Severe Bear Market of 2007–2009
Source: TC2000® chart courtesy of Worden Brothers, Inc.

supporting it (e.g., quantitative easing), the stock market has thrived in this environment rising on a sea of liquidity.

Fighting the trend and/or the Fed during this bull market would have been a losing proposition. At some point this bull market will end, as they all do; but until that time, the long-term trend is up. Having bet against this bull would have resulted in being trampled by it!

The Reversal from Bear to Bull Market

This market review begins with the conclusion of the 2007 to 2009 bear market and works through the evolution of the current bull market from its inception off the March 2009 low. As mentioned in Chapter 8, this bull market started from a single bottom reversal—a fairly rare "V" bottom.

During the devastating bear market that preceded this uptrend (see Figure 11.2), there was a meltdown of the financial markets. The U.S. housing market bubble burst and the credit markets were nearly frozen. That bear market was accompanied by the Great Recession. It was a bleak time in American history—the worst period of contraction since the Great Depression—and the effects are still lingering today.

The last leg down of that bear market was a dazzling display of capitulation. The ferocious bear growled loudly and clawed into the tender flesh and psyches of already-battered investors, taking one last big bite out of their portfolios. That sounds so dramatic, but it was! However, for those who were short, or utilizing the bear (inverse) exchange-traded funds (ETFs), there were plenty of profits to be had.

The market is anticipatory. The stock market tends to discount economic conditions up to several months in advance. It wasn't until later in 2009, a few months after the bull market was already under way, that the recession was officially called to an end. In addition, various economic reports began to reflect some improvement. There was a lot of talk about "green shoots" in the economy.

Many stocks had already been in an uptrend since the March 2009 low; and some had started to improve, or at least stopped falling, even before that bottom was formed. Price tends to lead the fundamentals; savvy investors help push prices up as they buy in anticipation of an economic recovery to come through the emergence of a new growth cycle.

Bull Market Observations prior to the Reversal

The concepts in this book are primarily based on technical analysis to help you build that important foundation for analyzing trends. However, when it comes to monitoring the movement of the broad market, it is important to expand the discussion. Recall from Chapter 8 that there may be advance signs that a market reversal could be forthcoming. Those signs may be in the form of one or all of the following:

- The Technicals
- The Fundamentals
- The Market Internals

The Technicals Technical events played a role in identifying the bear market reversal as the Dow plunged into the March 2009 low. Following are some important trend reversal warnings that occurred prior to the reversal:

- Divergence—There was a positive divergence between the Dow and various technical indicators.
- Volume—There was heavy volume during the final decline into the March 2009 low, suggesting capitulation (climax selling). Volume was also very high during the strong surge up from that low.
- Trendline Slope—The downtrend accelerated during the latter part of the bear market (from September 2008 to March 2009), requiring a steeper long-term down trendline be drawn.

- Base Building with OBV Rising—Even though the shift from bear to bull market occurred as a "V" bottom on the Dow, many stocks shifted from down to sideways prior to the bear market reversal. That set up rectangular-type bottom patterns on the charts of many stocks, with some of them showing OBV accumulation while price was still inside the base. An example was illustrated in Chapter 8.

The Fundamentals Fundamentals also played a role in identifying the 2009 bear market reversal. Following were some promising signs for recovery in the weeks prior to, during, and after the reversal:

- Copper Turned Up—Bottom reversal patterns formed between October and December 2008 on the daily charts of MG132 (a copper indicator in TC2000) and Southern Copper Corp. (SCCO). SCCO was already more than 50 percent off its 2008 low by March 9 when the Dow made its bear market low.
- Many industry groups bottomed out a few months prior to the Dow, including several technology and commodity-related groups.
- Upticks in ECRI's WLI—In March 2009, the WLI experienced upticks in its Annualized Growth Rate. In the following weeks, esteemed ECRI co-founder Lakshman Achuthan released more optimistic comments for the economy.

The Market Internals Market internals were also helpful in identifying a potential bottom:

- The number of NYSE stocks making new 52-week lows reached historic levels in late 2008. The number was still very negative going into the March 2009 low, but significantly better than at the prior correction low.
- The Advancers versus the Decliners had jumped to about eight to one within three days after the March 2009 low. Conversely, a few days prior to the March low the Decliners were outpacing the Advancers by about 10 to 1.

The Intermediate-Term Market Trends

Since the current bull market began on March 10, 2009, there have been several intermediate-term upward moves and several notable corrections; and potentially more to come since the major uptrend is still in force.

The Intermediate-Term Uptrends

Listed in Table 11.1 are the 11 intermediate-term uptrends that have occurred to date, including the one that was still in force at the time of this book's completion. The percentage rise indicated was measured from the prior correction closing low to the closing high of the intermediate-term uptrend using daily market data from TC 2000 (version 7).

The average duration of the completed uptrends was 77 trading days (labeled T-Days in Table 11.1), equating to an average length of 3.7 calendar months. The average advance was 19.24 percent calculated using the price percent change (PPC) method. Since it was still in force at the time of this analysis, the current upward move was not included in those averages.

The criteria chosen to identify an intermediate-term uptrend were a period where price trended up on the daily chart for more than three weeks, during which there were no declines in excess of 5 percent. There was one exception included in the table. During the first leg up of the new bull market, there was a

TABLE 11.1 Intermediate-Term Uptrends

Dates in Force	Duration	Percent Rise	Closing Low	Closing High
March 10 to June 12, 2009	67 T-Days 3.1 Months	34.40%	6,547.05 3/9/2009	8,799.26 6/12/2009
July 13, 2009 to Jan. 19, 2010	132 T-Days 6.3 Months	31.66%	8,146.52 7/10/2009	10,725.43 1/19/2010
Feb. 9 to April 26, 2010	53 T-Days 2.5 Months	13.09%	9,908.39 2/8/2010	11,205.03 4/26/2010
July 6 to Aug. 9, 2010	25 T-Days 1.2 Months	10.45%	9,686.48 7/2/2010	10,698.75 8/9/2010
Aug. 27, 2010 to Feb. 18, 2011	122 T-Days 5.8 Months	24.09%	9,985.81 8/26/2010	12,391.25 2/18/2011
March 17 to April 29, 2011	31 T-Days 1.4 Months	10.31%	11,613.30 3/16/2011	12,810.54 4/29/2011
Oct. 4 to Oct. 28, 2011	19 T-Days .8 Months	14.79%	10,655.30 10/3/2011	12,231.11 10/28/2011
Nov. 28, 2011 to May 1, 2012	107 T-Days 5.1 Months	18.23%	11,231.78 11/25/2011	13,279.32 5/1/2012
June 5 to Oct. 5, 2012	87 T-Days 4 Months	12.47%	12,101.46 6/4/2012	13,610.15 10/5/2012
Nov. 16, 2012 to May 28, 2013	131 T-Days 6.4 Months	22.86%	12,542.38 11/15/2012	15,409.39 5/28/2013
June 25, 2013 to TBD	Still in Force	6.8% to Date	14,659.56 6/24/2013	TBD

decline of 5.08 percent. However, it was only a two-day decline and it occurred during a strong surge off a major bottom. It was not a significant retracement of that first move up. Rather, it behaved more like a pullback within the trend.

Generally, there is not much disagreement of the start and end points of most bull and bear markets; after the fact, that is, when the major turning points are very clear. However, there may be several intermediate-term upward moves, and many declines of varying degree, within a prolonged bull market. Thus, there may not always be consensus as to their start and end points. So as you see, there is some subjectivity to these conclusions. They are based on my evaluation of the trends, but others may use different parameters for their own findings. I challenge you to go back to the start of the bull market and walk the daily chart forward. I believe you'll see why I designated the upward movements as I did, based upon the concepts described in Part I of this book.

The Market Corrections

Listed in Table 11.2 are the 10 declines I consider significant enough to be deemed as standard to deep market corrections. The percentage decline indicated was measured from the prior intermediate-term uptrend closing high to the correction closing low using daily market data from TC2000 (version 7).

The average duration of the completed corrections was 31 trading days (labeled T-Days in Table 11.2), equating to an average length of 6.2 calendar weeks, or 1.4 calendar months. The average decline was 8.81 percent calculated using the price percent change (PPC) method.

The criterion chosen to identify a correction was a market decline of at least 5 percent. There were two exceptions. The first was during the first leg up of the new bull market. There was a decline of 5.08 percent during that period, which was not included in Table 11.2. It was only a two-day decline and it occurred during a strong surge off the bear market low. In my view, it was not a significant correction in the context of that intermediate-term uptrend. It behaved like a quick pullbackwithin the trend rather than a significant retracement of the prior up move.

The second exception was the most recent correction, which was 4.87 percent; not quite 5 percent but it was included in Table 11.2. It occurred after price had advanced for more than six months. It was the first notable decline in an unusually long upward move and had the distinctive feel of a correction, albeit a relatively modest one given the length and percentage advance of the uptrend that preceded it. That correction lasted nearly a month and reached the 100-period simple moving average.

TABLE 11.2 Market Corrections

Dates in Force	Duration	Percent Decline	Closing High	Closing Low
June 15 to July 10, 2009	19 T-Days 3.7 Weeks	−7.42%	8,799.26 6/12/2009	8,146.52 7/10/2009
Jan. 20 to Feb. 8, 2010	14 T-Days 2.9 Weeks	−7.62%	10,725.43 1/19/2010	9,908.39 2/8/2010
April 27 to July 2, 2010	48 T-Days 9.6 Weeks	−13.55%	11,205.03 4/26/2010	9,686.48 7/2/2010
Aug. 10 to Aug. 26, 2010	13 T-Days 2.4 Weeks	−6.67%	10,698.75 8/9/2010	9,985.81 8/26/2010
Feb. 22 to March 16, 2011	17 T-Days 3.3 Weeks	−6.28%	12,391.25 2/18/2011	11,613.30 3/16/2011
May 2 to Oct. 3, 2011	109 T-Days 22.1 Weeks	−16.82%	12,810.54 4/29/2011	10,655.30 10/3/2011
Oct. 31 to Nov. 25, 2011	19 T-Days 3.7 Weeks	−8.17%	12,231.11 10/28/2011	11,231.78 11/25/2011
May 2 to June 4, 2012	23 T-Days 4.9 Weeks	−8.87%	13,279.32 5/1/2012	12,101.46 6/4/2012
Oct. 8 to Nov. 15, 2012	27 T-Days 5.6 Weeks	−7.85%	13,610.15 10/5/2012	12,542.38 11/15/2012
May 29 to June 24, 2013	19 T-Days 3.9 Weeks	−4.87%	15,409.39 5/28/2013	14,659.56 6/24/2013

In addition to the corrections listed in Table 11.2, there were many smaller declines ranging from just over 1 percent to almost 5 percent that I would consider to be pullbacks (about 1 to 3 percent) or minor corrections (about 3 to 5 percent), but not deep enough to cause much disruption of the trend.

Again, I wish to emphasize that the categorization of the various market declines is based on my evaluation of the trends; others may use different parameters for their own findings. Go back to the start of the bull market and walk the daily chart forward. I believe you'll see why I designated the corrections as I did, based upon the concepts described in Part I.

Evaluation of the Intermediate-Term Trends

Following is commentary on each of the intermediate-length upward movements listed in Table 11.1 that served to start, and then extend, the major trend. Each correction listed in Table 11.2 is also evaluated. To make for a smooth journey through the current bull market, the discussion begins with the first intermediate-term uptrend then moves forward through the subsequent correction. Then the next uptrend and subsequent correction are analyzed, and so on, all the way through to the intermediate-term uptrend that is currently still forming at the right edge of the chart.

All the illustrations are daily charts of the Dow Jones Industrial Average. The examples include horizontal lines drawn on the chart representing important support and resistance levels that formed as the trends developed. Oftentimes resistance levels reversed roles to that of support, and vice versa. For easy reference, all horizontal lines are labeled starting with the letter *H* for horizontal (e.g., H1, H2), and it is usually indicated at the left or right side of the line. All sloped trendlines are labeled starting with the letter *T* for trendline (e.g., T1, T2), and it is usually indicated at either the beginning or end of the line. *Note:* Primarily internal lines are used.

My primary chart template is used for the analysis with numbers located next to each simple moving average (SMA) in the chart window identifying its length as 20-, 50-, 100-, or 200-period. For all examples where a divergence is observed, or something particular is pointed out about the MACD, that indicator is shown in the lower panel. If there is no reference to that indicator, it is not shown in the example in order to allow for a larger chart.

As you review this case study, keep in mind the primary reasons for monitoring the up and down trends of the bull market:

1. Most stocks tend to move with the market. Thus, the broad market movement may have a strong influence on individual stocks' performance. Monitoring the broad market's trend guides the trader to the appropriate setups, and the strategies to employ at any given time.
2. Monitoring the intermediate-term uptrends allows traders to focus their efforts in the direction of the major trend. As an upward move progresses, watch for signs of a trend reversal in order to protect the capital invested in existing long positions, and to prepare to sell short (or stand aside if preferred) during a market correction.
3. Monitoring the corrections allows traders to profit from short positions (and/or inverse ETFs) during the declines. As a correction progresses, watch for indications of an impending reversal in order to protect the capital invested in existing short positions, and to prepare to go long again during a new upward move.

As you read the evaluation of each intermediate-term uptrend, be aware that while monitoring that trend in real time, I was watching for signs that the market was *done rising*. I watch for the early and later trend reversal warnings for an uptrend covered in Chapters 5 and 6, respectively. Additionally, as mentioned in earlier chapters, I monitor the market internals as part of my routine, and I run scans regularly for specific setups and/or market conditions. I watch those numbers for signs of excessive positive readings that may preclude a market top. I also watch them for signs of a negative divergence—the market is still rising but the market internals and/or number of scan hits suggest a loss of momentum.

While monitoring the market corrections as they developed in real time, I was watching for signs that the market was *done falling*. I watch for the earlier and later trend reversal warnings for a downtrend covered in Chapters 5 and 6, respectively. I also check the Fibonacci retracement levels, and look for small bottoming patterns (the double- and triple-tap action) that form at the ends of some corrections. Additionally, I watch for signs in the market internals and the number of scan hits that suggest the correction may be ending and another uptrend beginning. For instance, the number of hits in a breakout scan, or a scan for positive reversals (e.g., bullish candlestick or Western bar patterns), may start popping at/near a correction low.

Market Uptrend 1: March 10 through June 12, 2009

Figure 11.3 shows the first leg up of the new bull market, which was a rise of over 34 percent. Following are some factors to note regarding this uptrend:

- The first day up (March 10) was a high-volume long Bullish Engulfing candle shaven on both ends, meaning it had no upper or lower shadows (a very bullish bar).
- The initial move off the bottom was a strong surge. The Dow gained over 14 percent in the first seven trading days fueled by heavy volume.
- The 20-period SMA turned from down to up during that surge. And as the rise continued, the 50-period SMA also turned up and the 100-period SMA flattened out. The 20-period SMA crossed above the 50-period SMA, and the 50-period SMA crossed above the 100-period SMA. The 200-period SMA was still far above and still declining.
- The moving averages presented potential resistance above. However, price was able to push through each one on the way up, even closing just above the 200-period SMA, but not decisively.
- Note the downward slope of the MACD peaks as price was rising. There was a negative divergence at the top (labeled P1 to P2).

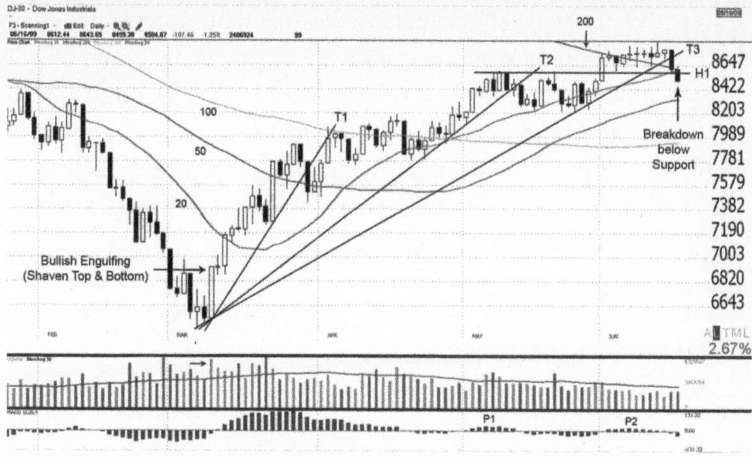

FIGURE 11.3 Intermediate-Term Uptrend: +34.4 Percent Rise March 10 through June 12, 2009
Source: TC2000® chart courtesy of Worden Brothers, Inc.

- As price moved sideways in a tight base during the last several days of the uptrend (holding just above the 200-period SMA), the trendline (T3) was extended upward closely to price. It was broken quickly when price turned down.
- The horizontal line (H1) and the 20-period SMA were broken the following day.

One of the primary reasons for drawing an intermediate-length up trendline is to recognize when the trend may be starting to reverse direction. However, just because a trendline is broken does not necessarily mean a trend reversal is imminent, which is why I suggest that a trendline break alone may not constitute a sell signal. When an up trendline is broken, look for additional signs that suggest a trend reversal may be under way. I emphasize this because it is not unusual for the up trendline to be broken during a pullback, or during a period of minor consolidation. For instance, in Figure 11.3 trendline T2 was broken as price moved sideways during May. However, that basing action only served to stall the trend temporarily and price broke out above the base on June 1.

When the uptrend resumes after a minor interruption, the up trendline is adjusted, or a new line drawn, to reflect the current length and slope of the uptrend as indicated by the lines labeled T1 through T3 in Figure 11.3.

Those were not the only adjustments made during this uptrend, but I think you get the idea.

The first up leg of the new bull market lasted just over three months. At its end, it was aging and overbought, and therefore becoming increasingly vulnerable to a correction. It ended with a breakdown in mid-June below the 20- and 200-period SMAs, the up trendline (T3), and the horizontal support line (H1).

As price turned down into a correction, it was not yet known if the uptrend the market had just experienced was the first leg up of a new bull market, or whether it was a bear market rally that had just topped out and price was resuming the major downtrend.

Market Correction 1: June 15 through July 10, 2009

Figure 11.4 shows the 7.42 percent correction that followed the initial uptrend. It was the first sizable decline of what would eventually be deemed a new bull market. Following are some factors to note regarding this decline:

- The decline began from a Bearish Engulfing candle, which formed after several Spinning Tops (indecision candles).

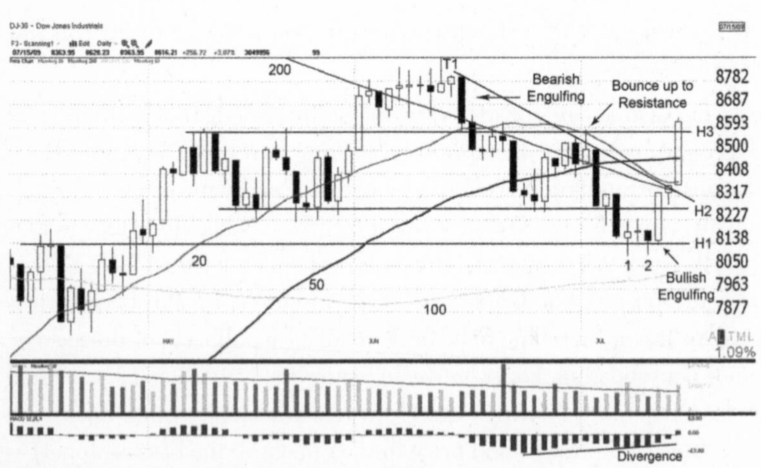

FIGURE 11.4 Market Correction: –7.42 Percent Decline June 15 through July 10, 2009
Source: TC2000® chart courtesy of Worden Brothers, Inc.

- After breaking down through the 20- and 200-period SMAs and line H3, price consolidated for three days just below that prior support level, using it as new resistance above.
- Price declined to line H2, then bounced back up to resistance at line H3 and the 20-period SMA. When price turned down from there it created a prominent lower peak. A downward-sloping correction trendline (T1) was drawn connecting the top of the intermediate-term uptrend to the lower peak.
- On the next swing down, price broke the H2 support level but found support at line H1. It consolidated there with a little double-tap (labeled 1 and 2), which would look like a double bottom on intraday charts.
- There was a positive divergence between price and MACD as the correction low formed.
- A Bullish Engulfing candle marked the end of the correction and the start of the next leg up, which soon broke up through line H2 and the 200-period SMA.

Market Uptrend 2: July 13, 2009 through January 19, 2010

Figure 11.5 shows the next leg up of the new bull market, which was a long run up (just over six months) and a rise of almost 32 percent. Following are some factors to note regarding this uptrend:

- The rise started from a Bullish Engulfing candle and was a strong surge up off the correction low with just brief pauses and very minor interruptions for the first few weeks.
- Early in the uptrend, price broke out above the high of the prior intermediate-term uptrend (H1) establishing a new bull market high.
- All the moving averages kept trending up, stacking one above the other.
- In October and again in early November, minor corrections (less than 4 percent declines) found support at the 50-period SMA.
- From mid-November to late December, price consolidated in a long base. Horizontal support and resistance lines (H2 and H3, respectively) identify the boundaries.

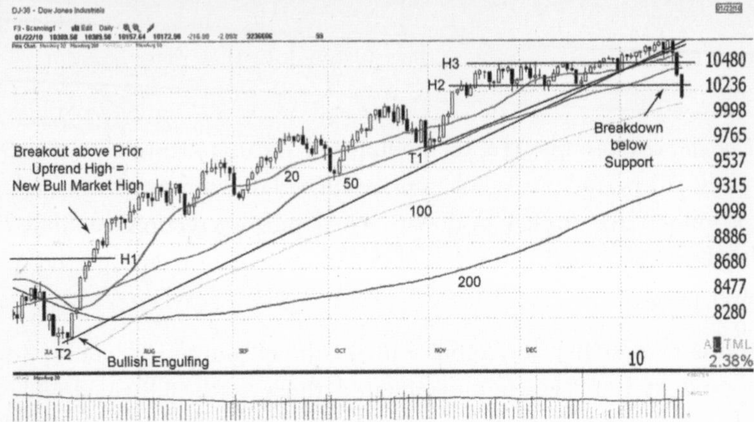

FIGURE 11.5 Intermediate-Term Uptrend: +31.66 Percent Rise July 13, 2009 through January 19, 2010
Source: TC2000® chart courtesy of Worden Brothers, Inc.

- During the first half of January, price moved up, slowly forming many narrow range bars. The up trendlines (T1 and T2) were extended up and both were fit tightly to price.

When the uptrend ended, the first push down off the top was sharp and fast. The 20- and 50-period moving averages were broken, as were the sloped trendlines. The horizontal lines H2 and H3 were also broken.

Market Correction 2: January 20 through February 8, 2010

Figure 11.6 shows the next correction of 7.62 percent. Following are some factors to note regarding this decline:

- The correction started from a sharp and fast decline off the top—three bearish candles from January 20 to 22 with strong volume. The peak it left behind is the current bull market high.
- After breaking a bit below line H1 at the end of January, price bounced for two days where it found resistance at line H2. Prior support reversed roles to that of resistance.
- Price plunged down through line H1 leaving a peak behind for drawing a correction trendline (T1).

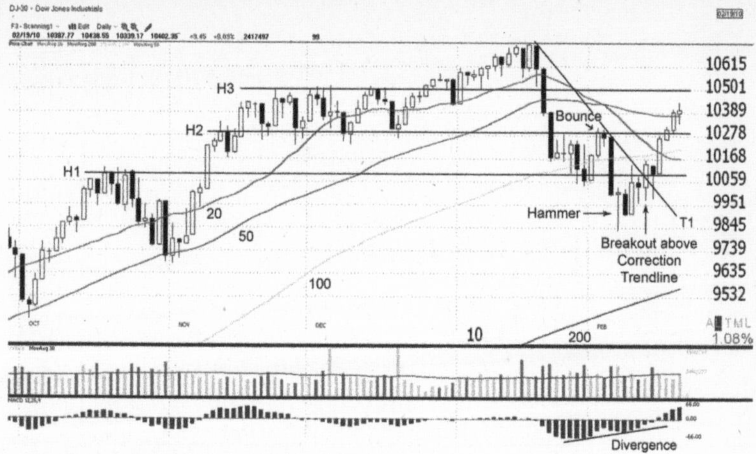

FIGURE 11.6 Market Correction: –7.62 Percent Decline January 20 through February 8, 2010
Source: TC2000® chart courtesy of Worden Brothers, Inc.

- The correction ended with a bullish Hammer. The following day was a bearish candle, but it held above the Hammer's low.
- There was a positive divergence between price and the MACD as the correction low formed.
- On February 11, price broke out above the down trendline and line H1.

Market Uptrend 3: February 9 through April 26, 2010

Figure 11.7 shows the next leg up of the bull market, which was a rise of just over 13 percent. Following are some factors to note regarding this uptrend:

- Price stalled at the 50-period SMA after the initial run up from the correction low.
- Price pulled back, dipping to the 20-period SMA intraday on February 25 (lower shadow), then turned up, leaving a bottom to start an up trendline. The trendline was later adjusted upward (T1).
- Price broke out above the prior intermediate-term uptrend high (H1) about midway through the uptrend, setting a new bull market high.

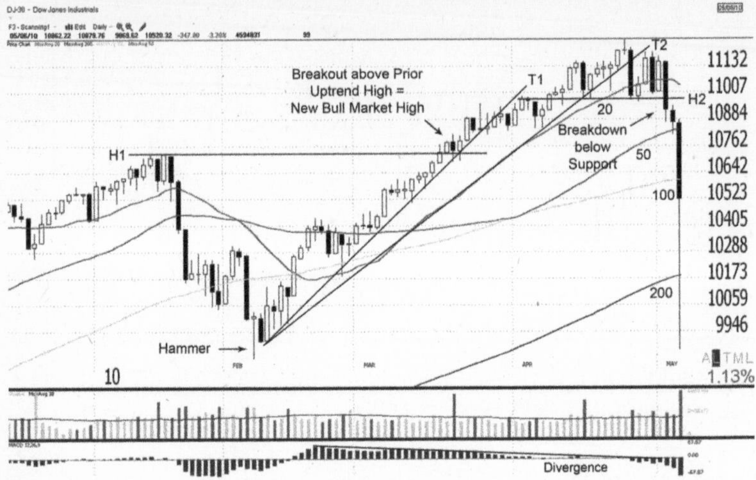

FIGURE 11.7 Intermediate-Term Uptrend: +13.09 Percent Rise February 9 through April 26, 2010
Source: TC2000® chart courtesy of Worden Brothers, Inc.

- The trendline (T1) had become tightly fit to price and was broken as price consolidated at the end of March. As price moved up again a new trendline was drawn (T2).
- Note the downward slope of MACD versus the price peaks during the entire uptrend (negative divergence).
- Price broke down through trendline T2 and closed just below the 20-period SMA.
- Price rallied back up for two days but found resistance at the up trendline—support reversed its role to resistance. That also constituted a failure to break above the prior peak.
- Price broke down through the 20-period SMA again, and through support at line H2.

In addition to the signs on the daily chart that the uptrend was breaking down, a quick look at the weekly chart would have revealed that the Dow had found resistance at the 200-week moving average. Many traders (including me) now monitor the 200-period moving average on all time frames. Additionally, a look at the market internals at that top would have reflected an overbought market. Thus, there were plenty of warnings that the prior uptrend was vulnerable to a reversal before the breakdown occurred.

Market Correction 3: April 27 through July 2, 2010

Figure 11.8 shows the next market correction. It was a very deep decline of more than 13 percent. Following are some factors to note regarding this correction:

- Two days following the breakdown through line H1, the Flash Crash occurred, declining intraday to the prior correction low at line H2 and leaving a very long lower shadow (more on this event later).
- From May 10 to 12, price rallied back up to just above the 50-period SMA but then turned down again. At that point, a correction trendline could have been drawn. That line is not shown, because other lines were subsequently drawn (T1 through T3).
- Price declined all the way back down to the prior correction low again (H2), breaking through the 200-period SMA on the way and ending with a bullish Hammer.

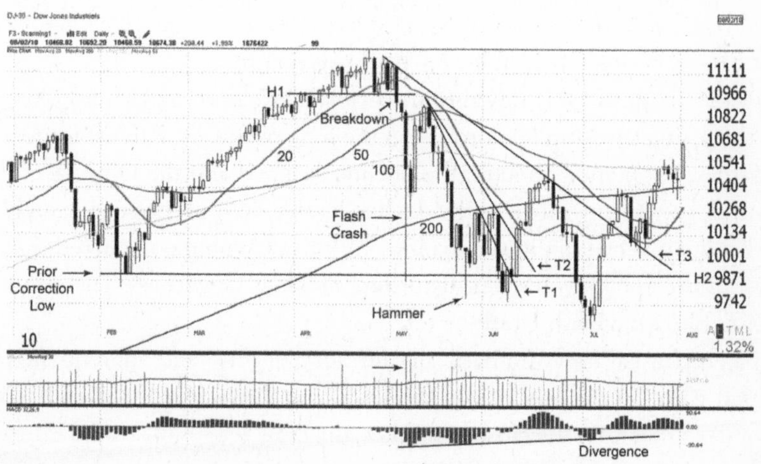

FIGURE 11.8 Market Correction: –13.55 Percent Decline April 27 through July 2, 2010
Source: TC2000® chart courtesy of Worden Brothers, Inc.

- Price turned up from that important support level on May 27, a long bullish candle, but was not able to get above the 200-period SMA. Price declined for a couple of days, leaving a peak that allowed for a steep correction trendline to be drawn (T1).
- Price turned up again and broke above the trendline (T1), but again failed to get over the 200-period SMA. When price turned back down, it closed below the prior correction's low. A new down trendline was drawn (T2).
- On June 10, price closed above the trendline (T2) and ran up to the 50- and 100-period SMAs where it found resistance.
- Price declined sharply again with just brief pauses along the way, ultimately closing below the prior bottom extending the correction. A new down trendline was drawn (T3).
- There was a positive divergence between price and the MACD as the correction low formed in early July.
- On July 12, price closed just above T3. The following day price found resistance at the 200-period SMA. Price declined back to the top of the trendline (T3) followed by a resumption of the new uptrend.

This correction merits more discussion—clearly it was not as orderly as the prior declines. An unusual, and spectacularly frightening event occurred after this correction had already gotten under way. On May 6, 2010, the markets were rattled as the Dow experienced an intraday decline of approximately 1,000 points! My eyes were glued to the intraday chart and CNBC that day—I could hardly believe what I was seeing.

Price ran all the way down to the prior correction low intraday, triggering the protective stop loss orders on the long positions of many traders and investors. Soon after, though, the decline stopped and the Dow raced back upward, recovering much of the decline by the close of the session and leaving behind a very long lower shadow. Very heavy volume occurred that day. It was a breathtaking and yet disturbing incident to witness. The event was later dubbed the Flash Crash.

To emphasize how dramatic the intraday decline and subsequent turnaround were, at the low of day the Dow was down *over 9 percent* from the prior day's close. By the close of market, the Dow was only down 3.2 percent from the prior day's close.

Note how the range (high to low) of the candles was much greater in the weeks following the Flash Crash than it had been during the prior run up. After such an event, it is not unusual for volatility to remain high for weeks, or even months in some cases. The Flash Crash was a significant event financially and psychologically; it kept traders on edge for quite some time.

Had you been monitoring the intermediate-length market trends as I've suggested throughout this book, you would have already seen the trend reversal warnings as the uptrend began breaking down, prior to the Flash Crash and subsequent deep correction. Refer back to the discussion associated with Figure 11.7.

At a minimum, those prior warnings would have suggested limiting exposure to further decline by reducing the size and number of open positions. Also, protective stops on long positions are often triggered as a correction begins. Thus, a trader's long positions may have already been stopped out.

The Flash Crash reinforced for me the benefit of closely monitoring the intermediate-term uptrend and taking defensive measures to protect capital and gains when negative signals occur. I'm not suggesting you'll never experience such an event but, in this particular case, the Flash Crash came after the earlier breakdown signals.

There were two other events that caused me some concern during this correction as they occurred at the right edge of the chart, aside from the craziness of the Flash Crash and the total depth of the decline. Looking back at Figure 11.8:

1. On May 20, the index closed below its 200-day SMA.
2. On June 7, price closed below the prior correction low from February 8 and broke through it again at the end of July.

Remember, those are technical signs traders look for as a dividing line between a bull and a bear market. However, after some additional volatile days, the index was able to recover and eventually moved on to a new bull market high.

Market Uptrend 4: July 6 through August 9, 2010

Figure 11.9 shows the next leg up of the bull market, which was a rise of almost 10.5 percent. Following are some factors to note regarding this uptrend:

- The first push up from the July low found resistance at the 200-period SMA (line H1). Note also the loss of momentum indicated by the small-bodied candles the following two days.
- Price pulled back to just below the 20-period SMA. When price turned back up, leaving a higher bottom, an up trendline was started (T1).
- On the next push up, price broke above the 200-period SMA (H1) but stalled at the 100-period SMA and the upper shadow of a Shooting Star that formed at the June high (H2).

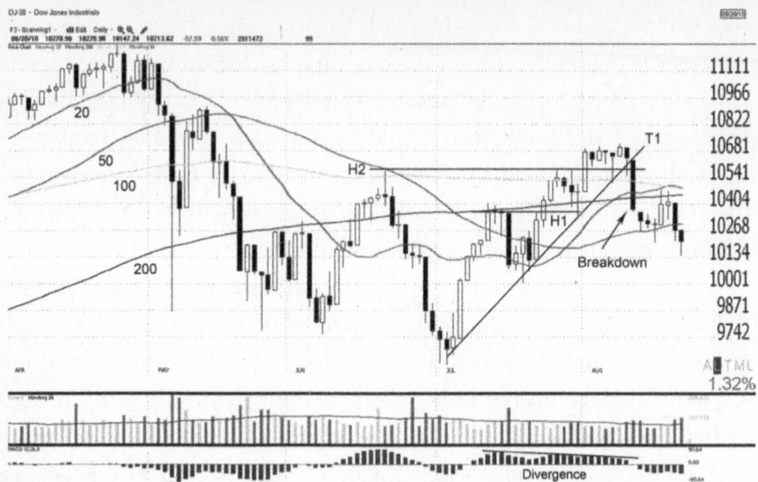

FIGURE 11.9 Intermediate-Term Uptrend: +10.45 Percent Rise July 6 through August 9, 2010
Source: TC2000® chart courtesy of Worden Brothers, Inc.

- Price dipped back and used the prior peak and the 200-period SMA (H1) as support before another swing up. The up trendline was extended upward, connecting to the low of that price pivot.
- Prior to the breakdown, there was a negative divergence between price and the MACD.

Although this uptrend did not last as long, nor was the rise as significant as many other advances during this bull market, price was finally able to break away from the choppy environment that had been the fallout from the Flash Crash.

Market Correction 4: August 10 through August 26, 2010

Figure 11.10 shows the next correction of 6.67 percent. Following are some factors to note regarding this decline:

- The first push down off the top was a swift drop through the 200-period SMA and line H1 down to the 50-period SMA. That down swing lost momentum, ending with a Dragonfly Doji.

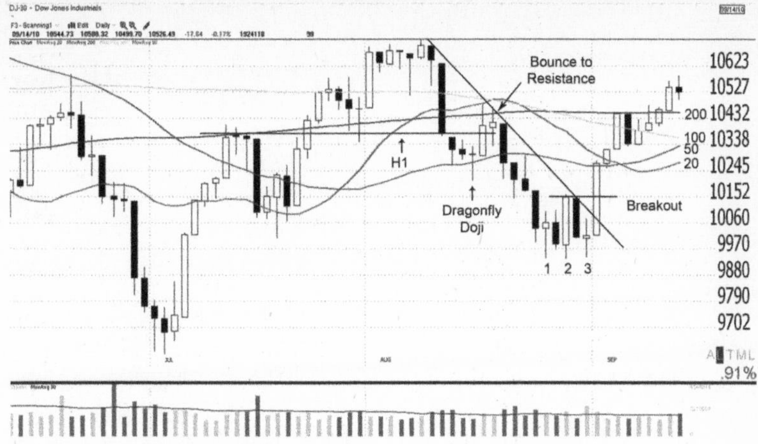

FIGURE 11.10 Market Correction: –6.67 Percent Decline August 10 through August 26, 2010
Source: TC2000® chart courtesy of Worden Brothers, Inc.

- Price bounced but found resistance at the 200-period SMA.
- Price turned down, closing below the 50-period SMA and leaving a peak behind to start a correction trendline.
- On August 25 price formed a bullish Hammer (number 1), followed by a Bullish Engulfing pattern (2) and a Spinning Top (3) followed by a long bullish candle. The combination created a small triple-tap bottoming action. It would have been an obvious triple bottom on intraday charts. The breakout from that minor bottoming action was the long bullish candle, which also broke decisively above the correction trendline and closed just above the 50-period SMA.

Market Uptrend 5: August 27, 2010 through February 18, 2011

Figure 11.11 shows the next leg up of the bull market, which was a long run up (almost six months) and a rise of just over 24 percent. Following are some factors to note regarding this uptrend:

- The move up began with a Bullish Engulfing pattern.
- Several weeks into the uptrend, price formed a base (H1) and broke out

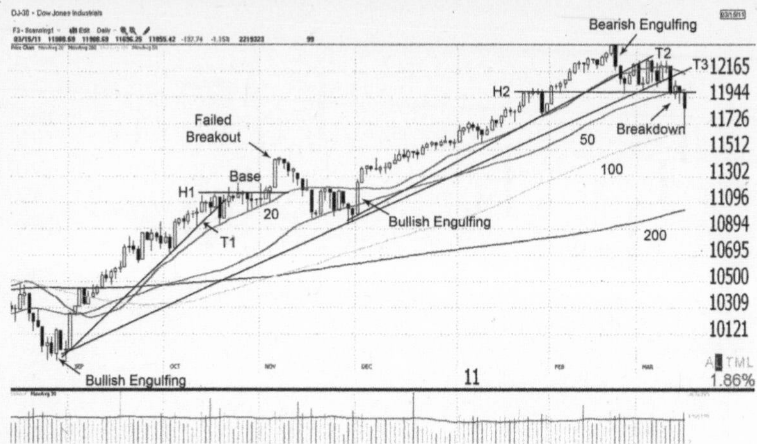

FIGURE 11.11 Intermediate-Term Uptrend: +24.09 Percent Rise August 27, 2010 through February 18, 2011
Source: TC2000® chart courtesy of Worden Brothers, Inc.

above it, but the breakout failed. It did, however, create a new bull market high having finally broken above the April 2010 high (not shown).

- Price declined below the base to the 50-period SMA. It was a minor correction of less than 4 percent, but enough to ease the prior overbought condition.
- As price tested the 50-period SMA, it formed a small triple-tap bottoming pattern. On intraday charts, it would have looked like a rectangular-type bottom after a downtrend.
- Price moved out of that base from another Bullish Engulfing pattern and reached another new bull market high several days later.
- A Bearish Engulfing pattern formed at the top of the uptrend, followed by a breakdown through the up trendline (T2) and a close below the 20-period SMA for the first time in a few months. Price consolidated below the broken trendline for several days, allowing a new up trendline to be drawn (T3).
- Price failed to move above the prior peak and, in fact, had formed a lower peak. It was followed by a breakdown through the new up trendline (T3), the horizontal line (H2), and the 50-period SMA.

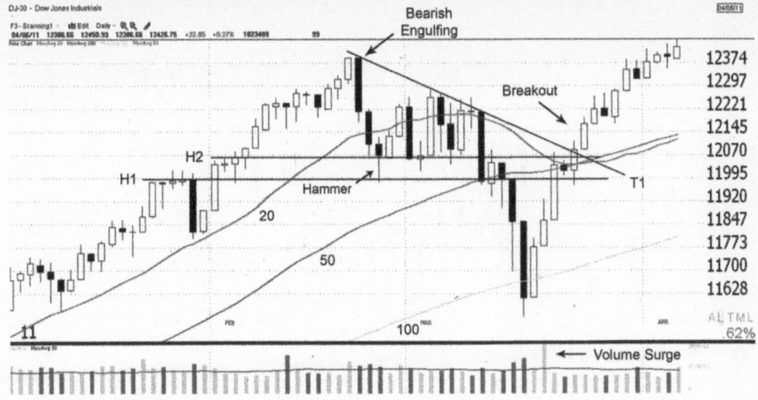

FIGURE 11.12 Market Correction: –6.28 Percent Decline February 22 through March 16, 2011
Source: TC2000® chart courtesy of Worden Brothers, Inc.

This run up was sort of a return to normal after a few months of high volatility following the Flash Crash in May 2010. Finally price was able to stabilize again—note how the candle bodies returned to a more normal size compared to the long candles of prior months.

Market Correction 5: February 22 through March 16, 2011

Figure 11.12 shows the next correction of 6.28 percent. Following are some factors to note regarding this decline:

- The correction started from a Bearish Engulfing pattern. It was a quick drop down to test the January high (H1) forming a bullish Hammer there.
- Price consolidated for several days forming a base. An internal horizontal line was drawn (H2) to identify its floor. The area between lines H1 and H2 formed a zone of support below price.
- Price broke down through the base bottom on March 10 but found support at the 50-period SMA and line H1. That left a peak behind for drawing a correction trendline (T1).
- After a one-day pause, price plunged down through that support and closed below the 100-period SMA in the following days.

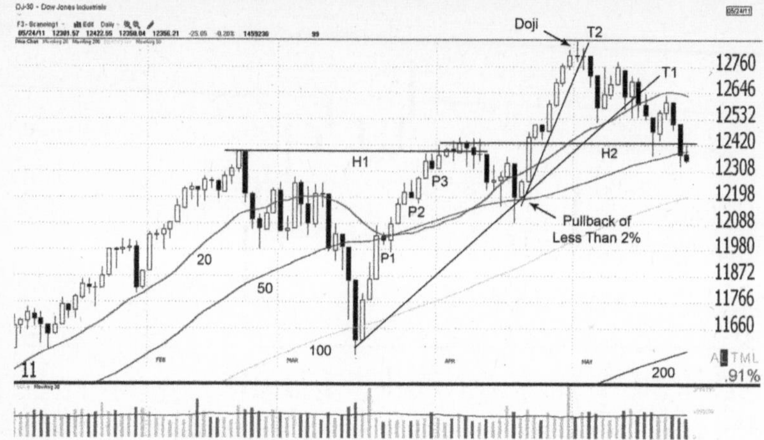

FIGURE 11.13 Intermediate-Term Uptrend: +10.31 Percent Rise March 17 through April 29, 2011
Source: TC2000® chart courtesy of Worden Brothers, Inc.

- Price bounced hard out of the correction low with a volume surge on the second day up, and a breakout above line H1 and the 20- and 50-period SMAs.

- Soon after, price broke out above the down trendline (T1). It took longer to break the trendline than in many of the past corrections. The sharp decline into the March low had left that line relatively far away from price.

Market Uptrend 6: March 17 through April 29, 2011

Figure 11.13 shows the next leg up of the bull market, which was a rise of more than 10 percent. Following are some factors to note regarding this uptrend:

- The initial run up was steep with only brief pauses (P1 through P3) along the way, creating one extended price swing. It wasn't really helpful to draw an up trendline yet (except for a short-term trader) because there were not any prominent rising bottoms—the line would have been broken by even just a minor dip or base.
- About halfway through the uptrend, price pulled back about 2 percent to the 50-period SMA. Normally, a decline to that moving average would equate to a percentage decline of about 3 percent or more (a minor

correction). However, the 50-period SMA had caught up closer to price. Thus, it didn't take much of a decline to reach that important support level in this case.

- When price turned up again, an up trendline was started (T1).
- Price accelerated, only pausing once during the next push up—it was another extended up swing. A very steep up trendline was drawn (T2).
- Two Doji candles formed at the top of the uptrend.
- When price turned down, the steep trendline (T2) was quickly broken.
- Price bounced for a few days but rolled over again leaving a lower peak and breaking the looser up trendline (T1) and the 20-period SMA.

Market Correction 6: May 2 through October 3, 2011

Figure 11.14 shows the next correction, which was the most significant one in this bull market. It was actually comprised of two down legs. The initial decline

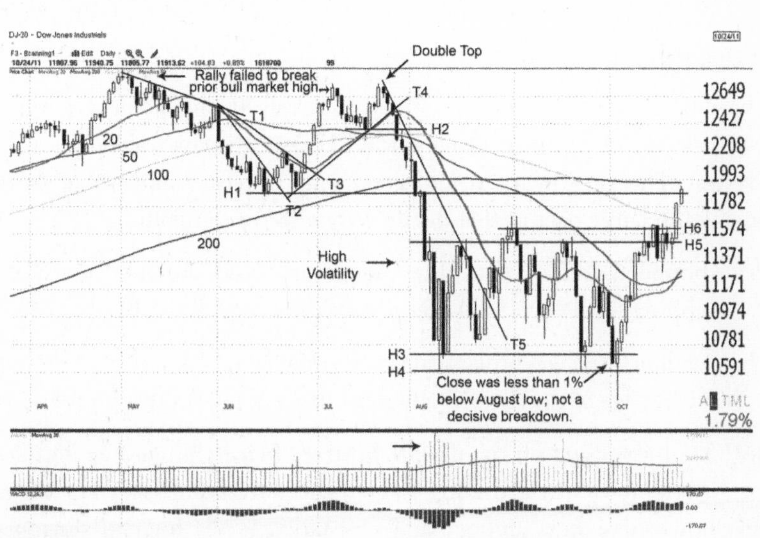

FIGURE 11.14 Market Correction: –16.82 Percent Decline May 2 through October 3, 2011
Source: TC2000® chart courtesy of Worden Brothers, Inc.

was from the April high, which was followed by a strong rally. The second leg down ended at the August low followed by several weeks of consolidation. Combined, these movements equaled a total decline of almost 17 percent.

The first leg down of this correction was a decline of just over 7 percent. At the time, I was monitoring that decline with down trendlines (T1 through T3) shown in Figure 11.14. Following are some factors to note:

- After a few weeks down, the decline accelerated, requiring a tighter trendline (T2).
- The trendline (T2) was quickly broken when price bounced.
- Price dropped back down for a test of the June low allowing for a new trendline to be drawn (T3).
- Price bounced again setting up a small double bottom (H1) and breaking the trendline (T3).

As price continued to rise out of the correction, at the right edge of the chart it appeared as if the next intermediate-term up leg of the bull market was under way. An up trendline (T4) was drawn. However, price failed to move up past the prior intermediate-term uptrend high (the April high). Following are some factors to note about the second leg down of the correction:

- A small double top formed and was confirmed with a close below the bottom between the peaks (H2). The up trendline (T4) was also broken during that push down, as were the 20-, 50-, and 100- period SMAs.
- The decline accelerated, falling precipitously through line H1 and the 200-period SMA into the August low (H3), with only brief pauses along the way. The very heavy volume and long bearish candles that formed during the latter part of that decline suggested capitulation.
- Price bounced off the August low then turned back down for a test of the new support level (at H3). A steep correction trendline was drawn (T5).
- The trendline (T5) was broken quickly during the next bounce. At that time, at the right edge of the chart, it appeared that a double bottom was forming.
- Instead of reversing off the double bottom, price chopped up and down for several weeks in a trading range. The horizontal lines H3 through H6 show some key support and resistance levels formed during the consolidation. *Note:* Don't look for divergence during this period because price already changed direction from down to sideways.
- On October 3, price closed just below the August low (H3), but by less

than 1 percent, so it was not a decisive break of that support. Additionally, it did not close below the lower boundary of the trading range (the external support line labeled H4).

- Price finally broke out from that choppy bottoming process in late October (H6), ultimately resuming the long-term uptrend.

When a period of consolidation occurs, it is typically considered to be a time of lower volatility. However, during the trading range that formed between August and October on the Dow, note the preponderance of long candles that formed—they kept the volatility quite high during that time. The period while price was trapped in that trading range was not kind to trend-following systems, but it afforded short-term traders plenty of opportunity to generate profits. Alternatively, there is no shame in sitting aside in the safety of cash during such a choppy period; in fact, for many novices doing so is advisable.

The Argument: Correction versus Bear Market The total decline of the two down legs that formed this market correction was so deep that many chartists, myself included, felt at the time the market was shifting from a bull to a bear. A gentleman whom I consider to be one of my mentors was also calling it a bear market. His market internals and scan counts were flashing bear market numbers.

Look at the chart again focusing from September, while price was still range bound, back to the April high. At that time, it appeared that the first move down off the top was the first leg down of a new bear market. It was followed by what appeared to be a bear market rally during June to July, and then another leg down into a bear market. In fact, that's precisely what it was if you consider this to be a baby bear market (a term I borrowed from strategist Sam Stovall) rather than a very deep market correction.

Following are some other charting factors I had considered at the time:

1. In order for a major uptrend to keep going, price must surpass the prior intermediate-term top to take the bull market to a new high. It had failed to do so when it turned down from the double top in July.
2. In order to remain in force, the prior correction low should provide support when tested. Not only was the June low broken, but on August 4 price plunged through the level that was the March 2011 correction low and closed far below it.
3. Additionally, price had long since closed below the 200-period SMA; and had also broken the very long-term 500-period SMA, which many of us chartists keep an eye on.

Perhaps you see why this decline had me more concerned than any of the others (the previous correction of some concern was the one from mid-2010). One promising technical note was that the Dow was holding near its 200-week SMA.

Beyond the chart itself, there were some things going on fundamentally. The power struggle in Washington, D.C. referred to as the debt ceiling showdown had been weighing on the market. The market did not rally right after the settlement of that issue. There were some poor economic reports suggesting slowdown or potential recession, and the market was reflecting those concerns. There was a lot of talk about a double dip recession at the time.

Following is some commentary from an e-mail I wrote on August 15, 2011, to a client in response to her question about the market environment:

"So far this looks like just a short-covering rally. These will happen in bear markets. In order for me to be convinced the bull is still intact, and what we've just experienced was an extremely deep correction versus a new bear market starting, the Dow and S&P would have to get back up through the 200-day SMA and then go on to eventually break the May high. Or the averages would have to chop around for a while, mostly sideways (holding above the August bottom) and then move up higher eventually taking out the May high. The August low is an important point—a close below that would increase my bearish stance. Unless the market pulls off a stunning reversal and upside move, I'll continue to approach it as a new bear market. If what we are seeing now is a budding new bear, we've likely only seen the first legs down so far. But since we don't have crystal balls to tell the future, we get to be patient and watch it unfold."

Well guess what, it did all of the things I said it would have to do to continue the bull market! I know better than to get dogmatic about what I think will or should happen. I learned a long time ago, through emotionally and financially painful lessons, to adjust to changes in the market environment and accept what it gives me. I adjusted my stance on it based on the market behavior. That is, I didn't doggedly short the market, I shifted focus back to the long side as the trend suggested I should. The market recovered and eventually moved on to make new highs.

Later that year, in an interview on CNBC on November 1, 2011, Sam Stovall, a very experienced and respected market strategist, referred to the sharp correction as a baby bear. In other words, a mild bear market, which I thought was an appropriate label.

In retrospect, we can look back at the April 2011 peak to the October 2011 closing low as either:

1. A very deep correction within a bull market.
2. A baby bear, as Sam Stovall referred to it.

It wasn't deep enough to match up to recent bear markets, but was definitely a very deep correction that was flashing bear market numbers.

With the benefit of hindsight, many analysts now refer to it as a very significant market correction rather than a bear market since the threshold of a 20 percent decline was not met. Therefore, most consider the current bull market to have been in force from the March 2009 low to present; and I can go along with that because the decline missed that threshold.

We can't ignore the fact, though, that there was what could be construed as a mild bear market within this bull market, which begets an argument for a *secular bull market*—a super cycle that lasts up to 25 years but includes some minor bear markets. If you think of a long-term uptrend as being strung together by a series of intermediate-length up moves and corrections against the major trend, a secular uptrend is one that is strung together by a series of bull markets separated by bear markets that are significant corrections of that prolonged uptrend.

I'm not making any predictions, but rather just pointing out another trending concept you'll inevitably come across in your market studies, or hear about periodically on financial shows. For an example of a secular bull market, look at the historic move up from 1982 to 2000. I would have no complaints about experiencing another glorious bull run similar to that during my lifetime.

Interesting Historical Note: In his November 2011 interview on CNBC, Mr. Stovall also indicated that after eight prior baby bear markets that he had analyzed, "...the S&P gained an average of about 13 percent three months after, about 23 percent six months after and 32 percent twelve months after." The movement following the 2011 baby bear was right in line with those historical averages. Three months later (January 3, 2012), the S&P 500 was up was up just over 16 percent. Six months later (April 3, 2012) it was up about 28 percent. One year later (October 3, 2012), it was up about 32 percent.

Market Uptrend 7: October 4 through October 28, 2011

Figure 11.15 shows the next leg up of the bull market, which was a rise of almost 15 percent. Following are some factors to note regarding this uptrend:

- The initial push up off the October low was an extended price swing with only brief pauses along the way. It would become the pole of a bullish flag. During that run up, price closed above the 50-period SMA for the first time in recent months.

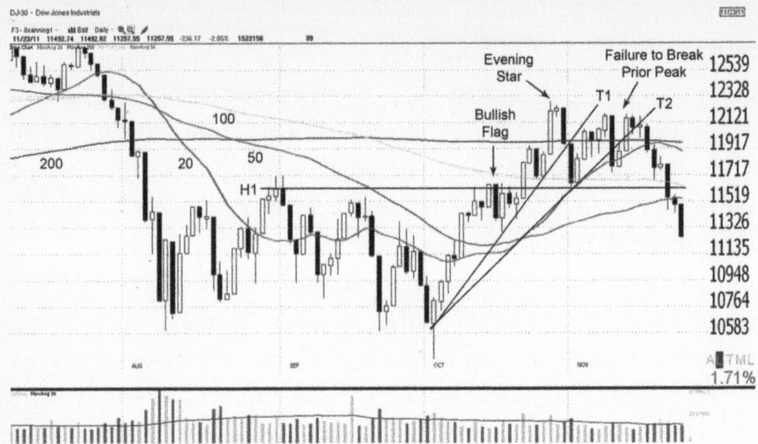

FIGURE 11.15 Intermediate-Term Uptrend: +14.79 Percent Rise October 4 through October 28, 2011
Source: TC2000® chart courtesy of Worden Brothers, Inc.

- From October 14 to 20, price stalled at the August high (H1), forming a bullish flag. An up trendline (T1) was started, and the slope was later adjusted. *Note:* When the Dow formed a flag, there were similar patterns (bases and flags) on the charts of many individual stocks providing good setups for potential long positions.
- On October 21, price broke out from the flag on above average volume, and above the trading range formed during the prior market correction. Price also closed above the 100-period SMA.
- Two days later price dipped back and tested the 100-period SMA as support. The up trendline (T1) was lengthened and adjusted to accommodate that new price pivot.
- Price closed above the 200-period SMA, but soon closed right back below it as a bearish Evening Star formed.
- The trendline (T1) was broken as price declined back to the top of the flag.
- Price rallied again allowing a new up trendline (T2) to be drawn, but price failed to break above the peak formed by the Evening Star.
- The trendline (T2) was broken as a new correction began its descent.

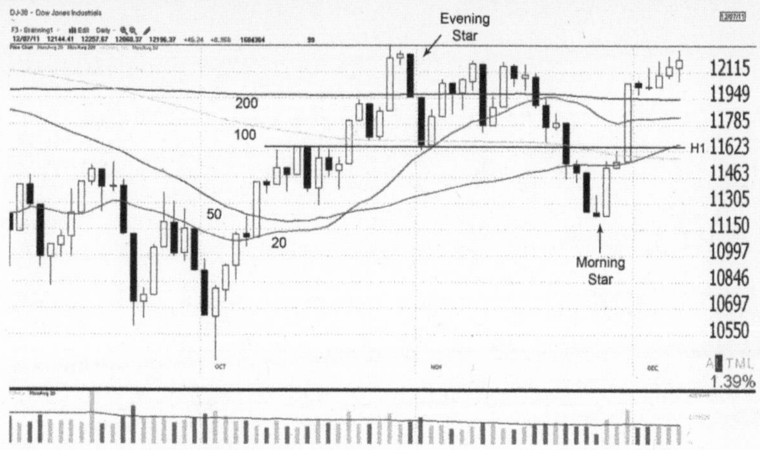

FIGURE 11.16 Market Correction: –8.17 Percent Decline October 31 through November 25, 2011
Source: TC2000® chart courtesy of Worden Brothers, Inc.

Market Correction 7: October 31 through November 25, 2011

Figure 11.16 shows the next correction of 8.17 percent. Following are some factors to note regarding this decline:

- The correction began with the bearish Evening Star that formed at the end of October.
- The trend accelerated down to the November low. That push down was interrupted by only brief pauses, so a correction trendline was not drawn.
- A bullish Morning Star formed at the correction low.
- As price pushed up from the low, it broke through the 50- and 100-period SMAs and the top of the bullish flag (H1) that had formed during the prior uptrend.

Market Uptrend 8: November 28, 2011 through May 1, 2012

Figure 11.17 shows the next leg up of the bull market, which was a rise of over 18 percent. Following are some factors to note regarding this uptrend:

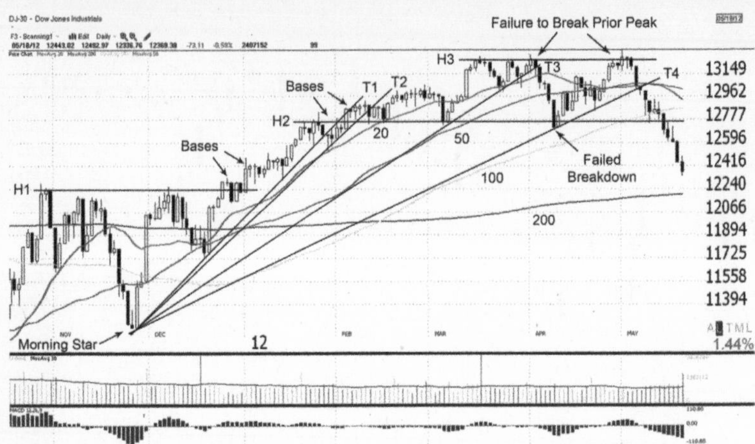

FIGURE 11.17 Intermediate-Term Uptrend: +18.23 Percent Rise November 28, 2011 through May 1, 2012
Source: TC2000® chart courtesy of Worden Brothers, Inc.

- The uptrend started from a bullish Morning Star. The first push up had only brief pauses along the way.
- Price found resistance at the October high (H1). Note the upper shadows on the candles as price approached that ceiling suggesting the upswing had lost momentum.
- Price pulled back to just below the 50-period SMA then turned up again allowing an up trendline (T1) to be started.
- The next swing up ended with a Doji. Price based for a few days near resistance at line H1, then pushed past it and based again for several days.
- Price rallied again, followed by the formation of another base that broke the up trendline (T1).
- Price moved up again, finally breaking above the April 2011 high (not shown), setting a new bull market high. That allowed a new up trendline (T2) to be drawn. It was broken when another base formed. This type of price action will keep breaking the up trendline without an actual breakdown of the trend.
- A horizontal line (H2) was drawn identifying the support and resistance created by that basing action.

- In early March, price pulled back to that horizontal line (H2) where it found support, and then rallied again, forming the March 2012 high.
- In late March, price was not able to break above the prior peak. The trendline (T3) was adjusted upward, fitting tightly to the price action.
- The trendline (T3) was quickly broken as price declined about 4 percent back to support at the horizontal line (H2), closing just below it (less than 1 percent). It turned out to be a false breakdown. Recall my earlier warnings about requiring that price break decisively beyond a barrier to consider it a valid break. I would not have considered this to be a significant enough close below the line.
- Price rallied, allowing a new up trendline to be drawn (T4). In late April another attempt to break above the prior peak failed (H3). By that point, it was clear price was trapped in a trading range. There's no use looking at MACD for a divergence at this point. Remember, look for divergence while price is still trending, not while it is consolidating.
- The uptrend ended in May as price broke down through trendline (T4) and the 20- and 50-period SMAs. Soon after, price broke down through the floor of the trading range (H2) and the 100-period SMA.

Market Correction 8: May 2 through June 4, 2012

Figure 11.18 shows the next correction of almost 9 percent. Following are some factors to note regarding this decline:

- From May 2 to May 18, price declined steeply with only brief pauses along the way. That slide would become the pole of a bearish flag. Only one very minor pivot formed about midway down, which made it difficult to draw a correction trendline. However, a very tight one could be drawn if desired (T1).
- Price turned slightly against the downtrend from May 21 through May 29 breaking the tight trendline and forming a bearish flag.
- Price broke down through the bottom of the flag leaving a peak behind to draw a new correction trendline (T2). The 200-period SMA was broken during that push down.
- There was a positive divergence between price and the MACD as the correction low formed.

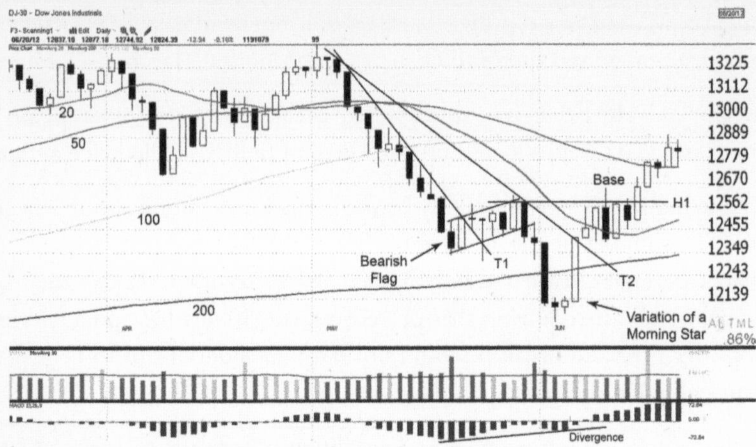

FIGURE 11.18 Market Correction: –8.87 Percent Decline May 2 through June 4, 2012
Source: TC2000® chart courtesy of Worden Brothers, Inc.

- On June 6, price closed back above the 200-period SMA and just above the correction trendline (T2) forming a variation of a bullish Morning Star.
- Price stalled for a few days forming a base below the prior peak (H1) and then pushed up through it. You may wonder why I didn't refer to this base as a bullish flag. You may certainly do so, but just keep in mind that, technically speaking, there must be a significant move (a pole) preceding a flag or pennant. But a launch from a base can be quite powerful, just like with an official flag.

Note: The Morning Star shown in Figure 11.18 is a variation because it has two small-bodied candles (the "star" portion) between the long bearish and bullish candles, where there is normally only one. However, in my opinion, this variation sends the same message—an abrupt turnaround in sentiment.

Market Uptrend 9: June 5 through October 5, 2012

Figure 11.19 shows the next leg up of the bull market, which was a rise of almost 12.5 percent. Following are some factors to note regarding this uptrend:

- The first half of this uptrend was fairly choppy. Note how the three

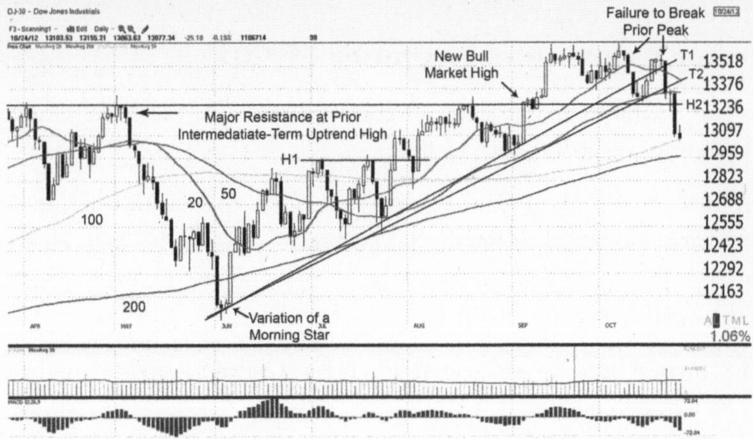

FIGURE 11.19 Intermediate-Term Uptrend: +12.47 Percent Rise June 5 through October 5, 2012

Source: TC2000® chart courtesy of Worden Brothers, Inc.

pullbacks from late June through late July each retraced almost the entire prior upswing.

- Price broke away from that choppy movement on July 27 (H1), then pulled back to the 20-period SMA.
- On September 6, price broke out just above a major ceiling (H2) formed by the top of the last intermediate-term uptrend. In doing so, it set a new bull market high.
- By the time the September 14 peak was formed, the uptrend was well over three months old—aging and vulnerable to a correction.
- Price failed to break above the September high during the next swing up. The decline from that peak broke the up trendline (T1).
- Price found support at the 50-period SMA and the prior strong ceiling (H2) and rallied again; but once again it failed to break the prior peak. That set up the potential for a shallow triple top (but it is just consolidation until confirmed). Here again, don't look to the MACD for a divergence as price is moving sideways.
- Price broke down through the trendline (T2), the 50-period SMA, and confirmed the triple top.

Market Correction 9: October 8 through November 15, 2012

Figure 11.20 shows a correction of almost 8 percent. Following are some factors to note regarding this decline:

- The push down through the 50-period SMA to the 100-period SMA was sharp and fast. The horizontal line (H1) was also broken. That is an important support and resistance line—it is the one that stretches back to the April high (not shown).
- Price turned back up and tested line H1 as resistance and formed a base below that ceiling.
- Price broke down through the bottom of the base (H2) and the 200-period SMA leaving a peak behind to start a correction trendline (T1).
- Price paused briefly (a Spinning Top followed by a Doji) then fell again, allowing for a very tight down trendline to be drawn (T2).
- Price quickly broke the tight trendline (T2). Such a tight line is prone to false breaks. However, in this case it was accompanied by a variation of a bullish Morning Star.

This correction was not surprising. From a technical standpoint, the prior intermediate-term uptrend was overbought and due to have a correction.

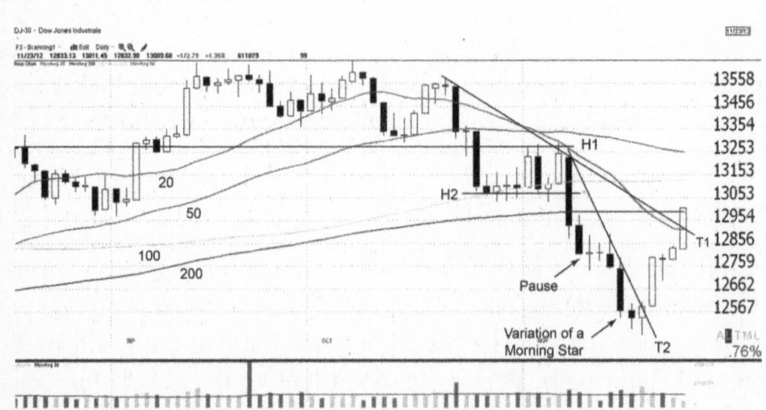

FIGURE 11.20 Market Correction: –7.85 Percent Decline October 8 through November 15, 2012

Source: TC2000® chart courtesy of Worden Brothers, Inc.

Add to that some fundamental issues putting pressure on the market, so there were many potential correction triggers:

1. The EuroZone was struggling. The economy was troubled, with negative growth in some European countries; plus their ongoing debt issues.
2. The looming fiscal cliff in America, which our elected officials (both parties played a role) avoided dealing with until the last minute.
3. The election was finally over and the market was digesting what the impact may be to business and the economy with four more years of the Obama Administration's policies.

Please understand that I don't refer to these events to spur political debate, but rather to point out the fact that global and political events and concerns impact the markets and the economy. These are big issues, so regardless of your political affiliation, try to look objectively at how the market reacts to certain events. The market will interpret such events either positively or negatively and price in (discount) those assumptions.

Market Uptrend 10: November 16, 2012 through May 28, 2013

Figure 11.21 shows the next leg up of the bull market. It was a very long run lasting over six months with a rise of almost 23 percent. I believe this trend

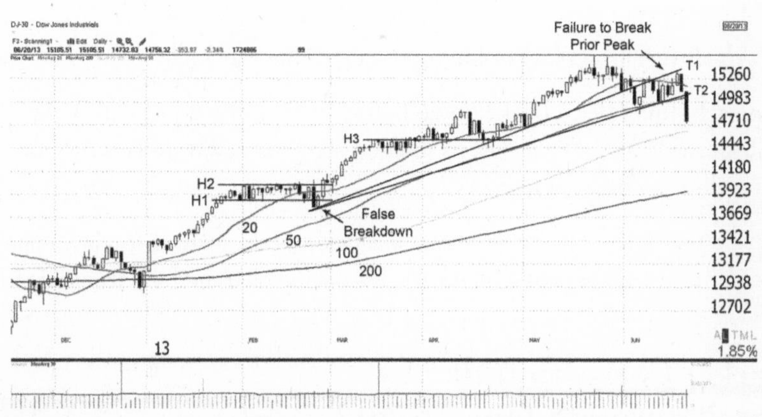

FIGURE 11.21 Intermediate-Term Uptrend: +22.86 Percent Rise November 16, 2012 through May 28, 2013
Source: TC2000® chart courtesy of Worden Brothers, Inc.

was able to continue on for so long because there was a fairly significant period of consolidation within it. Price consolidated for almost the entire month of February 2013 (between lines H1 and H2), which I feel served the purpose of easing the overbought condition enough to allow the uptrend to stretch on. There was no longer such a pressing need for a correction because the trend had a chance to rest. It continued on for about three more months after the formation of that long, narrow base. You could even look at it as two back-to-back intermediate-term uptrends with a period of consolidation separating them.

The February consolidation was important for another reason—it represented round number resistance. Price had stalled at approximately the 14,000 level. The thousand marks are important psychological numbers for the Dow, as are hundred marks for the S&P 500 Index. Once the Dow got above that level, it broke the 2007 high (the closing high of the prior bull market from 2002 to 2007) setting a new all-time high for the index. The Dow had the best first quarter of the year for the past 15 years.

Following are some additional factors to note regarding this uptrend:

- On February 25, the Dow closed below the bottom of the long base (H1). However, it was not a decisive break. I watched closely to see if it may be the start of a correction, but it turned out to be a head fake (false breakdown).
- Another fairly long base formed during the last two weeks of March. After the breakout above the base (H3), price immediately dipped back to the base top and found support there.
- During the next pullback later in April, price found support at the base top again (H3). That allowed an up trendline to be drawn (T1).
- A small variation of a double top formed the May high.
- In early June, price broke down below the trendline (T1) but held at the 50-period SMA where it consolidated for several days, allowing a new up trendline to be drawn (T2).
- Price was unable to break above the prior peak, instead leaving a slightly lower peak and breaking below the 50-period SMA and the trendline (T2).

Market Correction 10: May 29 through June 24, 2013

Figure 11.22 shows the next correction of almost 5 percent. Following are some factors to note regarding this decline:

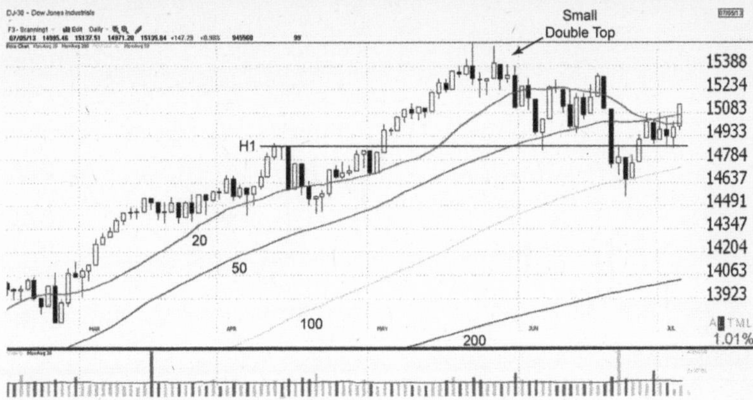

FIGURE 11.22 Market Correction: –4.87 Percent Decline May 29 through June 24, 2013
Source: TC2000® chart courtesy of Worden Brothers, Inc.

- The decline started from the small variation of a double top that formed the May high.
- The first push down found support at the 50-period SMA and the April high (H1).
- Price held above the 50-period SMA for several days before plunging through that moving average, as well as line H1.
- The decline ended right at the 100-period SMA, after which price bounced back above line H1 and based there for a few days before moving higher.

This was a modest correction, but it was the first notable decline in over six months. Because of the way this correction formed, it was awkward to draw a correction trendline so I did not do so. However, a break back above line H1 was encouraging, followed by a break above the 50-period SMA.

Market Uptrend 11: June 25, 2013 to Present

Figure 11.23 shows the next leg up of the bull market, which is still in force at the time of this writing with a rise so far of almost 7 percent. Following are some factors to note regarding this uptrend:

- The first strong push up from the 100-period SMA found resistance at the 50-period SMA where price formed a base.

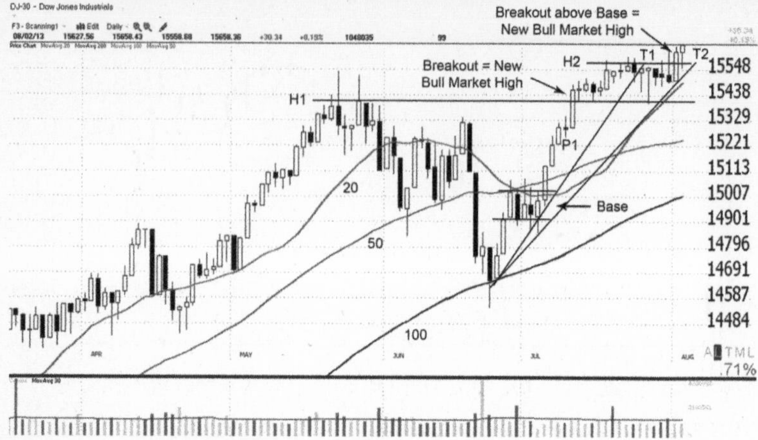

FIGURE 11.23 Intermediate-Term Uptrend: +6.8 Percent Rise as of August 2 June 25, 2013 to TBD
Source: TC2000® chart courtesy of Worden Brothers, Inc.

- Price broke out above the top of the base and the 50-period SMA for a several-day run slowed only by a one-day pause (P1).

- Price broke out above the May small double top that had formed at the end of the prior intermediate-term uptrend. That set a new bull market high.
- Price consolidated for four days, setting up a small base and using the prior ceiling as a new floor (resistance and support reversed roles).
- Price consolidated again for several days breaking the trendline (T1).
- On August 1, price broke out above the base top (H2), setting another new bull market high. A new up trendline (T2) was drawn.

The several narrow range bars that formed between July 12 and July 31, 2013, served to significantly decrease market volatility. I maintain an ongoing market study that tracks the average daily range (over a period of 14 days) for the major averages as a gauge of volatility. As of July 31, the average daily range of the Dow had declined to .62 percent. Compare that to, say, a period during April when the average daily range was 1.25 percent, almost double. I point this out because a move, up or down, from a period of such low volatility can sometimes be explosive. It will be interesting to see if the breakout follows through well in this case.

From a fundamental standpoint, following are some big issues on the horizon that may impact the bull market's progress:

1. To taper or not to taper: Will the Federal Reserve start pulling back on its $85 billion-a-month bond-buying program?
2. U.S. Government: The fiscal budget for 2014 (avoiding a government shutdown) and the debt ceiling issue will come to the forefront.

Conclusion

I've expressed a couple of times that novices must try to avoid becoming overwhelmed. As you review some of the chapters in this book, you may think it is all just too much to try to remember. But I hope that, as you review the discussion of each uptrend and correction illustrated in this chapter, you see that it really becomes quite repetitive. You'll regularly perform certain tasks and note certain technical occurrences. For instance, drawing and adjusting sloped trendlines and horizontal support and resistance lines becomes a quick but important task performed frequently.

In the instances where there may be a list of items to remember, such as the early and later warnings of a trend reversal outlined in Chapters 5 and 6, make a quick reference guide. Keep your quick reference materials close at hand until you know the information so well that you no longer need to refer to them. If you look back through all the chapters, in many of them you'll find tables and bulleted or numbered lists that can be very helpful in developing some quick reference guides.

In addition to monitoring the market's progress using the core tenets of technical analysis, pay attention to how news and certain catalysts impact the market. For instance, as you continue monitoring the current bull market to its eventual end, take note of how upcoming events like those mentioned above (tapering, budget and debt issues) influence market movement.

CHAPTER 12

Conclusion

Congratulations on reaching the end of this book. It must seem like a lot of information, and I'll agree that it is. But keep in mind it takes me many pages to thoroughly describe and illustrate each concept, especially in the structured way in which I do so. Remember, I don't just tell you what time it is—I show you how to build a clock.

It took me years to figure this all out. Much of what I know was learned from my own observations, experience, and revelations. But I also learned a tremendous amount through books, articles, and seminars, and from mentors. I am very grateful to those who have shared their knowledge, and I feel compelled to share my own understandings of the market in my way of portraying it. You can shave many months, and for some of you a few to several years, off your own learning curve by carefully studying the information provided in these chapters.

It required an entire book for me to impart to you what I know about trend analysis. In fact, I could probably go on for at least 100 pages more if the publisher wanted a 400-plus-page book! I've been told before that brevity is not my strong suit. Perhaps I do elaborate excessively; but when it comes to learning about charting and trading, most of my followers really appreciate the level of detail provided.

I suggest reading this book several times. If it is any consolation, there are a few trading books on my shelves with broken spines due to excessive reading and reference. I wouldn't ask you to do what I haven't done myself, or wouldn't be willing to do again, in order to learn what is needed to move down the path to trade mastery.

As you review the chapters again, focus on how the common concepts are categorized because that makes it easier to learn, absorb, and retain the information. Use the tables and the numbered and bulleted lists included in many of the chapters as quick reference guides. And finally, you'll need to do plenty of practice beyond the pages of this book.

Put what you've learned to work by analyzing, in your own charting platform, some past trends on the charts of stocks, market indices, sectors, and industry groups. Also analyze in real time some trends that are evolving at the right edge of the chart. Doing so will help you gain experience understanding and anticipating price movement, and recognizing specific chart formations, which you can respond to in order to generate profits.

Don't delay—start practicing right away. Don't make the mistake that so many aspiring traders do. They study a lot, but they don't take immediate and persistent action to utilize what they've learned. When knowledge is not put to work, it quickly diminishes. Don't let your mental muscles atrophy.

When you are ready, start putting on some trades. There is nothing that will teach you more than getting into the trading trenches. Mark Twain knew the importance of doing versus just learning as evidenced by this quote: "The person who has had a bull by the tail once has learned 60 or 70 times as much as a person who hasn't." But I do suggest starting with small position size and building up to larger size as you gain experience and confidence, and it is absolutely imperative to use prudent risk management techniques to protect your capital.

If you'll do these things I've suggested, I am confident it will begin to feel much less overwhelming; and you will eventually become skilled at analyzing trends. It is often said that knowledge is power, but it is actually the *application of knowledge* that is powerful.

A Strong Core of Knowledge Leads to Profitable Strategies

Included in this text are suggestions for trade selection and execution, and references to developing specific trading strategies. However, *the primary purpose of this instruction is to help you build a strong base of knowledge of trend analysis in order to increase profitability*. Attempting to jump right into taking trades without this strong charting foundation would be like putting the cart in front of the horse. That's precisely why the training I provide is broken down into a series of courses that are designed to build one upon the other.

This book is a crucial part of my charting instruction, and is part of the foundation from which successful trading strategies may be developed.

This instruction provides much of what you'll need to develop an essential knowledge base of charting. For those of you who wish to take more of my training after completing this book, you'll find courses that build upon this base on the Training & Products page on my website at www.tinalogan.com. Regardless of whether you choose to take more of my training or that of others, or continue your studies on your own, this book will help you progress down the path to becoming a skilled chartist and trader.

Understanding how trends evolve is very important because a large number of trading strategies are designed to capitalize on lucrative trending phases. Trend-following strategies can be very profitable. If you carefully review this instruction, and spend time applying what you've learned, ultimately you will be ready to implement trade management techniques and specific trading strategies. You'll have the knowledge and understanding of market movement that will help you implement a strategy you've been shown, or to develop your own unique trading strategies if you choose.

You may have noticed as you reviewed the chapters that there were certain concepts repeated and reiterated, sometimes many times. That was done intentionally to assist readers in retaining the information. As you continue your study and practice outside the pages of this book, browse through charts of stocks and indices until you are able to recognize the technical events listed in Table 12.1.

TABLE 12.1	Analyzing Trends
Trend Direction	The direction of the trend (up or down), or if it is in a trendless phase (sideways).
Trend Duration	The various lengths of trends: long-, intermediate-, and short-term.
Trend Interruptions	The interruptions that may occur within a trend: brief pauses, minor basing action, pullbacks or bounces, corrections and longer periods of consolidation.
Support and Resistance	The support and resistance levels formed on the chart by price pivots and moving averages; and how price reacts as it approaches round numbers, gap openings, trendlines, and known retracement levels.
Trend Reversal Warnings	The early warnings that a trend may be weakening, and later signs that a trend reversal may already be under way.
Broad Market Analysis	The trends, interruptions, and trend reversal warnings that occur on the charts of major market averages, as well as the messages provided by market sentiment indicators and market internals. Note how the movement of the broad market impacts the charts of many individual stocks.

The markets are in constant flux—always changing and evolving—so traders must adjust to those market shifts in order to maintain an edge. One of the challenging, yet stimulating, things about this business is that you'll always be learning. To this day, I am still continually reading, researching, and testing ideas in my ongoing studies of the markets with the goal of finding great trading opportunities. I don't consider these activities to be a burden. Rather, it is like mining for gold nuggets in a proven reserve. Trading and training are two of my greatest passions.

■ My Trading Philosophy

I sincerely hope you have learned much from this book. It was truly a labor of love for me to write. I'll leave you with my three-point trading philosophy:

1. Be steadfastly vigilant with money management. Controlling risk is crucial in order to survive, and ultimately thrive, in the marketplace.
2. Strive to capture a sizable portion of the trend you are trading, whether it is a short-, intermediate-, or long-term trend.
3. Let the broad market be your guide. Adjust techniques to meet the prevailing market conditions.

BIBLIOGRAPHY

Achuthan, Lakshman, and Anirvan Banerji. *Beating the Business Cycle*. New York: Random House, 2004.

Baumohl, Bernard. *The Secrets of Economic Indicators*. Upper Saddle River, NJ: Wharton School Publishing, 2005.

Bollinger, John. *Bollinger on Bollinger Bands*. New York: McGraw-Hill, 2002.

Bulkowski, Thomas N. *Getting Started in Chart Patterns*. Hoboken, NJ: John Wiley & Sons, 2006.

Covel, Michael. *Trend Following*. Upper Saddle River, NJ: Prentice Hall, 2004.

Hirsch, Jeffrey A., and Yale Hirsch. *Stock Trader's Almanac 2013*. Hoboken, NJ: John Wiley & Sons, 2013.

Logan, Tina M. *Getting Started in Candlestick Charting*. Hoboken, NJ: John Wiley & Sons, 2008.

Morris, Gregory L. *The Complete Guide to Market Breadth Indicators*. New York: McGraw-Hill, 2006.

——— *Investing with the Trend: A Rules-Based Approach to Money Management*. Hoboken, NJ: John Wiley & Sons, 2013.

Murphy, John J. *The Visual Investor*. Hoboken, NJ: John Wiley & Sons, 1996.

——— *Technical Analysis of the Financial Markets*. New York: New York Institute of Finance, 1999.

Person, John L. *Candlestick and Pivot Point Trading Triggers*. Hoboken, NJ: John Wiley & Sons, 2007.

Tainer, Evelina M. *Using Economic Indicators to Improve Investment Analysis*. Hoboken, NJ: John Wiley & Sons, 2006.

Tharp, Dr. Van K. *Trade Your Way to Financial Freedom*. New York: McGraw-Hill, 1999.

ABOUT THE AUTHOR

Tina Logan is the president of Tina Logan, Inc. (www.tinalogan.com). She has more than 22 years of combined experience as a trainer in corporate settings and as a coach for traders. For several years she has provided stock market training through private tutoring, books, e-books, and Internet sessions. Tina has mentored traders from across the United States and abroad. Her course attendees range from beginners who aspire to enter this challenging business, to more experienced traders who wish to improve their returns and fine-tune their chart analysis and trading skills.

Tina began trading by timing mutual funds in her retirement account before moving on to trading stocks. She left the corporate workplace in early 2000 in order to pursue her passion for trading, training, and continuous study and analysis of the stock market.

Tina was a contributing author to Stephen Bigalow's book, *High Profit Candlestick Patterns* (2005). She subsequently authored *Getting Started in Candlestick Charting*, published by John Wiley & Sons in 2008. She holds a bachelor of arts from the University of Nevada–Reno, where she majored in communications and minored in business administration.

INDEX

A

Accumulation, 168–171
Achuthan, Lakshman, 146, 233
Alert/alarm, 114–116, 120, 133–134, 218–222
Almanac. *See* Stock Trader's Almanac
Aluminum, 171
Arithmetic. *See* Scale/scaling
Asian financial crisis, 185–186
Associated Press (AP), 146
Average. *See* Index and Moving averages

B

Banerji, Anirvan, 146
Base/basing, 70–78, 219, 226, 265–266
Base building, 168–171, 233
Baumohl, Bernard, 160
Bear ETFs. *See* Inverse ETFs
Bernanke, Ben, 160
Best six months, 161
Black box, 137
Bloomberg, 161
Blowoff top, 95
Bollinger, John, 77
Bollinger Bands, 77–78, 155
  squeeze, 87-88
Bottom, 5, 10–18
  change in direction of, 21, 130–132
  definition of, 10
  divergence, 99–103
  double, 14–15, 21, 53, 87, 104–105, 122–123, 168, 214, 254
  failure to break, 103–105
  head-and-shoulders, 15, 130–131, 167–172, 214
  in downtrend, 22–24
  in uptrend, 21–22
  rectangular, 21, 168, 233
  rounded, 21, 168
  single (V), 167–172, 231–233
  small patterns, 214–215, 238, 266–267
  triple, 87, 105, 168
Bottoming process, 21, 94–96, 167–169
Bounce, 13, 34–35, 73–79, 191
  to resistance, 124–129, 210
Breadth. *See* Market Internals
Breakdown, 103, 120
  false, 266
  moving average, 127–129
  trendline, 107–108
Breakout, 103, 120,
  moving average, 129
Briefing.com, 158–159, 206
Bubble, 147
  housing, 231
Budget, 230, 269
Bulkowski, Thomas, 18, 25–26
Bureau of Labor Statistics (BLS), 160
Business cycle, 146–147, 167, 170–171
Buy-and-hold, 172, 183, 198

C

Candlesticks, 7–8, 69–70
  bearish, 67–68, 242, 254
  bearish reversal pattern, 5, 63,112–113
  body, 8, 17–18, 62–67, 141, 216, 251
  bullish, 62, 169
  bullish reversal pattern, 5, 68–69, 112–113, 216
  failed, 63, 68–69
  sentiment, 5, 207, 216, 262
  shadow/tail, 17–18, 42–47, 62–63, 84–85
    lower, 48–50, 212
    upper, 104, 260
  shaven, 238
  unconfirmed, 63, 68–69
  volume, 104, 216, 242
Capital preservation, 114–116, 165, 195, 247, 254
Capitalization, 149–150
Capitulation, 95, 106, 231–232
Catalyst, 177, 269
Channel, *See* Price channel
Chart
  candlestick. *See* Candlesticks
  line, 159–160
  platform, 47, 83, 95, 100–101, 137, 151–158
  template, 154–159
Chart pattern, 25–26, 157
  confirmation of, 87–88, 105, 125
  continuation pattern, 5, 15, 86–90
  intraday, 241, 249–250
  reversal pattern, 5, 15, 87–89
Choppy, 137, 186, 223, 248, 255, 262–263
Climax move, 95–98
Close, 18
Closing highs/lows, 41–48, 163–164
CNBC, 160–161, 176–178, 186, 246, 256–257
Coil. *See* Triangle
Commodities, 152–153, 170, 233
Components, 168
Consolidation, 28–38, 59, 86–90
  criteria for trendless phase, 24
  divergence, 102
  monitoring, 221–222
  trading range, 5, 9, 15, 88–90, 221–222, 254–255
  wide trading range, 36–38, 111, 189
Consolidation day. *See* Pause
Continuation pattern. *See* Chart pattern
Contrary/contrarian, 206–207
Convergence of signals, 114, 132–133, 220
Copper, 152, 171, 233
Core trade. *See* Trade
Correction, 5, 28–32, 157
  downtrend, 82–83
  duration of, 31–32, 226–227
  low/bottom of, 44–46, 179–188, 210–261
  magnitude of, 31–32
  reversal of, 120, 139, 177
  shift to consolidation, 89–90
  trigger, 110–111, 177, 210
  uptrend, 80–82
Covel, Michael, 138
Crash, 30
  1929 crash, 187
  1987 crash, 181, 186

D

Dark Cloud Cover, 97
Day trading. *See* Strategies
Death cross, 190
Debt ceiling, 223, 230, 256, 269
Decline. *See also* Correction and Pullback
  magnitude of, 90, 175–176
Deficit. *See* Budget and Debt ceiling
Depression, Great, 187, 231
Dip. *See* Pullback
Discounting, 145–146, 171–172, 232, 265
Discretionary strategy, 136–138
Distribution, 189
Divergence, 15
  bearish (negative), 99–101
  bullish (positive), 100–101, 215–216, 232
  guidelines for analysis, 101–103
  indicators, 5, 99–103
  market internals, 158–159, 205–208, 216
Doji, 61–62, 260–264
  Dragonfly, 68, 112–113, 248
  Gravestone, 68
Double tap, 214–215, 238, 241
Dow, Charles Henry, 27
Dow Theory, 3, 27–28
Downtrend, 5, 12, 15
  criteria for, 22–24
Drawdown, 136–138, 173, 183–184, 198

E

Earnings, 177
Economic cycle. *See* Business cycle
Economic Cycle Research Institute (ECRI), 171, 233
Economic reports, 148, 160, 172, 177, 232, 256
Economy, 146–152, 171–172, 230–232
Edge, 9, 136, 148, 159
Employment reports, 160, 172
Engulfing pattern
  bearish, 68, 112–113, 191–194, 238–251
  bullish, 68, 193–194, 238–251
eSignal, 95, 151
ETFs. *See* Exchange-traded funds
Europe/EuroZone, 160, 230, 265
Evening Star, 258–259
Exchange-traded funds (ETFs), 156–157, 168
  inverse, 165, 183–189, 226, 237
  leveraged/ultra, 184, 226–227, 231–232
  SPDRs, 44–50, 151–153
  watchlists, 42–48

F

Falling knife, 68–69
Federal Open Market Committee (FOMC), 160
Federal Reserve, 145–147, 160, 177, 230–231, 269
Fibonacci, 81–86, 213–214, 238
  as support-resistance, 111, 157
Financial crisis of 2008, 231
Fiscal cliff, 265
Flag, 5, 74–76, 88. *See also* Base/basing
  bearish, 192–194, 261–262
  bullish, 257–262
Flash Crash, 47–48, 50, 214, 223, 245–251
Fox Business Network (FBN), 161
Fundamentals
  company, 177, 204
  market, 9, 145–148, 160–172, 232–233

G

Gap, 5, 199
  breakaway, 5, 89–90
  continuation, 5, 97
  exhaustion, 5, 97–98, 132
  gap down, 96
  gap up, 96
  morning/opening, 5, 96–97, 141
  support-resistance, 98, 132, 212
Golden cross, 170
Government shutdown, 269
Gross Domestic Product (GDP), 160, 172
Guidance, 177

H

Hammer, 68, 112–113, 193, 243–251
Hanging Man, 112–113
Head fake, 266
Healthcare, 230
High
  52-week, 14
  all-time, 14, 89–90
  bar, 12, 14, 18
Horizontal line. *See* Trendlines

I

Index, 148–150. *See also* Market
  housing sector, 29, 33, 154
  Nikkei, 30
  semiconductors, 154–156
  volume, 156
Indicators, 5, 100–101, 155. *See also* Market internals
Indices. *See* Index
Industry Groups. *See* Sectors
Initial Claims, 160
Intermediate-term trend. *See* Trend, intermediate-term
Inverted Hammer, 193
Investopedia.com, 11
Investor's Intelligence, 207

J

January effect, 161

K

Key reversal, 96–97, 216

L

Leading
  divergence, 99

Leading (*continued*)
  indicators, 207
Line chart, 159–160
Logarithmic. *See* Scale/scaling
Long-term trend. *See* Trend, long-term
Low
  bar, 12, 18

M

MACD, 99, 155, 261–263
Margin, 209, 226–228
Market
  averages, 149–150
  broad market, 145–161
  Dow Jones Industrial Average, 27, 148–150, 157
    all-time high, 181
    inverse ETFs, 184
    past bear markets, 185–186
    past bull markets, 163–164
    resistance, 177, 266
    support, 177
  impact on trading, 69–70, 91, 109–110, 147–158, 195–196, 208–224, 237
  major market average, 6, 108, 148–149
  monitoring of, 147–149
  long-term trend, 120–121, 157
  intermediate-term trend, 157–158
  opening bell, 135, 140
  pullback, 175–178, 196, 210, 216-217, 227, 235
  relationships, 161, 216
  reversal warnings, 204–209
  rhythm, 222–224
  Russell 2000, 150
  S&P 400 midcap, 150
  S&P 500, 44–46, 111, 148–157, 177, 213–223, 256–266
  S&P 600 smallcap, 150
  Transportation average, 150
  Utility average, 214
  volume, 169, 232, 246
Market, bear, 30, 146–147, 164–165, 183–194
  2000–2002, 120
  2007–2009, 120, 147, 166, 183–188, 191–197, 231–233
  baby bear, 163–164, 176, 255–257
  correction, 165–166, 187–194, 211, 217–218, 240
  development of, 187–194
  duration of, 186
  magnitude of, 186
  of past 50 years, 185–187
  reversal of, 165–174, 191, 231–233
Market, bull, 30, 146–148, 163–184
  2002–2007, 120, 168, 181, 188–189, 197
  2009 to Present, 91, 163–164, 229–269
    2011 correction, 81, 176, 186–188, 198, 214, 223–226
    corrections of, 235–236
    extensions of, 233–235
  bull market high, 179–181, 241–268
  consolidation, 176–178
  correction, 175–177, 187–192, 209–222
  correction versus bear market, 255–257
  declines within, 175–176
  development of, 165–178
  duration of, 164–165
  magnitude of, 165
  of past 50 years, 163–165
  prior bull market high, 181, 266
  surge, 169–174, 232–241
  reversal of, 182, 187–190
Market, secular bull, 257
Market average. *See* Index and Market
Market breadth. *See* Market internals
Market indicators. *See* Market internals
Market internals, 5, 148–152, 158–160, 196–199, 204–208, 237–238. *See also* Sentiment
  Advance/decline, 152, 158, 233
  Arms Index (TRIN), 158
  divergence, 158–159, 205–208, 216
  McClellan indicators, 152
  New highs-lows, 158, 205–206, 233
  Up-down volume, 158
  Tick, 158
  Zweig indicator, 152
Mean reversion, 76–79
Mechanical system, 136–138
Metals, 171
MetaStock, 95, 137, 151
Minor trend. *See* Trend, short-term
Money management. *See* Risk management
Monetary policy, 145–147, 160, 230–231
Morning Star, 216, 259–264
Morris, Gregory, 159

Moving Average Convergence Divergence. *See* MACD
Moving averages, 19–20, 79–84, 157, 238–268
10-period
mean reversion, 77–78
trend direction, 19–25, 169, 190
20-period
as support-resistance, 82, 126–128
break of, 128
in consolidation, 24–29, 87, 128
mean reversion, 76–77
trend direction, 19–25, 154, 169, 190
50-period, 80
as support-resistance, 82, 111, 122–126, 154, 182, 190, 212
trend direction, 190, 238
100-period, 80
as support-resistance, 82–83, 111, 129, 154, 182, 212, 235
trend direction, 170
200-period, 80
as support-resistance, 111, 129, 133, 154, 182, 190–193, 212
close above, 166
close below, 187–188, 247, 255
trend direction, 170, 190
500-period, 255
break of, 126–129
crossover, 169–170, 190, 238
exponential, 127
in consolidation, 132
weekly, 80, 182, 244, 255
Murphy, John, 9, 166
Mutual funds, 184

N

NASDAQ
composite index, 120, 150
stock exchange, 158
New York Stock Exchange (NYSE), 158, 206, 233
News, 38, 91–93, 109–110, 160, 168, 177, 210
earnings release, 93
sell the news, 145

O

Obama, President 146, 265
October, 186
On-Balance Volume (OBV), 99, 155, 170, 233
Open, 18
Opportunity cost, 209
Oscillator, 99, 155
Outside day, 96–97, 216
Overbought, 39–40, 91
intermediate-term basis, 32–33, 60, 82, 176–178, 199–210, 221, 226–228
short-term basis, 34–35, 60–63, 72–77
Oversold, 80, 91, 209–210, 227–228
intermediate-term basis, 32–33, 60, 82
short-term basis, 34–35, 47, 60, 76–77

P

Parabolic. *See* Vertical
Pause
downtrend, 67–69, 126
uptrend, 62–66
Peak, 5, 10–18
change in direction of, 130–132
definition of, 10
divergence, 99–103
failure to break, 103–108, 244, 263
in downtrend, 22–24
in uptrend, 21–22
Pennant, 5, 74–76, 88, 262
Percent change, 39–48, 234–236
Percent rule, 103
Person, John, 11
Piercing pattern, 97
Pivot. *See* Price pivots
Pointer, 100–101, 218
PPC. *See* Percent change
Presidential cycle, 161
Price bar. *See* Bar and Candlesticks
Price channel
ascending, 22
descending, 186
horizontal, *See* Consolidation
Price percent change (PPC). *See* Percent change
Price pivots, 10–16, 64–65
for measuring trends, 41–48
intermediate-term trends, 178–179
other terms for, 11
roles of, 15
short-term trends, 53–55
Price scale. *See* Scale/scaling
Price swing. *See* Trend, short-term
Priced-in. *See* Discounting
Probability, 78–79, 133

Profit-taking, 5, 34
at ceiling-floor, 108–109, 182
partial profits, 39–40, 65–73, 108–115, 133
Protect capital. *See* Capital preservation
Pullback, 34, 71–79, 226
Put/Call ratio, 207

Q

Quantitative easing. *See* Monetary policy
Quick reference guides, 141–142, 269

R

Range, 62, 97, 246–247
average daily, 223, 268
narrow, 62, 242, 268
Reaction. *See* Correction
Recession, 147
double dip, 256
Great Recession, 187, 231–232
Rectangle. *See* Consolidation
Relative Strength (RS), 99, 155
Relative Strength Index (RSI), 99, 102, 122, 155
Relief rally. *See* Bounce
Resistance, 5–6, 15, 25, 90–91, 178–182. *See also* Trendlines
at consolidation, 86
at gap opening, 98
at major ceiling, 110–111
at moving average, 79–83
at price pivot(s), 74, 103–105, 191
at round number, 181, 266
break of, 122–124
reverse roles, 123–124, 193
Retail Sales, 160, 172
Retracement. *See* Correction
Returns, 136
Reversal pattern. *See* Chart pattern
Reversion to the mean. *See* Mean reversion
Risk management, 135–138, 163, 183, 209, 272–274
Rotation. *See* Sectors
Routines, 145, 195–198, 206, 220, 237–238

S

Santa Claus rally, 161
Scale/scaling, 39–40, 84–85, 159–160
Scans/scanning, 149, 196–199, 207–208, 216, 237–238
Seasonal, 145, 161
Secondary Trend. *See* Correction
Sectors, 109–110, 146, 177
impact on stocks, 91
industry groups, 6, 233
monitoring of, 6, 44–48, 116, 148–154, 217
Selling climax, 95
Sentiment, 148, 157, 204–208
candlesticks, 5, 207, 262
Sequestration, 230
Shooting Star, 47, 63, 112–113, 247
Short-covering rally. *See* Bounce
Short selling, 34, 40, 68–76, 115–125, 133, 139, 183–191
correction, 210–211, 226–227, 237
Short-term trend. *See* Trend, short-term
Slippage, 39–40, 135, 209
Spinning top, 62, 240, 249, 264
Standard & Poor's, 223
Statistics, 76–79, 161
Stochastics, 99, 102, 155
Stock Trader's Almanac, 161–164
Stockcharts.com, 154, 158
Stop and reverse, 115–116
Stops, 16, 39–40, 65–66, 220–221
as exit strategy, 134–136
manipulation of, 40, 135
mental, 120, 134–135
orders, 115, 134–135
proximity, 61, 70
tighten, 115
trailing, 131–134, 198
triggered, 39–40, 81, 87, 104, 114–115, 120, 131, 209
Stovall, Sam, 255–257
Strategy/strategies, 3, 6, 79, 199. *See also* Swing trading
adjusting, 176–177, 208–209, 237
buy-the-dip, 72, 175, 215
day trading, 196, 223
development of, 3–8, 116–117, 138, 161, 272–273
Lock and Reload, 61, 135, 196
long, 199, 210–212, 225–228
short. *See* short selling
trend-following, 6, 81, 115, 136–138, 198, 223, 255

Supply-demand, 86, 145, 160
Support, 5–6, 15, 25, 178–181. *See also* Trendlines
at consolidation, 86, 212
at correction low, 81
at gap opening, 97, 212
at major floor, 110–111
at moving average, 72, 79–83, 212
at price pivot(s), 65, 71–72, 103–105, 178–179, 191, 212
break of, 122–124
reverse roles, 123–124, 193, 201–203
Swing. *See* Trend, short-term
Swing high. *See* Peak and Price pivots
Swing low. *See* Bottom and Price pivots
Swing trading, 34, 47–48
entry, 61, 70, 78
intraday trends, 53–57, 73, 139–140
management of, 65–76, 195–196
swing-ending warning, 112–113, 140–141
trading tips, 138–141
Symbol, 151–159

T

Tail. *See* Candlesticks
Tainer, Evelina, 160
Taper/tapering, 269
Target, 108–110, 117, 177, 140–141
Taxes, 230
TC2000, 95, 151–156
custom date sort, 42–48
Technology, 154
Tharp, Van, 138
Time frames, 12, 19
intraday, 39–40, 47–48, 54–57, 139–140, 196
multiple, 110–111, 197–198
weekly, 37, 55, 157, 170
divergence, 101
moving averages, 80
support-resistance, 110–111, 197
trendline, 49–51, 124
trend-end warnings, 95
Top
double, 5, 23, 52, 87, 103–105, 189
confirmation, 88–89, 105, 116–125
divergence, 102
head-and-shoulders, 5, 15, 130–131, 189
rectangular, 189
rounding, 189
single, 188–189
triple, 87, 105, 189, 263
Topping process, 23, 94–96, 182, 188–190
Trade. *See also* Swing trading and Trade management
long-term (core), 5, 61, 72, 110
adding to, 61, 70–73, 115, 133–134, 172, 191, 222
entry, 198
exiting, 131, 198
profits, 114, 135
selection, 10
short-term, 5, 158, 223, 227, 255
Trade management, 10
cash, 176, 183, 209, 223–227, 255
entry, 72–79, 114–116, 123–124
exit into strength, 39–40, 47, 110
number of positions, 209, 228, 247
orders, 220
overextended, 39–40
position size, 228, 247, 272
price pivots, 15
response to warnings, 113–117, 208–209
trigger, 115–116
TradeStation, 137, 151
Trading range. *See* Consolidation
Trading strategy. *See* Strategy
Trend. *See also* Trend, short-, intermediate- and long-term
broad market, 6
building blocks of, 5, 14, 30-35
definition of, 3, 9
development of, 5, 10
direction of, 9–26
dominant, 35–36
duration of, 6
identification of, 6
interruptions of, 15, 28, 59–92, 157
measurement of, 41–48
momentum of, 15, 99–104, 130
monitoring of, 134–138, 156–157
other trends, 4
questions asked about, 3–4
reversal of, 5–6, 15, 90–94, 120–121
reversal warnings, early, 93–117, 199–209, 226, 237–238
reversal warnings, later, 119–142, 199–209, 226, 237–238

Trend. (*continued*)
  strength of, 4, 6, 61, 147–148, 158, 196–199, 204–207
  trends within trends, 55–57
  trendless period. *See* Consolidation
Trend, intermediate-term, 21, 30–42, 195–228
  building blocks of, 5, 34, 139
  duration of, 31–32
  high/top of, 41, 166, 179, 230, 254–263
  in wide trading range, 36–38
  interruptions of, 33–35, 61–76, 157
  magnitude of, 31–32
  monitoring of, 138–139, 172–174
Trend, long-term, 21, 28–38, 196–198
  building blocks of, 28–32, 196–197
  correction of, 28–32, 191, 196, 209–222
  extension of, 30–32, 191, 196–199
  interruptions of, 79–90, 157
  investing in, 29
  major peaks-bottoms, 29, 41, 49–51, 230
  reversal of, 95–96, 231–233
Trend, major. *See* Trend, long-term
Trend, minor. *See* Trend, short-term
Trend, primary. *See* Trend, long-term
Trend, short-term, 12–13, 21–22, 33–38
  downswing, 67–74
  duration of, 34–35
  in intermediate-term trends, 33–34
  in trading range, 36–38, 89
  swing-ending warnings, 112, 140–141
  upswing, 62–65, 71
Trendlines, 5, 15–17
  adjusting, 23–24, 48–53, 105–107, 200–204
  break of, 5, 16, 19, 107–108, 124–126, 260
  converging, 24–25, 86–88
  correction, 216–219, 240–267
  drawing, 16–17, 26, 155
  external, 17–19
  intermediate-term, 48–53, 124–126, 156–157, 200–204, 239–268
  internal, 17–22
  horizontal, *See* Trendlines, horizontal
  long-term, 48–51, 156, 202–203
  resistance (down) line, 16–23, 130, 192
  short-term, 53–55
  slope change, 48–53, 105–107, 232
  steep line, 38
  strength of, 16
  support (up) line, 16–22, 130
  tight, 107–108
Trendlines, horizontal, 5, 17, 156, 201–204
  break of, 126–127
  correction, 218–219
  trading range, 36–38, 221–222
Triangle, 5, 15, 86–88
  ascending, 87–89
  descending, 88
  symmetrical, 24–25, 88, 131
Triple tap, 214–215, 238, 249–250
Twain, Mark, 272
Tweezers, 10
Twitter, 145

U

Unemployment, 230
Uptrend, 5, 12, 15
  criteria for, 21–22

V

Vertical, 38–41
Volatility, 5, 62, 79
  decline of, 86, 268
  increase of/high, 39–40, 223–224, 246–247, 255
  stops, 132–135, 198
Volatility index (VIX), 207
Volume, 5, 79
  confirmation, 216
  decline of, 65, 87
  during a pullback, 73
  heavy, 96–98, 104–106, 254
  moving average of, 87, 155
  trend of, 4

W

Wachtel, Larry, 167
Watchlists, 42–48, 151–154
  review daily, 151–152
  review weekly, 152–154
  trade candidates, 114, 220
Wedge, descending, 192
Weekly. *See* Time frames
Weekly Leading Index (WLI), 171, 233
White space, 70–71, 89
Wilder's RSI. *See* Relative Strength Index

Y

Yahoo! Finance, 206